THE WILDER HOUSE SERIES
IN POLITICS, HISTORY,
AND CULTURE

The Wilder House Series is published in association with the
Wilder House Board of Editors and the University of Chicago.
A complete list of titles appears at the end of this book.

David Laitin, *Editor*
George Steinmetz, *Assistant Editor*

Editorial Board:
Leora Auslander
Prasenjit Duara
Ira Katznelson
William Sewell
Theda Skocpol
Susan Stokes

DC
33.7
.43
1992

MIDDLEBURY COLLEGE LIBRARY

TRUE FRANCE

The Wars over Cultural Identity,

1900–1945

Herman Lebovics

Cornell University Press

Ithaca and London

Copyright © 1992 by Cornell University

All rights reserved. Except for brief quotations in a review, this book, or
parts thereof, must not be reproduced in any form without permission in
writing from the publisher. For information, address Cornell University
Press, Sage House, 512 East State Street, Ithaca, New York 14850.

First published 1992 by Cornell University Press
First printing, Cornell Paperbacks, 1994

Printed in the United States of America

Library of Congress Cataloging-in-Publication Data

Lebovics, Herman.
 True France : the wars over cultural identity, 1900–1945 / Herman Lebovics.
   p.   cm. — (The Wilder House series in politics, history, and culture)
 Includes bibliographical references and index.
 ISBN 0-8014-2687-1 (cloth : alk. paper)
 ISBN 0-8014-8193-7 (pbk. : alk. paper)
   1. France—Civilization—20th century. 2. Politics and culture—France—
History—20th century. 3. France—Colonies—History—20th century.
4. France—Cultural policy—History—20th century. 5. France—Ethnic
relations—Political aspects—History—20th century. I. Title. II. Series.
DC33.7.L43   1992
944.081—dc20   91-44697

Cornell University Press strives to use environmentally responsible suppliers
and materials to the fullest extent possible in the publishing of its books. Such
materials include vegetable-based, low-VOC inks and acid-free papers that are
recycled, totally chlorine-free, or partly composed of nonwood fibers. Books
that bear the logo of the FSC (Forest Stewardship Council) use paper taken
from forests that have been inspected and certified as meeting the highest
standards for environmental and social responsibility. For further information,
visit our website at www.cornellpress.cornell.edu.

Cloth printing   10 9 8 7 6 5 4 3 2 1
Paperback printing   10 9 8 7 6 5 4 3 2

For Jesse and Ethan

Contents

Illustrations

Preface

This book is about the creation of a certain idea of Frenchness in the first fifty years of this century. My concern is to assess the penalties of incorporating people in a narrowly defined construction of the French cultural world; I wish to understand what it meant for French people of Paris and the provinces and for colonial people to be included within an imagined (and therefore powerful and, like the Old Testament God, jealous) French identity.

When television or a newspaper carries a story about an act of cultural chauvinism—a racial incident, an instance of xenophobia, discrimination against some domestic minority—we feel a sense of outrage that someone we think *belongs* is being labeled as not one of us. In the United States the people among whom we wish to be counted see African Americans, Asian immigrants, and homosexuals as unfairly excluded from a commonality we all share. And in France, too, good people reject discrimination against people of African and Jewish heritage. Think of the prominence of the French civil rights organization called SOS Racisme at its height in the late 1980s, and of the rush of public figures from almost all points on the political spectrum to associate themselves with it.

These histories of exclusions are matters we have studied so that we can enhance our ways of overcoming them. We have to learn much more about the history of discrimination and how people are marginalized in their own societies, but the project is well launched in the West—if not yet in Eastern Europe—both in scholarship and in social practice.

We know little, however, and have thought less about the tyranny of solidarity. We have many excellent studies of attempts to expel Protestants, immigrants, Jews, and Arabs—to name just a few of the categories—from modern France.[1] Yet the idea embodied in Jesus' "Compel people to come in" also expresses a potential source of oppression. That text served as the scriptural basis of the Inquisition. What I will try to comprehend in this book is how the embrace of a culture and what Gérard Noiriel has termed "the construction of the 'sense of belonging'" not only can give a sense of orientation and coherence to the lives of its members but also can appear in the form of the iron maiden.[2]

I describe the construction of a French cultural identity in the first half of this century as it was manifested in the discourse of the nascent cultural sciences and in important institutional expressions in museums, expositions, colonial education and pacification, and, most important, politics. In one sense I deal with a uniquely French notion of identity which, beginning in the years around 1900, marked all those who were French or might become part of the nation; it allowed both local identities and the single national identity of Frenchness. This definition encountered difficulties as it was played out in twentieth-century French politics, cultural and otherwise, because, finally, one's *petit pays* had to yield to the requirements of the *grand pays,* or rather, and more precisely, the *petit pays* became a pawn in national struggles for power.

Philip Schlesinger has concluded that "national cultures are not simple repositories of shared symbols to which the entire population stands in identical relation. Rather, they are to be approached as sites of contestation in which competition over definitions takes place."[3] I argue, accordingly, that (1) from the turn of the twentieth

---

1. Gérard Noiriel suggests we reserve the word "category" for human collectivities created outside the group, by bureaucratic fiat, as in the case of refugees; then "group" would designate self-created social entities. See his *Tyrannie du national: Le Droit d'asile en Europe, 1793–1993* (Paris, 1991), 320.

2. Ibid., 311.

3. Philip Schlesinger, "On National Identity: Some Conceptions and Misconceptions Criticized," *Social Science Information,* 26 (1987), 219–64, esp. 260–61.

century, when the new leaders of the Third Republic seemed to have succeeded in consolidating a new polity, to at least 1945, the key move of the discontented right was to avoid politics by shifting its ground—and the field of contestations—to culture; that (2) French cultural universalism, as inherited from Gallican Catholicism, absolutism, the Enlightenment and Jacobinism, and finally conservative republicanism, bore within itself an often contested but never-defeated logic of convergence and conformism; and (3) that beginning around the turn of the century, the new French right, building on this peculiarity of the French, promoted a deadening hegemony of the idea and practice of a True France as the only hope for national renewal, the power of that idea and practice coming from the right's claim to be the sole representative of the French heritage.

The idea of an exclusive identity of France was the chief strategy, the hegemonic project, of conservative cultural thought and practice from the time of the Dreyfus affair to the end of World War II. The left upheld, albeit differently, this same cultural imperative. Nevertheless, the paradigm of an exclusive French identity was, and is, profoundly reactionary both in culture and in politics. It holds that there can be only one way to participate in the culture of a country and only one natural political organization that fits the society. It has led to struggles in the zero-sum combats between left and right for the right to speak in behalf of True France in anthropological discourse, in colonial ideology, in folklore theory, in the 1920s, during the Popular Front, under Vichy rule, and even today.

The idea of a True France was cultivated and disseminated in political rhetoric, in public monuments, in the arts (especially literature), in academic philosophy, in historical works, and throughout all levels of French schooling. It saturated all the "places of memory," in the sense in which Pierre Nora uses the term, in the first half of this century. I have chosen to follow the construction and workings of the ideology in the borderlands of social science and politics for two reasons. First, I have had the good fortune to find fine sources, even fascinating ones, about groups and key individuals who worked in the fields of both cultural theory and public policy. Thus I could practice that opportunism of the archives which has proved so rewarding in the historian's craft and pose questions for which available materials offered especially rich responses. Following the traffic of ideas about practice to the practice of ideas and back, I did not have to be content with just Michel Foucault's social sciences of results; I found information and employed theoretical approaches that let me say something about intentions.

Second, the concept of cultural or national identity, as employed in most of our contemporary discussions and certainly in the discourse of the interwar years, serves more to stake ideological claims than as a useful analytical tool. We must find a way to enter the ideological world of French identity without losing ourselves in a cloud-cuckoo-land of national character or being taken in by political-theological nonsense. We need a subject of manageable scale and an entrée to it which allows us the possibility, if not of objective judgment, at least of a judgment that is not preordained. So my strategy is to make "identity" the problem, not the solution. And the field of cultural anthropology, taken in the broadest sense to include some of its important institutional manifestations, as the emerging discipline of the topic in the years between World Wars I and II, is the ideal ground to determine the dimensions of the problem. I certainly do not propose to cover the whole intellectual and institutional spectrum pervaded by the discourse of foundationalist and exclusivist identity or to provide a history of the origins, growth, ascendancy, and demise of an idea and its related practices, though elements for such a history may be found here.

Rather than take a genetic, linear approach that links one idea or practice to preceding ones on a unitary time curve running from origins through development to denouement, I have chosen to follow Foucault's genealogical method, which looks to the confluence of discursive formations, or ideologies, and power-saturated practices at different moments in different settings. Each chapter, then, addresses a key aspect of an essentialist way of thinking and doing in the conservative discourse about French cultural heritage: representations of other peoples to the French, of colonized people to themselves in metropolitan-controlled education, of the French of the provinces to Parisians and themselves; and finally the contested practices of the state during the 1920s, the Popular Front, and Vichy in efforts to realize certain visions of the national cultural heritage. This mode of presentation, I hope, will come across to the reader as a coherent rendering of a certain way of thinking about and acting in society which takes account of beginnings and causes, chronology and development. But it does not pretend to take up the metaphysical task of capturing an essence or of telling the whole story. Those operations, in cultural theory and in practice, are precisely what I am analyzing.

Although it will become evident as we go along, it is worth alerting the reader to my view of what constitutes explanation in cultural history. For the sake of clarity, we might distinguish two poles of thought. First, some cultural analysts, as Paul Rabinow characterizes them, "attributed a significant degree of autonomy to culture (and character) from the social and economic circumstances in which they arose."[4] Perhaps Clifford Geertz and many of his students have given us the most creative examples of work arising from such assumptions.

Pierre Bourdieu, in contrast, writing here on identity and representation, proposes that "the political boundary, this product of a legal act of delineation, produces cultural differences quite as much as it results from them."[5] Similarly, Luc Boltanski warns against a "substantialist" view of social groups; I would mention cultures as well. He urges us rather to see a social phenomenon—in his case, white-collar employees, called in France cadres—as a core, a paradigm, or even a field of activity with an extensive periphery filled with ambiguities, possibilities, spaces for the play of forces, permitting, in short, easy passage to ideology and politics.[6]

As I will not be explaining cultural developments by other cultural developments, this book comes closer to the social science of Bourdieu than to a narrow culturalist position. Now that we have escaped

4. Paul Rabinow, "Beyond Ethnography: Anthropology as Nominalism," *Cultural Anthropology*, 3 (1988), 357.

5. Pierre Bourdieu, "L'Identité et la représentation: Eléments pour une réflexion critique sur l'idée de région," *Actes de la Recherche en Sciences Sociales*, 35 (1980), 66.

6. Luc Boltanski, *The Making of a Class: Cadres in French Society* (1982), trans. Arthur Goldhammer (Cambridge, 1987), 27–37, 145–83, 279–96. In the succinct words of the anthropologist Claude Rivals, "The cultural is not the totality of the social": *Ethnologie folklorique et politique: À propos du livre de Christian Faure, "Le Projet culturel de Vichy"; une lecture . . . autobiographique*, Toulouse Institut de Sciences Sociales, Université de Toulouse, Le Mirail (Toulouse, 14 July 1989), 25.

from the tunnel visions of economic determinism and more recently from social-historical determinism, it ill behooves us to worship the idol of the all-pervasiveness of culture.

Readers will find the political, in often recognizable historical forms such as the Beaux-Arts administration, the Colonial Ministry, and police agencies, to be important in these discussions of social science and cultural practice. In a word, they will find cultural history with the state not only left in but with a commanding presence, rather than playing the role of just another confluence of cultural practices. Certainly, this state—the political—was as much constructed as were cultural policies. I have no intention of reifying politics, but it does not aid understanding of twentieth-century history or of empowerment to deny the workings of political agency at moments in history.

I confess that I am critical of the idea of France fostered by the right, and the particulars of my animosity toward the construction of that identity will become evident in the chapters that follow. This work takes a direction Foucault charted: "The purpose of history, guided by genealogy, is not to discover the roots of our identity, but to commit itself to its dissipation. It does not seek to define our unique threshold of emergence, the homeland of which metaphysicians promise a return; it seeks to make visible all those discontinuities that cross it."[7] Despite my admitted values, I hope to describe a certain idea of France, follow the playing out of that idea in French social science and cultural policy, and, above all, reveal the political meaning of the cultural attitude under study in an honest and helpful way. This work of demonstration, I believe, is new, and my finding—that a conservative construction of a True France played a major deleterious role in French thought and cultural practice in much of the twentieth century—is a product neither of pluralist attitudes nor of antiauthoritarian political proclivities.

This is just another way of saying that a book, at least one that might be worth reading, links honest explication with partisan passion, not so that readers are compelled to concur with the thinking of the author but so that they can now participate in the discussion,

7. Michel Foucault, "Nietzsche, Genealogy, History" (1971), in *The Foucault Reader*, ed. Paul Rabinow (New York, 1984), 95.

knowing what is at stake. Such a book, this book, cannot be a lone venture. Ideas, formulations, chapters, and drafts must be tried out on people concerned with the issues, individuals in many cases more knowledgeable about them than the author. These colleagues, critics, readers, even kibitzers suggest new sources, the works of other authors, and perhaps other perspectives that require the aid of archivists, librarians, staff people at institutes, research centers, universities. The injustice—or limited liability, might be the better term—is that the book's spine bears the name of the author and omits the names of the individuals whose criticisms helped shape the book. I acknowledge and thank those people.

First I thank the most tried—in several senses of the word—and the most helpful. My friend and colleague Richard Kuisel once again demonstrated his mastery as a critical reader who reads to make the author's ideas work better, not to impose his own. Bonnie Smith read an early draft as well as nervous last thoughts and deftly pointed me in the direction she realized, better than I did at the moment, I wanted to go. David Prochaska's unique combination of historian's skills, knowledge of colonialism, and sophistication on aesthetic questions was beneficial at several junctures. The criticisms I received from the readers for Cornell University Press and for Wilder House, Loic Wacquant, Leora Auslander, and Robert O. Paxton, were models of sharp, useful readings. I appreciate the intellectual enthusiasm, engagement, and support David Laitin, Wilder House director, gave me from the time he first saw the manuscript to its finished form.

Brigitte Howard helped me puzzle out Paul Rivet's handwriting. I thank Brooke Larson for our fruitful dialogues on how to study the oppressed and Barbara Weinstein for her good criticisms of early drafts of sections of the book. Jack J. Spector shared his knowledge of the art and politics of surrealism with me. Charles Rearick gave me sound criticism on how I was treating the cultural politics of the Popular Front. Caroline Ford offered me perspective-opening criticisms of the first parts of the manuscript; she saved me from walking out on some rather thin limbs. Patricia Mainardi helped me with my design idea for the cover of the book and made valuable suggestions for better reading the images from the Colonial Exposition of 1931 in Chapter 2. I thank Ian Lustick for allowing me to see a draft of his "Where and What Is France? Three Failures of Hegemonic Construction."

In France, Jean Jamin of *Gradhiva* and the Musée de l'Homme was always ready with decisive aid and encouragement. Isac Chiva of the Laboratoire d'Anthropologie Sociale and the Ecole des Hautes Etudes en Sciences Sociales, although sometimes not in agreement with what I was saying about the political history of his discipline, was always welcoming when I saw him and generous with his aid. Marcel Maget's willingness to talk with me put the chapters on Louis Marin and Georges-Henri Rivière on much firmer ground. Laurence Bertrand-Dorléac and Gérard Noiriel both by their reactions to the work and in more free-ranging conversation gave me reassurance that what I was writing might make sense to French readers. I acknowledge, too, the aid of Marc Augé, Jean-Pierre Rioux, Pascal Ory, and the good angel of many American researchers in Paris, Patrick Fridenson. The professionalism and friendship of Floréal Jimenez combined to make my research in the library of the Musée National des Arts et Traditions Populaires both a productive and a pleasant experience. Bernard and Marcia Scholl, my good Parisian friends, were generous with nourishment for my body and soul. And the graciousness of Nicole Gênet facilitated my summers' work greatly.

Dean Andrew Policano, in collaboration with Provost Tilden Edelstein, has been generous in finding funds for unexpected expenses incurred in the preparation of this book, in particular for the rights to reproduce the photographs from *L'Illustration*. John Gillis's invitation to spend the spring semester of 1991 at the Rutgers Center for Historical Analysis came at a moment when the discussions in which I participated and the criticism of my own work could translate into significant improvements in the final drafts. Finally, I acknowledge the support of the National Endowment for the Humanities, which on two occasions awarded me Travel-to-Collections fellowships to enable me to work in the Archives Nationales in Paris and Aix-en-Provence.

Earlier drafts of three chapters have appeared in journals. A version of Chapter 1 was published as "The Discourse of Tradition in French Culture: The Rightist Social Science and Political Practice of

Louis Marin, 1890–1945," *Historical Reflections/Réflections Historiques,* Winter 1991, 45–75. Some sections of Chapter 2 appeared in the article "Donner à voir l'empire colonial: L'Exposition coloniale internationale de Paris en 1931," *Gradhiva: Revue d'histoire et de l'archives de l'anthropologie publiée par le Musée de l'Homme* (Paris), 7 (Winter 1989–90), 18–28. An early draft of Chapter 3 appeared as "Assimilation ou respect des différences? La Colonisation du Vietnam, 1920–1930," in *Genèse: Sciences sociales et histoire,* May 1991, 23–43. The sections that first appeared in journals are used here by permission.

HERMAN LEBOVICS

Stony Brook, New York

T R U E   F R A N C E

Introduction

At the end of *L'Identité de la France,* Fernand Braudel's majestic two volumes of historical reflections on the long, great, and complex transformations he credited with the creation of modern France, Braudel meditated on the future of the large North African population in contemporary France. A curious topic for the conclusion to so sweeping and magisterial a book, a reader might judge. Writing in the first person and with a sense of urgency—this was his last book—Braudel tried to puzzle out the way Arabs living in France, both those born there and immigrants, might be assimilated in *"la communauté."* He dismissed the cultural pluralism of "the American way of life" as a possible model for France (which, in any case, he believed did not really work to ease tensions among the cultures in the United States), because "here in France, the situation is much more tense and unstable than it is in the United States, and more subtly so; *for we are an old country;* for the home of our guests, an old country also, is near ours, adjoins ours." In a few hours French Arabs could return to their past lives, their old joys, their nostalgia; they could renew their ties with their ancestral culture. Americans, in contrast, he wrote, went back to the old country only after they had made their fortune. Cortez burned his boats upon reaching the Mexican shore.

What then were Braudel's hopes for this large, fertile, and largely unassimilated population that was today testing the historic identity of his *patrie?* He wanted those who wished to live in France to choose: to burn their boats—that is, to accept French citizenship, to accept membership in the French community, and in so doing modify their culture, especially by rejecting any lingering devotion to integralist Islam so that they might accommodate to their new homeland. France, he observed, although historically a Christian civilization, had become tolerant and had put its wars of religion behind it. It could absorb this population too, as it had absorbed others before it: Catalans, Bretons, Alsatians, Martiniquais, and the other peoples who found themselves in the political and cultural entity called France.[1]

This "old country" of which Braudel had a certain idea did not come into existence all at once. The violent conquest known in history as the Albigensian Crusade brought a great part of the South under the sway of the kings of France. In many ways North and South are truly reconciled by now, although a local society maintains the monument to the martyrs of northern might at Montségur, and visitors still place fresh flowers upon it as they pass on the steep path leading to the top of the Albigensian refuge. Brittany did not come under the rule of the French crown until 1532; Metz, Toul, and Verdun were annexed only in 1648. The Treaty of the Pyrenees of 1659 made the Catalan regions of Roussillon, Conflans, and Cerdagne politically French. Lille and Tournai passed under French rule in 1668, but Flanders was annexed only during the French Revolution (1795). Napoleon Buonaparte, born in 1769, managed by just a year to be French, for Corsica was seized by French arms in 1768. Retroactive nationalism notwithstanding, neither the history of Alsace nor even that of Lorraine lends itself to Braudel's reading of French history. Savoy and Nice, the latter Garibaldi's hometown, became French territory only in 1860, and then as a political payoff by the house of Savoy to Napoleon III for not interfering with Cavour's plans for the Italian peninsula. With the exchange of territory was negotiated a dynastic marriage between the two houses. Algeria, as a future part of France, came under French rule in 1830; much of the Asian part of the colonial empire, destined by support-

---

1. Fernand Braudel, *L'Identité de la France*, 2 vols. (Paris, 1986), vol. 2, pt. 1, *Les Hommes et les choses*, 193–99. Italics mine.

ers of a large vision of France in the 1930s to become part of the nation, was fully annexed only in the last part of the nineteenth century. In short, a great deal of old France has not been so long a part of the French state.

The myth of what Raoul Girardet has called "a kind of geographic predestination of the French nation," the idea of a virtual France existing before the historical France, which pervades Michelet's historical works, was invented by the writers of nineteenth-century schoolbooks. Vercingetorix and his band have been perennial ancestors in old textbooks.[2] So have been the Celts, especially in the eyes of the first students of folklore early in the nineteenth century. In a 1948 book that is still in use, written to prepare students for the CAPES, the graduate-level teacher qualification examinations, Ferdinand Lot attributed the paternity of France to Clovis.[3] If one desired, one could make a case for the French version of the Oath of Strassburg (843), or a few centuries later for the Song of Roland, with its evocations of "sweet France," as the origin of the idea of France as we think of it today. In the nineteenth century Ernest Renan, who greatly influenced republicans but also such far rightists as Charles Maurras, theorized on what was truly French. In Lavisse students read that to hearten Charles VII, Joan of Arc spoke to him of Charlemagne and Saint Louis: "this daughter of the people knew that France had existed for a long time." High school students learned in Albert Malet's textbook that the Capetians who found France broken up into independent states, each with its own government, "*recreated* the political unity of France."[4]

It might be argued that, although as a political entity France as we know it today is not so old, the cultures of the regions that came to constitute modern France are surely ancient. So in a sense there has always been an Old France; just the present political boundaries are relatively modern. But Marc Bloch's insight in his *Feudal Society*, that

2. The playful ironies of the comic-book hero Asterix the Gaul would not be so amusing to French adults and children alike if the latent sacrilege were not there. For the right feel, American readers might imagine Washington and the Continental Army at Valley Forge presented as a musical winter carnival.

3. Ferdinand Lot, *Naissance de la France*, ed. Jacques Boussard (Paris, 1970).

4. Raoul Girardet, *Mythes et mythologies politiques* (Paris, 1989), 156–57; Pierre Nora, "Lavisse, instituteur national," in *Lieux de mémoire: La République*, ed. Nora (Paris, 1984), 247. Italics mine.

cultures of oral traditions can change greatly and rapidly, is compelling; it is not very accurate to apply the word "old" to them. Nor is there anything especially unique historically about peasants manifesting loyalty to their village. Loyalty both to region and to France, however, was ideologically universalized only in the beginning of the twentieth century.

It is as hard to believe in a French manifest destiny as in the American one. Because of the accretions of territory in the nineteenth century alone, the national myth manufactories of Europe went into full production to generate the "retroactive nationalism" that Robert S. Lopez deplored in the writing of medieval history. Although Nice and Savoy became French as part of a trade between king and emperor (very much in the style of those made by contemporary Monopoly players), at the same time the French-speaking Valle d'Aosta became part of unified Italy. At various moments in European history the Rhineland, Freiburg im Breisgau, parts of Spain, Holland, and Belgium were candidates for inclusion in the French realm. Even this enumeration omits both the New World of the western hemisphere and Napoleon's attempt to redraw the map of France and that of Europe. Alsace and Lorraine, having become part of a newly invented Germany in 1871, became French again in 1918, German once more in 1940, but French after the defeat of Germany in World War II. To the chagrin of some French nationalists, however, just after the end of that war the people of the Saar voted to become part of West Germany.[5] Both the wars of decolonization and the unforced French grants of independence to parts of the colonial empire reversed a French policy that some supporters of the empire saw as making natives into Frenchmen. Today Guadeloupe has a serious separatist movement while nearby Martinique does not; both are Caribbean departments of France. Just to mention New Caledonia, where the indigenous population now makes up a minority but wishes national autonomy, is to evoke the question of French colonial—and certainly New Caledonian— identity. The recent work of Hervé Le Bras and Emmanuel Todd has further emphasized the regional—even biological, they insist— diversity of France. One need not accept their improbable thesis,

5. It is said that, as an act of reprisal, the university cafeteria changed its cuisine from French to German the day after the vote.

that this diversity, above all in its political manifestations, rests on differing regionally specific kinship systems, to concur that French society manifests more diversity ethnically, regionally, and culturally than many of its European neighbors.[6]

Yet despite strong evidence for alternative readings of the creation of modern France—perhaps *because* possibilities for different outcomes were always present—this sense of *a single identity* of France, a national character, persists among contemporary students of French history both at home, as in the case of Braudel, and among methodologically conservative foreign historians. In his fine study of the (neglected) importance of immigrants in French history, Gérard Noiriel criticized Braudel's approach in *L'Identité de la France*, with its thirty-five pages out of nearly a thousand devoted to the immigrant population, as "holist." Theodore Zeldin essayed to capture the national character in his book *The French;* Eugen Weber performed double ontology in showing us how peasants became Frenchmen.[7] Both works start out implicitly from the founding myth of nineteenth-century nationalism: the belief that there existed, or should exist, a functional relation between political unity and unity of culture.

The contemporary search for France is not confined to historical ontologists alone; it represents a widespread puzzlement to those who look to history to situate themselves in the world. Never before have we seen on the market so many handsome multivolume works offering the French panoramic visions of the history of their revolution, or the peasantry, or the countryside, or daily life, or even historical memories. It does not matter that, at best, most of these volumes will only be read in, not read through. Their very bulk, their representations, be they paintings, photographs, charts, or his-

6. Hervé Le Bras and Emmanuel Todd, *L'Invention de la France: Atlas anthropologique et politique* (Paris, 1981), 8–10. They make a case for a France "condemned" to racial, religious, and regional tolerance because of the heterogeneity of the population. See also Maurice Agulhon, "La Fabrication de la France: Problème et controverse," in *Anthropologie sociale et ethnologie de la France: Colloque du Centre d'ethnologie française et du Musée national des arts et traditions populaires, Paris, 19–21 novembre 1987* (Paris, 1989), 1–21.

7. Gérard Noiriel, *Le Creuset français: Histoire de l'immigration, XIXᵉ–XXᵉ siècles* (Paris, 1988), 50–67, esp. 59; Theodore Zeldin, *The French* (New York, 1983); Eugen Weber, *Peasants into Frenchmen: The Modernization of Rural France* (Stanford, 1976).

torical facts, offer readers and authors a sense of coherence, of centeredness, perhaps even a surreptitious teleology of historical destiny.

Can people really practice historical hermeneutics by plumbing the depths of a national existence and surfacing with a deeper understanding of what is France? Is such knowledge scientific; is it value-free? What can identity—or some suitable coding for that idea—mean as applied to so many and such diverse groups? Or is the attempt to come to an understanding of *the* meaning of so great and so complex a bundle of interrelated lives as are lived in France, as a way of thinking about France, as a manner of looking at France, seriously flawed? Do searches for *France* embody beliefs, values, *projets*, in short, ideologies of what France should be? Have the seekers discovered the truth before departing on the quest? Most important, finally, is there not a danger that a question about essences could kill the cultural development of which it seems so solicitous? These are the questions that started me on this investigation.

As the most newly professionalized social discipline in the years after World War I, French anthropology offers an especially useful window on the *sciences humaines* and beyond onto the modes of the mental creation of France in the society. The need socially to stabilize the new republic after its political consolidation and the task of governing a new colonial empire encouraged the development of disciplines that studied how humans whom nature had brought together organized their social existences. In the early decades of the century, both on the right (the followers of Fréderic Le Play and of Catholic social teachings) and on the left (the Durkheimians), intellectuals with no formal training in the social sciences worked to create sciences around their social visions. Because of its heterogeneous origins, wrote Jean Jamin, "ethnology found itself in an equivocal situation epistemologically, one in which ideology coincided with science, the subjective with the objective, participation with observation."[8] Jamin was speaking about one specific strand of the discipline, but his sense of the liminality of that moment applied equally to all strands, in particular to the conservative tradition.

8. Jean Jamin, "De l'humaine condition de 'Minotaure,'" in *Regards sur Minotaure,* ed. Charles Georg (Geneva, 1987), 79.

Cultural liminality is the phenomenon of crossing a cultural threshold; those who cross over suffer a deep sense of the danger, the loss, and, if successful, the accomplishment of moving from one state of being to a new one. It is an idea that Arnold Van Gennep first theorized in his work on rites of passage, but it can be expanded to include the cultural passage of France in the twentieth century. What Clifford Geertz has observed about the tensions between essentialisms of threatened historic cultures or national character or race and the drive toward modernity and cosmopolitanism in the cultures of new states describes the dialectic of French anthropology, colonial thought, and folklore studies in the years between the wars. Such transitional historical moments are dangerous to a society.

> The tension between these two impulses—to move with the tide of the present and to hold to an inherited course—gives new state nationalism its peculiar air of being at once hell-bent toward modernity and morally outraged by its manifestations. There is a certain irrationality in this. But it is more than collective derangement; it is a social cataclysm in the process of happening.[9]

For France that cataclysm, beginning around the turn of the century with the final victory of the Republic, its attack on clericalism, and the Dreyfus affair, reached a crescendo in the social struggles of the 1930s with the triumph of the Popular Front, its fall, the strange defeat of 1940, and the coming of the Vichy regime. In France the traditional impulse came from the politically conservative side, and the cosmopolitan one was the position of the left—at least some of the left in the 1930s.

However ancient reflections on a possible French identity may have been, the last decades of the nineteenth century formed an intellectual and political watershed in the quest for France. Sentiments, ideologies, even words came into intellectual use in ways that continue to operate powerfully today. First, whatever may have been the status of the *Ding-an-sich* of French culture, that moment is identified by later questers after national identity *in their theories and histories* as the turning point of a new France of disappearing peas-

9. Clifford Geertz, "After the Revolution: The Fate of Nationalism in the New States," in *The Interpretation of Cultures: Selected Essays* (New York, 1973), 234–49.

ants and threatened regionalisms. At the same time it was the period when the new colonial empire was consolidated, and questions about the relation of all those people who had just passed under French rule to the people of European France were inevitably raised. Moreover, in those years was forged the historic alliance of members of the industrial bourgeoisie and growers which refounded and stabilized the Third Republic and thereby for the first time connected a capitalist society to a republican state in an enduring fashion.[10] And because of the implantation of republican rule and, most crucially challenging to the old politics, of universal male suffrage, we witness not only the birth of a right-wing going-to-the-people on the part of disaffected monarchists and neo-monarchists, especially those in the train of the Le Playists Maurice Barrès and Charles Maurras and the larger intellectual milieu of the Action Française, but also, and not unconnected, the birth in France of the disciplines of ethnography and folklore studies.[11] From approximately the turn of the century, at the time of the Dreyfus affair, the search for French identity takes on a new integralist form, at the same time deeply cultural and politically conservative, which permits us to distinguish it from anything that came before; it was nothing less than the construction of a moral majority, when a political one was wanting. It also—the other key historical beginning—takes on a scientific mantle with the organization of these new social sciences as systematic professionalized disciplines. The new politics and the new anthropology were connected.

Geertz contends that "the pull of the indigenous tradition is felt most heavily by its appointed, and in these days rather beseiged guardians—monks, mandarins, pandits, chiefs, ulema, and so on." For the first half of this century, the French development followed this scenario. The church had lost much status by the early twentieth century; the anticlerical republic had driven back its enemy. The indigenous tradition was defended most militantly by its conservative would-be mandarins, pandits, and chiefs, by an old order attempting to hold onto its shrinking power and finally, under Vichy

10. On this theme see my *Alliance of Iron and Wheat: Origins of the New French Conservatism in the Third French Republic, 1860–1914* (Baton Rouge, 1988).

11. On how universal suffrage elicits the need for hegemonic projects, see Gérard Noiriel, *La Tyrannie du national: Le Droit d'asile en Europe, 1793–1993* (Paris, 1991), 309.

rule, to regain eroded national traditions and the social statuses they validated.

It is useful to explore the links of personality with history in this story. In some deeply embedded manner, human experience explicated in narrative, as story, satisfies in ways the most elegantly theorized social science statements cannot.[12] I think historians can very well enhance understanding of complex and murky historical phenomena, especially where intellectual history touches the study of power in society, by continuing to tell stories with people in them, as long as they remain clear in their own minds, as I have tried to be, that there are many stories, and "people" may be most safely understood as a useful heuristic device to advance the story's plot. Individuals who figure in this story—the anthropologist and politician Louis Marin, the colonial hero Marshal Lyautey, the Vietnamese radical student Nguyen Van Tao, the Socialist director of the Musée de l'Homme Paul Rivet, the folklorist Georges-Henri Rivière, and the others, some important, some just bit players in the history of the construction of conservative identity—help us to understand what the story is about. People speak discourses, after all, even if they do not necessarily invent them.

The seduction of the vision of True France is that it may be found everywhere, in every aspect of French life. That poses, of course, the problem of deconstructing an idea that is half cultural style, half political project. As a preliminary, so as not to be essentialist about an essentialism, let me not try an inappropriate feat of definition, but instead, as it were, rotate a representation of True France and describe briefly what we might see on the various facets as they appear in historical settings.

The discourse of True France employs the essentialist, determinist language of a lost or hidden authenticity that, once uncovered, yields a single, immutable national identity. The idea of France it consecrates is profoundly static and ahistorical, indeed antihistorical, for despite all vicissitudes of history—monarchy, republic, empire—a vital core persists to infuse everything and everyone with the undying if seriously threatened national character.

12. An unpublished paper by Rhys Isaacs helped me think about this issue: "Telling Ethnography: Some Meetings and Mixing of History and Anthropology" (April 1991).

This conceit is idealist in metaphysics. Its epistemology is dualistic: revealed truths dominate the spiritual realm, but it is strongly empiricist in the human sciences. Ethics are, of course, Catholic, and therefore both God-given and formalistic. In aesthetic matters, True France celebrates high culture and absolutist judgments of art. The golden age was the seventeenth century. Creativity is a deep mystery; but the worth of its artistic creations is endorsed by the (right) state.

Life, when authentically lived, is regional, rural. The social structure should be seen as hierarchical, with authority very clearly spelled out. Yet society is also tradition-laden and organic. France is a nation of patriots—or renegades. And everyone has two *pays:* each has roots in his own *petit pays* and all share the destiny of eternal, potentially greater France.

A last word about beginnings. Historians sometimes share with the partisans of the famous proof for the existence of God via the First Cause an exaggerated sense of the need to go back in time in the search for origins. Late-nineteenth-century anthropologists, colonial thinkers, and folklorists were hardly the first to pose the question of French cultural identity. Pierre Nora locates the great watershed of national identity at the French Revolution, for at that moment, he argues, there crystallized the idea of the existence of two French nations: a monarchical and a republican one.[13] Although the judgment of the contested society is surely right, the idea of a monarchical *nation* fits neither the theory nor the practice of traditional nineteenth-century monarchists, and it is not the most interesting thing about the new right of the twentieth century. I hypothesize but one nation, the republic, which at a certain moment the right attempted to redefine as its own, especially in the cultural realm. In the first fifty years of this century progressive France disputed the right's grand maneuver but accepted its definition of the cultural heritage at issue and much of its language. The new nationalism of the decades around 1900 cannot, I think, be understood as simply the renewed assertion of claims by the monarchical

13. Pierre Nora, "Nation," in *A Critical Dictionary of the French Revolution*, ed. Mona Ozouf and François Furet, trans. Arthur Goldhammer (Cambridge, Mass., 1989), 742–49. Taking a parallel line, but more cautious, is Colette Beaune, *Naissance de la nation France* (Paris, 1985), 7–11, 337–51.

nation. This vision of national identity represents something new, certainly with origins in monarchism but with claims about the True France, claims upon a republican France, more compelling than nineteenth-century monarchism could be.

One way to start a visit to a new country is to learn the language. Let us begin, then, with a look at the vocabulary and idioms of this metaphysical France. For this purpose the career of Louis Marin, one of the most powerful figures both in the new conservative *sciences humaines* and in interwar French politics, can instruct us. How did Marin describe the essential France?

CHAPTER ONE

Integral Culture: Louis Marin and the Conservative School, 1890–1940

W e might get a first sense of the anthropologist-politician Louis Marin by knowing his totems. In the course of excavations for a building near his apartment in the Latin Quarter the workmen unearthed the skeleton of an ancient Gaul, a warrior perhaps. "The engineer," reported Marin, "knew my anthropological tastes"; he gave Marin the skull. Upon measurement, its proportions turned out to be exactly those of Marin's skull. There was a comforting sense of the racial continuity of French life over the centuries in those numbers. He placed the skull in his study between busts of Joan of Arc, the heroine of the new right cultic nationalism that had came out of his native Lorraine at the end of the century, and Saint Louis, patron of scholarship and champion of Christian might in the Crusades. He could look up at the skull and the heads as he sat at his desk preparing his weekly lectures on anthropology, conferring with political colleagues in the Fédération Républicaine, studying ways to strengthen and expand the French colonial empire, preparing his parliamentary speeches on the danger on the left, German aggressiveness, and the needs of his Lorraine homeland.[1]

1. Gaëtan Sanvoisin, "Le Parlement et la menace extérieure: L'Oeuvre de M. Louis Marin," *Revue hebdomadaire,* 41 (27 February 1932), 473–93.

Louis Marin, the head of the two leading French anthropology societies, president for many years of the most powerful colonial society, and chief, if not of a tribe of Gauls, at least of the major far-right party in the Chamber, embodied in his historical personality the major qualities of the far right of the Third Republic in the interwar years. His career offers us a paradigm of that political and intellectual right before its simultaneous fulfillment and dissolution in the Vichy regime. Most important, it introduces us to the master discourse *and* the political blueprint for the construction of an essentialist French national identity promoted by Marin and his friends in the first half of this century. Marin spoke and wrote of his vision of the complex modern nation of the twentieth century as if it were a large village community held together by a common faith, family, habitual obligations, and deference. His work, his institutional power, his political voice challenged opponents who, both in the realm of the social sciences and in political life, sought to win France to a modern democratic consciousness and practice. In public life and in the *sciences humaines* he spoke for the authentic and eternal France.

The Field

The literature on the proximate origins of French *sciences humaines* in the 1890s and the decades thereafter describes the epic struggles of Emile Durkheim and his circle with philosophical enemies and bureaucratic prejudice in the faculties and the world of the Latin Quarter to create a new socially conscious sociology for a reestablished republic. Anthony Giddens, for example, writes of the Durkheimians' opposition to the "strongly entrenched forces on the Right," and their dedication to studying ways of transcending "the traditional forms of society which the conservatives defended."[2] But who these rightists were is not always so clear.

2. Anthony Giddens, *Emile Durkheim* (Harmondsworth: Penguin, 1978), 14. It is generally understood that "Durkheim felt that it was his central task to contribute to the development of a new French republican moral order": Lewis A. Coser, "Durkheim's Conservatism and Its Implications for His Sociological Theory," in *Emile Durkheim, 1858–1917: A Collection of Essays with Translations and a Bibliography*, ed. Kurt H.

Aside from cursory, dismissive references to the school of Fréderic Le Play, we learn almost nothing about any rival schools of social science. From the Durkheim hagiography we could not guess that in the first decades of the century there flourished in France organized and active *sciences humaines*—with societies, annual meetings, and periodicals—dedicated to studying ways of keeping alive a conservative vision of French identity.[3] Nor do we learn the reasons for the ultimate eclipse and disappearance of this social science tradition in the years after World War II. We know enough about the history of social ideas to eschew the explanation that somehow the best ideas won out.[4]

The intellectual and political career of Louis Marin, then, affords us the opportunity to explore the thought and practice of one of the gatekeepers of the French conservative social science. In this instance at issue is the development and transformation of French

---

Wolff (Columbus, 1960), 213. Steven Lukes, *Emile Durkheim: His Life and Work, a Historical and Critical Study*, 2d ed. (Stanford, 1985), esp. 497–529, has little on this dominant conservative tradition. See further Ernest Wallwork, *Durkheim: Morality and Milieu* (Cambridge, Mass., 1972), 151–59, where Wallwork discusses ethical theories that rivaled those of Durkheim but refers neither to works by authors Durkheim opposed nor to the historical setting for his concern about ethics.

3. Victor Karady puts the apogee of the Durkheimian tradition in the 1930s, but points out its marginality in French academic life even then. The creative heyday of the first generation of Durkheim's circle (he died in 1917) was the 1920s and 1930s, it is true. When Georges Davy retired from his post at the Sorbonne in 1955, the reign of the first generation ended. But it was after the war, in the 1950s, that Karady believes that "all the major developments in the discipline that were realized since the beginning of the century came to fruition." Understandably focusing on new theories and the winners, he has nothing to say about the other tradition except that up to World War II its appeal was "limited" to the upper classes of the provinces and the conservative bourgeoisie, with strongholds in the law faculties and certain institutions such as the Ecole Libre des Sciences Politiques! See Victor Karady, "The Prehistory of Present-Day French Sociology (1917–1957)," in *French Sociology: Rupture and Renewal since 1968*, ed. Charles C. Lemert (New York, 1981), 33–47. See further the two special issues of the *Revue Française de Sociologie*, 17 (1976) and 20 (1979), devoted to Durkheim and the Durkheimians, and Claude Lévi-Strauss's 1945 overview, "French Sociology," in *Twentieth-Century Sociology*, ed. Georges Gurvitch and Wilbert E. Moore (New York, 1945).

4. See Victor Karady, "The Durkheimians in Academe: A Reconsideration," in *The Sociological Domain: The Durkheimians and the Founding of French Sociology*, ed. Philippe Besnard (Cambridge, 1983), 72. In *Scientific Knowledge and Sociological Theory* (London, 1974), Barry Barnes is, I think, on the mark with his suggestion that "if alleged scientific knowledge is mobilized by intellectuals and used to attack the legit-

anthropology—divided in France before World War II between *anthropologie*, the study of what in Anglo-American science is called physical anthropology, and *ethnographie*, systematic description of the life of extra-European tribal cultures—in the first half of the twentieth century and the place of that group of disciplines in the elaboration of a conservative idea of French identity.

The theoretical contents of Marin's anthropology are of little concern to us. As we shall see, his theoretical endeavors were trivial efforts, primarily post-Dreyfus neo-conservative ideas organized in Le Playist structures. Rather Marin was the genius of the intellectual, organizational, and political promotion of the conservative essentialist discourse in anthropology. Propitiously, because he functioned in a leadership role both in public life and in his area of anthropology, Marin's biography permits us to follow the dialectic of values and action, scholarship and state policies, ideology and outcomes in that discourse and its practices.[5]

The little that has been published about him treats either one or the other of two Marins: the active conservative politician or the leader of a notable tradition of French social science. Historians of French anthropology have recently become interested in such organizations as the Société d'Anthropologie, the organization founded by Paul Broca, and the Société d'Ethnographie, France's leading prewar ethnographic society, started by Claude Bernard.[6] The re-

---

imation of institutions they seek to undermine, opposing pressures will be generated. Their own mythology will be attacked in turn, and that of their opponents will be elaborated, supplemented, and more heavily defended. Such intellectual jousting can never result in any 'real' outcome, determined by the 'inherent worth' of the ideas involved and the positions defended, or by what 'science really says,'" (p. 150). For an excellent case study of the vital linkages between the development of French physics and politics, including the role of political ideology, in the period under study here, see Spencer R. Weart, *Scientists in Power* (Cambridge, Mass., 1979), esp. vii–ix.

5. In a most uncommon gesture, soon after the Marin Papers were deposited at the Archives Nationales, Madame Fernande Marin opened them to qualified scholars to use without special permission, thereby making available a wonderful source for the study of social science organizations and conservative politics in the Third Republic. I will hereafter cite them as A.N. 317 AP.

6. Donald Bender, "The Development of French Anthropology," *Journal of the History of the Behavioral Sciences*, 1 (1965), 139–51; Michael Hammond, "Anthropology as a Weapon of Social Combat in Late-Nineteenth-Century France," *Journal of the History of the Behavioral Sciences*, 16 (1980), 118–32; Elizabeth A. Williams, "An-

search on the role of the cultural sciences in the management of the colonial empire is well under way.[7] In all these spheres Louis Marin appears as a leader or intellectual spokesman. From 1920 he served as president of the Société d'Ethnographie, from 1923 as director of the Ecole d'Anthropologie, from 1906 as president of the Fédération Régionaliste Française, in 1930 (elected by 233 votes out of 244 cast) as president of the Société de Statistique, and from 1925 until his death in 1960 as president of the Société de Géographie Commerciale de Paris.

Yet the other Louis Marin is better known. Deputy from Nancy and sometime cabinet minister, friend and political ally of the powerful industrialist François de Wendel, in the late 1920s and 1930s he led the far-right Fédération Républicaine, which spawned fascists without itself going that extra distance. In the last hour he redeemed himself politically by rejecting collaboration with the Germans and finally joining another French patriot, Charles de Gaulle, in London.[8]

How did these scholarly concerns connect with his political ones, if they did? Alternatively, was there anything in either the method of Marin and his scholarly collaborators or the content of their anthropological interests which suggests a political agenda? Fernande Marin, his widow, argued that "for Louis Marin, ethnography, so-

---

thropological Institutions in Nineteenth-Century France," *Isis*, 76 (1985), 331–48; and "The Science of Man: Anthropological Thought and Institutions in Nineteenth-Century France" (Ph.D. diss., Indiana University, 1983), 130–75; Terry N. Clark, *Prophets and Patrons: The French University System and the Emergence of the Social Sciences* (Cambridge, Mass., 1973); Joy Harvey, "Evolutionism Transformed: Positivists and Materialists in the Société d'Anthropologie de Paris from the Second Empire to the Third Republic," in *The Wider Domain of Evolutionary Thought*, ed. D. Oldroyd and I. Langham (Dordrecht, 1983), 289–310; Francis Schiller, *Paul Broca: Founder of French Anthropology, Explorer of the Brain* (Berkeley, 1979), 130–35. See esp. the valuable work of Marc Knobel, "De l'étude en France des types judaïques et négroïdes (1930–1945)," contribution to the round table Racisme et ethnologies européennes. Les Recherches africanistes européennes de 1920 à 1945: Une Réflexion épistémologique, Paris, 16–18 March 1988, mimeo.

7. See, e.g., Mohamed C. Sahli, *Décoloniser l'histoire: Introduction à l'histoire du Maghreb* (Paris, 1965); P. Lucas and J. C. Vatin, *L'Algérie des Anthropologues* (Paris, 1982), 11–86.

8. The important study of this political side of Marin's career is William D. Irvine, *French Conservatism in Crisis: The Republican Federation of France in the 1930s* (Baton Rouge, 1979); for the end phase see 159–230.

ciology were the bases for his future political activity," and that his politics informed and guided his scholarly activities.[9] Those conservative political convictions oriented Marin toward an especially unfruitful variety of cultural˙science which came under attack from progressive-minded social scientists in the 1920s and 1930s and finally expired with the death of Vichy, its last crutch and refuge. The political disgrace of association with the conservatism of the last days of the Third Republic and the consequent exhaustion of its remaining symbolic capital killed off Marin's kind of social science tradition more than narrow methods or meager fruits. As we will see, however, he and his friends—Le Playists and Maurrasians—kept alive both intellectually and politically the ideology of a True France and left it as a legacy of cultural prejudice in contemporary life.

The Lorraine Homeland

Born in the village of Faulx on 7 February 1871, the year of Prussia's defeat of France and the annexation of much of his natal province by the German Empire, Marin—like his friend and contemporary Maurice Barrès—grew up with a keen sense of loyalty to his French Lorraine homeland and an unrelieved sense of the dangers to its borders and its French culture.[10] His mother died two weeks after his birth. His father, an attorney, remarried six years later, and the child lived first with his father's sisters and then briefly in the Marin household while attending the village school. In 1881 the elder Marin decided that his son should be sent off to the prestigious Catholic Collège de la Malgrange, outside of Nancy. There the young student met and befriended François de Wendel, future powerful industrialist and supporter of far-right movements. In this last year at Malgrange Marin became friendly, too, with le père Schwalm, a young Dominican, who first introduced him to the social ideas of Fréderic Le Play, an intellectual influence that would hold

---

9. Fernande Marin, *Louis Marin, 1871–1960: Homme d'état, philosophe et savant* (Paris, 1973), 122.

10. Unless otherwise specified, biographical information is from ibid., 47–87.

Marin for the rest of his life. Something of the nature of that influence may be gathered from the title of the work Le Play published in the wake of the Prussian defeat and the Paris Commune: *L'Organisation de la famille, selon le vrai modèle signalé par l'histoire de toutes les races et de tous les temps* (The organization of the family, according to the true model demonstrated throughout the entire history of all the races). The young man was learning to think about social institutions and social organizations as capable of being true or false.[11]

From the *collège* he moved to Saint-Sigisbert, the section of Malgrange that prepared students for the entrance exams to the *grandes écoles*, the special institutions of higher learning where an elite was trained for careers in the higher reaches of public administration and education. Marin, however, remained in Nancy to study for his *license ès lettres*, which he obtained in 1890, and the exams for a law degree, which he passed that same year. As a student Marin went out out into the streets to demonstrate with other student supporters of General Georges Boulanger in Nancy. In later years he recalled his first memory of active involvement in politics as his work with Maurice Barrès in the campaign on behalf of the general's political rise.[12]

---

11. See André François-Poncet, "Notice sur la vie et les travaux de Louis Marin, 1871–1960," in *Institut de France, 1964* (Paris, 1964), 8. On Le Play see his works, in particular the influential *Les Ouvriers européens* (Paris, 1855), *L'Organisation de la famille, selon le vrai modèle signalé par l'histoire de toutes les races et de tous les temps* (Tours, 1871), *La Paix sociale après le désastre* (Tours, 1871), *La Réforme en Europe et le salut en France* (Tours, 1876), and *Instruction sur la méthode d'observation dite des monographies de famille* (Paris, 1862; new ed. rev. A. J. Focillon, 1887), published in English as "Instructions in the Observation of Social Facts According to the Le Play Method," trans. C. A. Ellwood, *American Journal of Sociology*, 2 (1897), 662–79. For secondary works one may begin with Catherine Bodard Silver, *Frédéric Le Play: On Family, Work, and Social Change* (Chicago, 1982), esp. her most valuable introductory essay, 3–134. For an attempt to situate Le Play's work politically by a sympathizer see L. Dimier, *Les Maîtres de la contre-révolution au dix-neuvième siècle: Leçons données à l'Institut d'Action Française, Chair Rivarol* (Paris, 1907), 255–78. Also Fernand Auburtin, *Frédéric Le Play d'après lui-même: Vie, méthode, doctrine* (Paris, 1906); Edmond Demolins, "L'Etat de la science social," *Science Sociale*, n.s. 15 (1893), 5–20; Edmond Demolins, Robert Pinot, and Paul de Rousiers, "La Méthode sociale," *Science Sociale*, n.s. 1 (1904), 1–92; and the volume of studies celebrating the centenary of Le Play's Société d'Economie Sociale, Roger Grand, ed., *Recueil d'etudes sociales publié à la mémoire de Frédéric Le Play* (Paris, 1956).

12. Marin, *Louis Marin*, 94–96; Sanvoisin, "Le Parlement et la menace extérieure," 476–77.

Paris

In 1890, like many ambitious and talented provincials before him, Marin moved to Paris. In the capital he soon made the acquaintance of Edmond Demolins, a follower of Le Play. In 1899 Demolins founded a school, the Ecole des Roches, near Verneuil in the Eure, to carry on the teachings of the master. Demolins introduced him to another young Le Playist just embarking on a career as one of the leading organic intellectuals of French industrialists, Robert Pinot, the future secretary general of the Comité des Forges.[13] In the rich intellectual climate of the fin de siècle, Marin developed the qualities of a polymath. In these early years he read widely and deeply in the new outpouring of far-right literature: Leconte de Lisle, Paul Bourget, Alphonse Daudet, Charles Maurras, and Maurice Barrès, whose *Leurs Figures* he reread often. He recalled also the pleasures of Guy de Maupassant and Anatole France, the latter, perversely, a favorite of Charles Maurras, too.

Marin even tried his hand at fiction as a means of exposing the evils of society and promoting good social values. In 1905 he published a short didactic novel depicting the horrors engendered by the vacuum of moral education. Echoing the anti-Semitism that had grown on the far right in the wake of the Dreyfus affair, *Le Triomphe du vice: Etude réaliste et sociale* portrays one Ismaël Jacob, a small-town moneylender, as "an old scoundrel, an unspeakable usurer" who pursued his debtors relentlessly and without pity. The moneylender's deepest convictions were (in English in the text), "business are [sic] business, les affaires sont les affaires."[14] Marin pursued his fascination with other (non-French) cultures in formal studies, too.

Rejecting the "new Sorbonne," as rightist intellectuals termed what they believed to be the overly theoretical, Germanized institution,[15]

13. François-Poncet, "Notice sur la vie," 8.

14. Louis Marin, *Le Triomphe du vice: Etude réaliste et sociale* (Paris, 1905), 105. It should be pointed out that after World War II Marin worked closely with Jewish members of organizations to which he belonged. His papers from that period contain several letters from individuals with Jewish surnames expressing confidence and friendly feelings toward him. See A.N. 317 AP, cartons 170 and 171.

15. Henri Peyre, "Durkheim: The Man, His Time, and His Intellectual Background," in *Emile Durkheim: 1858–1917*, ed. Kurt H. Wolff (New York, 1979), 3–31, esp. 14, evokes the moment in French intellectual culture and the ideological currents.

he enrolled in the Ecole Libre des Sciences Politiques to continue his legal studies. The next year he was "received" at the conservative Catholic social research and reform organization that Le Play had founded, the Société d'Economie Sociale. He also attended classes at the Ecole Pratique des Hautes Etudes, Broca's Ecole d'Anthropologie, the Ecole du Louvre, and the Ecole des Langues Orientales. He began to participate actively in the meetings of the Société d'Ethnographie.[16] Although he brought his legal studies to a successful close in 1892 with his admission to the bar, Marin's heart lay rather with his ethnographical studies and with politics.

When opportunity permitted, he pursued his anthropological education and engaged in a particularly gentlemanly style of research. Marin took trips all over the world to study rural life in cultures at all levels of development. His travels constituted a kind of Grand Tour *cum* research trip of the sort Fréderic Le Play had taken to compile information on the life of workers in industrial societies. He stayed with the local inhabitants when he could and took extensive notes on their customs, mores, technologies, and languages, great compendia of untheorized social facts—the stuff of late-nineteenth-century French ethnography. In the ten years between 1891 and 1901 he and his friend Georges Ducrocq visited Germany, Algeria and Tunisia, Siberia, Hungary, Romania, Poland, Russia, Scandinavia, England and Ireland, Turkestan, Central Asia, and China. In 1901 he took the Trans-Siberian Railroad across Russia and then proceeded on to Mongolia, Manchuria, China again, and Korea.[17] Rather than making Marin "cosmopolitan"—a negative, possibly Jewish trait in the judgment of his ultranationalist friends in late-nineteenth-century France—these voyages reinforced his Lorraine and French patriotism. Indeed, in public life he came to be known above all for his fierce and unwavering loyalty to place and to kind.[18] These qualities appeared both in his teaching and in his scholarly contributions to the social sciences. In these early years

16. Marin, *Louis Marin*, 99–107. Marin published his accounts of some of these study journeys: *Voyage de 1901 en Russie, Sibérie, Mongolie, Mandchourie, Chine et Corée* (Paris, 1911). After his death Madame Marin published additional materials: Louis Marin, *Voyage de 1899 en Orient, Constantinople, Caucase, Arménie, Asie Centrale, Turkestan, Russie et Chine* (Paris, 1978).

17. Marin, *Louis Marin*, 142.

18. "Infinitely the patriot," according to the sarcastic judgment of one contemporary, Emmanuel Berl, *La Politique et les partis* (Paris, 1932), 32.

Marin was preparing himself for his future role as a modern-day French J. G. Fichte, the professor searching for the peculiarity of the people, the chauvinist denouncing the enemy who had invaded the homeland. But unlike Fichte the philosopher, Marin searched for the essence of France in anthropology.

Les Sciences Humaines in 1900

At the turn of the century the young nationalist from Lorraine came upon the French anthropological scene at a moment of crisis in the development of both the discipline and republican politics.[19] The Dreyfus affair, which began, we should recall, when General Staff officers thought Captain Alfred Dreyfus's Jewish origins a plausible ground for suspecting him of treason to France, was deeply troubling public life.

The issue of identity played a role, too, in the troubled organizations for social studies. The Le Playist tradition as carried on in the organization he had founded, the Société d'Economie Sociale, and the circle of contributors to the review *Réforme Sociale* had begun to splinter and weaken immediately upon the death of Le Play in 1882. One wing joined the Musée Social at its founding in 1895 and there both undertook morally informed empirical investigations and mooted moderate schemes to improve the lot of workers and peasants in ways short of interfering with either the labor market or the privileged relation between employer and employee.[20] A more investigative and less socially activist Le Playist splinter group around the journal *Science Sociale* continued until the death of its leading light and financial patron, Henri de Tourville, in 1904.[21] With as yet

19. For this turning point, which might be considered the moment of the "second founding" of the Third Republic, see Herman Lebovics, "La Grande Dépression: Aux origines d'un nouveau conservatisme français, 1880–1896," *Francia*, 13 (1987), 435–45.

20. On the Musée Social, see the excellent study by Sanford Elwitt, *The Third Republic Defended: Bourgeois Reform in France, 1880–1914* (Baton Rouge, 1986), 155–69.

21. On Henri de Tourville, see Terry N. Clark, "Henri de Tourville," in *International Encyclopedia of the Social Sciences* (New York, 1968). For politics and theoretical differences in the scholarly society, see Clark, *Prophets and Patrons*, 104–11.

no academic recognition and organizationally divided into rival bodies—the Société d'Anthropologie, which sought explanations for cultural differences in physiological evidence, and the Société d'Ethnographie, which encouraged nontheoretical descriptive studies—French anthropology was in disarray. The founders had died (Bernard in 1878, Broca in 1880) and their successors were unable to carry on at the same level of creativity or indeed academic visibility. For two decades after Broca's death the Société d'Anthropologie tore itself apart in disputes over evolution, materialism, and political persuasion; only the death of the chief rivals at the end of the century brought the turmoil to a halt.[22]

At this point the Société d'Ethnographie, without the reflected prestige of the Ecole de Médecine, which hosted the other organization, began to gain a reputation for amateurism and nonseriousness.[23] It also took on an openly conservative coloration. In his last book a leader and one of its founders, the linguist Léon de Rosny, linked ethnography directly with the contemporary explosion of rightist French nationalism. He still wanted to hold to the ultimate goal of the universal fraternity of the world's peoples, he averred, but now he privileged national renewal as the first step in that direction.[24]

In effect, both disciplines, as they approached the turn of the century, were torn by disputes over the object of their researches and, in a wider sense, over the essential features of French society which needed to be better understood and, if necessary, to be shored up by social policy. This was the moment, too, where the Le Playists

22. See Hammond, "Anthropology as a Weapon," 128–29; Williams, "Anthropological Institutions," 337. Gabriel de Mortillet, Broca's left-leaning successor as head of the Ecole d'Anthropologie, wished to employ research to advance social causes dear to him, such as anticlericalism. He died in 1898; with him expired the radical tendency in the school and movement. On Mortillet, see Williams, "Science of Man," 231–78; Bernard Kalaora, "Paul Descamps, ou La Sociologie leplaysienne à l'épreuve du Portugal de Salazar," *Gradhiva*, 6 (1989), 50–64; Bernard Kalaora and A. Savoye, *Les Inventeurs oubliés: Fréderic Le Play et ses continuateurs aux origines des sciences sociales* (Paris, 1989).

23. See Léonce Manouvrier, "La Société d'Anthropologie de Paris depuis sa fondation, 1859–1909," *Bulletins et Mémoires de la Société d'Anthropologie de Paris*, 11th ser., 10 (1909), 309; Williams, "Anthropological Institutions," 338.

24. Léon de Rosny, *Traité d'ethnographie théorique et descriptive*, 2 vols. (Paris, 1900, 1902), 1:33–35.

began their investigations of the social life of the colonial empire.[25] As we would expect in the case of such passionate commitments in a new field, a major consequence was intellectual and organizational fragmentation.[26] It was at this moment and into this field of petty contending factions that Durkheim and the Durkheimians attempted to move with their multifaceted "sociology" for a progressive republic.[27] This was the intellectual milieu in which Marin found a place in fin-de-siècle Paris.

First Social Agenda

By 1895 he had proved himself sufficiently proficient in his anthropological studies to be invited to lecture on ethnography—Marin was one of the first academic lecturers on this subject in France—at two important strongholds of Le Playist social science, the Collège Libre des Sciences Sociales and the Ecole Libre des Sciences Poli-

25. See Elwitt, *Third Republic Defended*, 82–83.

26. Elizabeth Williams counted nine or ten groups or organizations that conducted anthropological work on the eve of World War I: there were remnants of Gabriel de Mortillet's group in both the Société and Ecole d'Anthropologie; Léonce Manouvrier's people at his laboratory at the Ecole Pratique des Hautes Etudes; the newly founded Institut Français d'Anthropologie; the Institut de Paléontologie Humaine, which the prince of Monaco encouraged; the Muséum d'Histoire Naturelle; Rosnay's ethnographic Alliance; Ernest-Théodore Hamy's Musée d'Ethnographie; and the new Institut Ethnographique. In the politics of the field, however, few could exert directional force. The attempt to create an umbrella organization for both anthropology and ethnography with the founding in 1911 of the Institut Français d'Anthropologie gained few supporters. See Williams, "Science of Man," 270–75.

27. From 1887 Durkheim had taught social science and education in Bordeaux. He published his dissertation and chief work, *The Division of Labor*, in 1893, *Rules of Sociology* in 1895, and *Suicide* in 1897. With the beginning of the journal *L'Année Sociologique* in 1897 it becomes appropriate to speak of a Durkheimian school. Finally, in 1902, after fifteen years in the provinces, he was invited to join the pedagogical faculty at the Sorbonne. Giddens suggests that hostility aroused by his theoretical and political views delayed his call to Paris: *Emile Durkheim*, 20. This judgment is correct, but it can now be nuanced. There were two kinds of conservative responses to what he was doing: to be sure, individuals in the educational establishment were troubled by his leftist republicanism, but as Marin and his associates found too, the structure of French higher education was not hospitable to the new social sciences. On this second kind of conservatism see Clark, *Prophets and Patrons*, esp. 162–95.

tiques.[28] According to surviving course listings, between 1895 and 1911 he lectured on methods of ethnographic research, social geography and national psychology, methods of detailed examination and description, survivals of earlier patterns in the French provinces, the physical anthropology of Western Europe, the family in Western civilization, and the relation of ethnic and social studies to the practices of morality, among other topics.[29] Between 1895 and 1923 at the Ecole d'Anthropologie, which for a generation after its founding in 1876 was the only center for the study of physical anthropology in France, Marin regularly offered evening courses for Parisian primary school teachers training for higher degrees. In other series offered there Marin lectured on themes as topical as the crisis of Western civilization (1929), and after World War II on the contemporary crisis of traditions (1950) and the ethnic philosophies of the totalitarian regimes.[30] His scholarly lectures and articles manifested the same conservative patriotism, with the focus always on the maintenance of culturally conservative institutions.

In 1908 Marin offered the Twenty-seventh Congress of the Le Playist Société d'Economie Sociale his views on "the depopulation of the countryside and the return to the land," a domestic concern that, along with the Social Question, was most vexing to contemporary conservative social scientists. He had spoken several times in the past before this conservative social reform society dedicated to maintaining the vitality of such moral guides as the family, country life, and religious practice.[31] Indeed, as he reminded his auditors, he had made his first appearance as president of the Fédération Régionaliste Française to argue for the cause of French regionalism.[32]

28. For an argument as to the widespread academic and intellectual influence of Le Playist teachings in the late nineteenth century, see the article, admittedly by a follower of Le Play, Pierre du Maroussem, "Soixante Années d'enquêtes et de doctrine," in a journal of the movement, La Réforme Sociale, 73 (1917), 37–73. See further Clark, Prophets and Patrons, 104–21.

29. A.N., 317 AP, carton 196; Marin, Louis Marin, 218.

30. Marin, Louis Marin, 212–24. In the course of this work Marin imbued several generations of teachers with his views on the cultural sciences.

31. On the history of this Le Playist organization, see Elwitt, Third Republic Defended, 26–38.

32. Marin assumed that post in 1903. On this organization, which united individuals interested simply in preserving what survived of the local cultures of France

The regionalist movement is concentrating its efforts on the countryside: by institutional means, by promoting changes in rural social
practices, and by encouraging new legislation, it aspires to bring people
back to the land, to keep them there, and, the better to accomplish the
task, to multiply the resources available to our countryside.

But especially now Marin felt more serious thinking was
needed.[33] To be sure, he remarked, there was ample public
awareness of the problem. The newspapers, reviews, and books
were full of tales and lamentations about the terrible fate of country
people transplanted to the cities. But the nonspecialists of the everyday press "cannot structure their reflections, cannot organize their
ideas in systematic form, cannot manage in an orderly fashion to
study and logically articulate all the questions touching this return to
the fields." Using the term that the right then preferred to refer
to the peasantry, Marin saw "the rural democracy" improving economic life on the land by means of its associations, rural credit
institutions, and cooperatives. In his capacity as president of the
Fédération Régionaliste Marin urged the Société d'Economie Sociale
to study and work to do its share of this task, so crucial for the
survival of the France they all loved.[34]

What was needed above all, Marin argued, was theoretical direction in the investigations of what was happening. He liked the ideas
that the former Opportunist premier Jules Méline developed in his
recently published *Retour à la terre* (1905). In this book, which was

---

with opponents of modernity and of the republic's efforts to create a national culture,
see Thiébaut Flory, *Le Mouvement régionaliste français: Sources et développement* (Paris,
1966). The name of Frédéric Mistral, leader of the Provençal revival, is only the most
famous in the movement.

33. See the fascinating reports on the conservatives' perception of the flight from
the land by Urbain Guérin, Le Playist researcher and librarian of the Musée Social,
delivered to the General Assembly of the Société des Agriculteurs de France in 1894
and 1895, in *Bulletin de la Société des Agriculteurs de France*, 25 (1894), 235–42, and 26
(1895), 150–53. See further J. Guillou, "L'Emigration des campagnes vers les villes"
(thèse de droit, Caen, 1905), and Herman Lebovics, *The Alliance of Iron and Wheat:
Origins of the New Conservatism in the Third French Republic, 1860–1914* (Baton Rouge,
1988), chap. 4.

34. Louis Marin, "Le Dépeuplement des campagnes et le retour aux champs:
Communication faite au xxviie congrès de la Société d'Economie Sociale," *Réforme
Sociale*, 16 September 1908, 6–7, 14.

reissued several times, Méline urged immediate state intervention to improve rural life to keep the peasants from continuing their out-migration and even to encourage the repatriation of urban workers to the countryside. To the mind of the former conservative premier, a return to the soil was a necessary policy for France, "for its tendency is to maintain the equilibrium of the country, both socially and politically; it serves to protect us from the troubles which result from the too exclusive development of manufacture."[35] Of course, both Méline and Marin understood "too exclusive development of manufacture" to mean worker radicalism, but they also meant the threat to regional uniqueness and variety and to the continuation of rural patterns of custom, morality, and hierarchy.

Even in his activities in the Société de Statistique Marin focused on issues important to national, indeed nationalist, politics. Statistics, he was persuaded, not only were useful for evaluating and manipulating cultural data but were especially valuable for establishing precise and extensive data on the human resources at the disposal of France in its overseas possessions, and on their most efficacious use. It would be valuable, he argued in a lecture before this body, to know with some accuracy the number of French people living in the colonial possessions and something about the populations under French rule. But even more, statistical studies, he believed, could yield valuable information on the strengths and weaknesses of the metropolitan authority not just in the economic realm but socially and politically.[36] After World War I he was especially eager for refined data on wartime damages and losses to France to serve as a solid basis for French claims on the German enemy for restitution.[37]

---

35. Jules Méline, *Retour à la terre* (Paris, 1905). I have used the wording of Justin McCarthy's translation, *Return to the Land* (London, 1907), 220–21. For more on Méline's work, first as minister of agriculture and then as premier, to create a stable conservative republic, see my *Alliance of Iron and Wheat*, 1–3; and on his social agenda for stabilizing French society, chap. 7.

36. These views, presented in a lecture before the Société de Statistique, may be found in the *Revue de l'Union du Commerce et de l'Industrie*, March 1916.

37. See the Preface to Edmond Michel, *Les Dommages de guerre de la France et leur réparation* (Paris, 1932), the basic ideas of which Michel first worked out (and Marin heard) soon after the war in a paper given at the Société de Statistique de Paris, "La Réparation des dommages de guerre, contribution à l'étude des dommages des guerre (suite), communication faite à la Société de Statistique de Paris, 21 février

Marin wrote, too, on the need for educational reforms that would emphasize practical and moral training in the service of cultural integrity. In 1922 he criticized the domination of the dead classical languages in French secondary schools and championed their replacement by the "mother tongue," here meaning French, for the sake of strengthening what Marin was already calling "the national culture." Here Marin's thinking showed the influence of the *Psychologie de l'education* of Gustave Le Bon, with whom he was in frequent contact in this period.[38]

After he had become sufficiently prominent in Parisian intellectual and political life—approximately after World War I—he began to appear regularly at Le Bon's weekly intellectual luncheons, where the social theorist served his distinguished guests lavish meals and directed the flow of conversation in an effort to spread his own ideas among the elite members of French society. These *déjeuners* put Marin in regular contact with the leading figures in literature, the sciences, politics, and diplomacy on the republican right. They were an efficacious means for him—always a gregarious spirit—to bridge the distance between the sciences and the realms of public life in which he was concerned.[39] Marin saw his methods of anthropological inquiry, then, as tools to render architects' drawings of conservative moral orders both for France and for colonial societies. He rooted his approach in a tradition of ideological social inquiry, a mode of investigation that paradoxically combined the most narrow of em-

---

1923": Marin, *Louis Marin*, 229. At the Congrès International de Géographie Economique et Commerciale in 1900, when a German academic participant questioned the value of statistical studies in economic geography and called for more historical and specific investigations, Marin turned the ensuing debate about method into a national confrontation. He angrily challenged the German's arguments from the floor and moved a resolution against his thesis. See *Procès verbaux, congrès international de géographie économique et commerciale, 27–31 August 1900*, ed. Georges Foucart (Paris, 1901), 44–46.

38. Louis Marin, *La Nécessité en France d'un enseignement secondaire fondé sur la langue maternelle et la culture nationale à l'exclusion des langues mortes* (Paris, 1922); Robert A. Nye, *The Origins of Crowd Psychology: Gustave Le Bon and the Crisis of Mass Democracy in the Third Republic* (London and Beverly Hills, 1975), 161.

39. Nye, *Origins of Crowd Psychology*, 83–85. Le Bon hoped by his luncheons to overcome the disadvantage of having no formal connection to the academic world. For a list of those who attended—truly an impressive assemblage of remarkable and powerful persons—see ibid., 113n.

piricisms in ethnographic investigation with a concern for maintaining conservative institutions.

The *Table d'Analyse en Ethnographie*

To understand Marin's method it is important here to recall that French conservative thought characteristically embraced methodologies aimed at eliciting factual information while positing ethical norms drawn from both secular conservative tradition and Catholicism. Inspired by Auguste Comte, Charles Maurras, for example, worked with the notion of an "organized empiricism" (*l'empiricisme organisateur*), which would result in our "putting the happiness of the past to the profit of a future that all wellborn spirits desire for their nation."[40] From Father Schwalm and Le Play's followers Marin had learned to value an applied social science that rejected the deductive and socially critical theorizing of radical social analysts in the mode of the Enlightenment rationalists and the Revolution for ideas that were at the same time descriptive and tradition-maintaining.

In 1935 Marin's friends and students feted him for his forty-two years of devotion to the teaching of ethnography. The intellectual leaders of the republican right of the Third Republic or the offspring who carried on for them gathered to honor one of their most powerful and visible spokesmen. Jacques Pinot, nephew of Robert, who had led the Comité des Forges, was there, as were P. Le Play, grandson of Frédéric; Pierre Lyautey, nephew of the great figure of French colonialism; René Verneau, recently replaced by Paul Rivet as head of the ethnology museum; Jean Charles-Brun, founder of the Fédération Régionaliste; and representatives of the Playist Société d'Economie Sociale and of the Institut Catholique, to name the most significant.

In his address of thanks Marin reflected upon his spiritual and scientific itinerary. The ideas of Le Play, he testified, had been "the [most] profound inspiration for us." He recalled that he had been

40. François Bourricaud, *Le Retour de la Droit* (Paris, 1986), 143.

drawn to the Fédération Régionaliste, for example, because of its interest in gathering and preserving knowledge of provincial life and its role in correcting for the too-rapid march of progress and the introduction of foreign ideas to France, a "reaction especially against the zealots, the parties, and Marxist and internationalist doctrines." In his life politics and ethnography had been his two concerns, he told his friends. Morality guides politics into correct paths; ethnography shows us how other civilizations have solved parallel problems, and gives us new ideas to guide our moral decisions. In his own writings he had kept distinct *ethnography*, which, however usable in generating normative ideas, was itself descriptive and value-free, and *ethnology*, which—he had his left intellectual opponents in mind—too often theorized ethnographic data beyond reasonable limits.[41]

The scientific instrument that Marin expected to contribute most to the development of methodology and of theory was an ethnographic questionnaire he had begun to develop in 1897 and had continued to elaborate. This method of eliciting information to inform social policy proposals was a common feature of nineteenth-century social investigation.[42] Its empiricist value-free format appealed especially to conservative social investigators of the late century. Tourville had devised an ethnographic questionnaire he called "La Nomenclature," which was current when Marin began his studies in Paris and which was probably the model for Marin's own first effort.

The most elaborate version of his *Questionnaire d'ethnographie*, expanded from a few pages in a journal in 1897 to a 127-page book by 1925, contained a discussion of a "Table d'analyse en ethnographie" (table of ethnographic analysis). Here he distinguished between "speculative studies" and "applied studies," "the object of which is to act upon civilizations or their components, to transform them, and

41. *L'Ethnographie*, n.s. 30 (1935), 84–111. For the list of guests see 82–84. On the influence of Le Play on Marin, see the obituary by A. Rosambert in ibid., n.s. 55 (1961), 5.

42. See, e.g., how the leading Le Playist social investigator, Urbain Guérin, employed this method to investigate the situation of rural laborers during the agricultural depression of the early 1890s at the request of the Société des Agriculteurs de France in my *Alliance of Iron and Wheat*, 112–16.

therefore, as a necessary requirement, first to assess them." He divided the speculative aspect of the discipline into descriptive investigations (ethnography), which generalize the vital concepts found among the bulk of the population, and explicative ones (ethnology), which look for causes and effects.

Descriptive studies, the heart of ethnography, neither explain nor evaluate. They aim to understand civilizations through their elements, their evolution, or "their concrete realizations, that is, the different peoples." "The process of analysis is basic to the methods of this kind of study," as well as to those of other disciplines; "it helps political or colonial practitioners quite as much as it does scientists." And the fundamental instrument of analysis is the table.

Ethnographic information elicited by detailed questionnaires and arranged in systematic arrays permit a comparative study that reveals cultural differences and nuances that are of interest to us, he explained. With the social transformation of many foreign cultures today and even of "the great civilizations" and with the rapid disappearance of the historic culture of provincial life everywhere, collecting and organizing ethnographic data are urgent tasks for pure science. In addition, "all the achievements [*conquêtes*] of Western civilization" require us to reflect on how they differ from those of other cultures and to recognize "them not only as good but as *the best*." With this knowledge we can know what in the culture is essential to our lives, which aspects of our civilization "*unquestionably represent progress*," and which features "we cannot abandon at any price." In brief, he sought a science that would guide us to the essence, the truth, of a culture.

Contact with the West through missionaries, travelers, colonizers, and improved means of communication has radically changed the civilizations outside the West. The recent war accelerated the process. The world beyond Europe was beginning to resent Western domination; the native peoples themselves had begun to seek major changes. "Naturally, their movements of resentment will multiply not only in this nationalist form of aggressions against Europe in the name of its own principles, but also in the form of a return to their roots [*du retour aux conceptions indigènes*]."

In this upcoming "great duel" it is essential for us to know both our own civilization and the cultures of our antagonists. As "trustees of Western civilization" we have to maintain its purity yet seek progress. "To be able to judge innovations or projects with greater certainty, not only must we know the cultural values of our own past and those of foreigners," he concluded, "but also we must be able to employ one and the same method of comparison." Therein lay the value of Marin's questionnaire and his *table d'analyse en ethnographie*.

The questionnaire, all 125 pages of it, was divided into three major sections: Material Life, Mental Life, and Social Life. The first two categories were not unusual, but the pages devoted to social life represented Marin's modernization of the tabular method, so that his school of ethnography might more readily compete with the new breed of investigators who called themselves sociologists. Le Play's influence is evident in the focus of the first array of questions on social life, in "the social facts." His political concerns can be seen most clearly at the end of the form, which poses questions on property relations, the state, and relations with other societies.

The questionnaire, if faithfully executed by an ethnographic investigator, Marin believed, would permit one to read, know, and act on any culture. His students had been using it even before the first version was published, and he had made successive revisions available to them. Because currently (in 1925), he wrote in the Introduction, "no *table d'analyse* is on sale in France," the Société d'Ethnographie thought it useful to publish Marin's.[43]

Soon after he published his chief contribution to methodology he manifested a new interest in bridging the conceptual gap between ethnographic studies and French anthropology, in effect in unifying the two anthropological organizations over which he presided. In 1927 he suggested to an international anthropological congress the study of systems of versification in poetry as one possible way to begin to link the physical with the cultural. But even here he wished to keep in focus "the possibility for the practical use of the results of this research."[44]

43. Louis Marin, *Questionnaire d'ethnographie: Table d'analyse en ethnographie* (Paris, 1925), 1–3, 93–124, esp. 94, 122–23.

44. Louis Marin, *Unité et unification des tables d'analyse en ethnographie. Un exemple des rapports entre les études ethniques et anthropologiques: Les Systèmes de versification*, address presented at the Third International Congress of the Institut International d'Anthropologie, Amsterdam, 20–29 September 1927, 1–9.

In May of the next year he warned the annual meeting of the Société d'Ethnographie both of the error of the sociologists who wished to employ ethnological data as raw material for sociological theorizing and of the need to maintain the integrity of the ethnographic method. The proposition that he advanced, that "ethnological data [*le phénomène ethnique*] can be explained in their own terms," strikes us as inadequate if not charged with a hidden agenda.

Why suddenly from 1925 to 1928 did Marin, whose strength, we have seen, was not in the area of theory, put out a series of publications on methodology all of which focused on defining—we could even say fencing off—*l'ethnographie* and *l'anthropologie* as distinct from any other discipline? To understand this uncharacteristic preoccupation with seemingly theoretical questions, we must recall Marin's *political* agenda of preserving anthropology and ethnography as the dominant social science disciplines for *his* France. But by the mid-1920s Marin's was not the only claim to lead French social science, nor was his the only vision of France held by practitioners of *les sciences humaines*.[45]

Democratic Social Science

In 1925 Marcel Mauss, Durkheim's intellectual heir and nephew; Lucien Lévy-Bruhl, dedicated disciple too and an early biographer of Jean Jaurès; and Paul Rivet, an active member of the socialist party (SFIO) and a kind of scholar-politician opposite number of Marin, joined together to form an Institute of Ethnology within the University of Paris. They thereby gave this discipline a firm place in the French academic world, which significantly increased their holdings of symbolic capital.[46] By employing the term "ethnology," Mauss, Rivet, and Lévy-Bruhl made clear their intention of pursuing interpretive and theoretical work while pushing out the boundaries of the field to suit their needs.

45. Marin addressing the General Assembly of the Société d'Ethnographie, 18 May 1928, at the Musée Social, *L'Ethnographie*, n.s. 18 (1928), 143.
46. See Pierre Bourdieu, "Le Champ scientifique," *Actes de la Recherche en sciences sociales*, 2/3 (1976), 88–104, esp. 89–94, and "Les Conditions sociales de la production

For us the most interesting figure of the group was Paul Rivet, who performed a role in science and politics somewhat parallel to that played by Marin. Trained originally in medicine, Rivet was interested in New World archaeology and cultures, especially in (physical) anthropology. But already in the 1920s he was beginning to have doubts about the utility of cephalic measurements as a scientific way to classify human races. Measurements of various dimensions of parts of the skull, however precise, gave no certainties, he argued. Moreover, peoples with similar nasal or cephalic indexes or similar in height might be otherwise vastly different and distant from each other. He found, for example, that ancient Pompeians and certain California native Americans shared the same nasal index. Later Rivet manifested some hope for new methods of anthropological classification via seriology, but his instinct was to retain a pro-culture agnosticism in human classification.[47]

Upon the retirement of René Verneau three years after the founding of the Institute of Ethnology, Rivet, the best organizer and politically the most active of these three men on the left, assumed the directorship of the Museum of Ethnography, housed in the old Palais du Trocadéro. The building had been erected as a temporary exhibition hall to house ethnographic displays at the Exposition of 1878, and like many such creations—the Eiffel Tower is only the most famous—it continued in use. In the years of Verneau's direction the museum had been allowed to become sadly understaffed, underfunded, stagnant in acquisitions, and increasingly shabby.[48] Upon his appointment and throughout the early 1930s Rivet, a decisive and powerful personality, championed rebuilding on the site

sociologique: Sociologie coloniale et décolonisation de la sociologie," in *Cahiers Jussieu* nº 2, *Université de Paris VII: Le Mal de voir: Ethnologie et orientalisme. Politique et épistémologie, critique et autocritique*, ed. Bourdieu (Paris, 1975), 416–27; in the same volume see Fanny Colonna, "Production scientifique et position dans le champ intellectuel et politique, deux cas: Augustin Berque et Joseph Desparmet," 398–414. For an introduction to Bourdieu's theoretical framework, see his *Outline of a Theory of Practice* (1972), trans. Richard Nice (Cambridge, 1977), 164–97.

47. See William H. Schneider, *Quality and Quantity: The Quest for Biological Regeneration in Twentieth-Century France* (Cambridge and New York, 1991), 218–19.

48. See Elizabeth A. Williams, "Art and Artifact at the Trocadero: Ars Americana and the Primitivist Revolution," in *Objects and Others: Essays on Museums and Material Culture*, ed. George W. Stocking, Jr., vol. 3 of *The History of Anthropology* (Madison, Wis., 1985), 162–63. See further her "Science of Man."

and reorganizing and expanding the collection to create a new museum that would house both general ethnological exhibits and specifically French materials.[49]

He also worked actively to bring all French ethnological research under the aegis of one organization, where, with the prestige of the connection to the Sorbonne and the control of the nation's major ethnology museum, Rivet and his friends would become hegemonic in their field of the *sciences humaines*. The chief rival to Rivet's Institute of Ethnology was of course Marin's older and more prestigious Société d'Ethnographie.

In October 1928, immediately upon assuming his new post at the museum, Rivet wrote Marin, then serving in Poincaré's cabinet, to ask for his support in restoring a cut in the museum's budget. In November he sent Lévy-Bruhl to see Poincaré to press the case. The cut was restored. A few days later Rivet wrote an extremely respectful note to Marin thanking him for his good offices and offering Marin his services if he ever needed them. What Rivet had in mind became apparent in January 1929, when he suggested to Marin the fusion of the two anthropological societies of Paris. Marin was not forthcoming. Rivet again raised the fusion in another letter to Marin dated 31 March 1930, in which the ethnologist-politician offered to visit the politician-ethnographer for "a little chat" about the question. Rivet's scheme came to nothing at that time, but the episode reveals the prestige and power, the capital in the field, still retained by conservative anthropology in the interwar years.[50]

49. In an official report requesting funds for the reconstitution of the museum, the ever politically astute Rivet argued that France needed a museum appropriate to its status as a colonial power and for the sake of its scientific reputation. Foreign visitors should not be able to say, as recent eminent scientific visitors were heard to say, that the current museum was "'a disgrace' for France": "Rapport sur l'état du Musée d'Ethnographie du Trocadéro et projet pour son organisation," A.N. 317 AP, carton 170. The report, a carbon of the original, bears no date or signature. In correspondence with Marin in 1928 (discussed below) Rivet enclosed the document and stated that they were his views. The holdings of the Archives Nationales on the reorganization are not fulsome. They may be found in F21 4906–8 and 6136–58.

50. P. Rivet to L. Marin, 20 October, 21 November, and 28 November 1928; 12 January 1929; 31 March 1930, A.N. 317 AP, carton 170. Unfortunately, only Rivet's side of the correspondence is on file. Even so, Marin's pointed rejection of the proposed merger in his writings from 1925 to 1928 make many of his reservations clear enough.

Only after the conservative Poincaré fell in July 1929, the left parties won a majority in the Chamber in the May 1932 elections, and the more responsive Herriot ministry was installed in June could Rivet elicit enough sympathy from the keepers of the government's budget for the actual reconstruction, despite serious state fiscal problems in the years of rebuilding.[51] Rivet's victory coincided with the triumph of the Popular Front. In August 1935 the Trocadéro Museum closed its doors and construction of the Palais de Chaillot began on the site. In May 1937, under the auspices of Léon Blum's first Popular Front ministry, an ethnology museum bearing the new name that Rivet had insisted upon, the Musée de l'Homme, opened its doors. Rivet, a socialist, had been one of the founders of the Vigilance Committee of Antifascist Intellectuals.[52] He and the co-workers he had gathered around him wanted the new museum's title to strike the note of universalist and egalitarian humanism that pervaded the contemporary discourse of the left and democratic alliance in that highly politicized moment of French life and thought.[53]

51. On 24 June 1928 the franc was devalued to a level that wiped out roughly 80% of the national debt, embittering rentiers and pushing many of them further to the political right. The franc was once again devalued on 2 October 1936 by Léon Blum's Popular Front ministry.

52. Mauss and Lévy-Bruhl were long-time active socialists. See James Clifford, *Person and Myth: Maurice Leenhardt in the Melanesian World* (Berkeley, 1982), 151. With Alain-Paul Langevin and Henri Bouché, leaders of Le Comité de Vigilance des Intellectuels Antifascistes, Rivet wrote a number of political pamphlets in that highly politicized era which bear such titles as *La Jeunesse devant le fascisme* (1934), *Non! La Guerre n'est pas fatale* (1936), and *Les Prétentions sociales du fascisme* (1937). See Nicole Racine-Furland, "Le Comité de vigilance des intellectuels antifascistes (1934–1939): Antifascisme et pacifisme," *Mouvement Social*, 101 (1977), 87–113.

53. In a press release prepared for the opening, Georges-Henri Rivière, Rivet's co-worker and the head of the new Museum of Folklore, Arts, and Popular Traditions (of France), housed in the Palais de Chaillot, wrote of the intention of the newest of the national museums to "situate itself harmoniously in the synthesis of peoples [*races*] and of human cultures": A.N. F21 4906. The Marin Papers contain a series of bitter complaining letters by one of his protégés who sought entré to a position at the Musée de l'Homme and was blocked by Rivet. Despite his standing both in the social sciences and in public life, Marin of course could not help him. See A.N. 317 AP, carton 195. Lest we dismiss the interpenetration of social science and politics in France as a result of the softness of these disciplines, we should note the parallel relationship of political principles and funding for physics research in the period of Léon Blum's Popular Front ministry; see Weart, *Scientists in Power*, 24–36.

The Musée de l'Homme staff firmly aligned itself on the left in the political arena. In November 1940, a few months after the defeated republic had been replaced by Vichy in the south and by the Germans in Paris, the new government removed Rivet from the directorship of his museum. Alerted that the Gestapo was about to arrest him, he escaped to Spain, and from there, in May 1941, reached Bogotá, Colombia, to take up a museum post that the nation's president, Eduardo Santos, had offered him. Between the defeat of France and his flight, the staff he had assembled at the Musée de l'Homme organized, first under his protection and then on their own, the first important resistance group. Known as the Vildé Circle, after the linguist Boris Vildé, the group, among other achievements, published the first resistance newspaper. After the war, those who had survived betrayal, exposure, and capture by the occupying Germans resumed their museum posts. Rivet returned from South America to take up the directorship once again.[54]

It should be clear that we are not concerned here with an increasingly rightist anthropological tendency matching itself against value-free social scientists. By the era of the Popular Front, France's intellectual and cultural life had become as polarized as its politics. To politics we must now turn, then, to complete our understanding of the development of Marin's anthropology.

The Politics of True France

By the 1930s Marin was at the height of his career both intellectually and politically. He led the major party of the far right in the

---

54. In *The Vildé Affair: Beginnings of the French Resistance* (Boston, 1977), based on interviews with living participants and surviving personal papers, Martin Blumenson has given us the first study of the resistance efforts of the group. On individuals in the group see Patrick Ghrenassia, "Anatole Lewitzky: De l'ethnologie à la résistance," *Liberté de l'esprit: Visages de la résistance*, no. 16 (1987), 237–53, and in the same issue of this magazine (which appears three times a year) Yves Lelong, "L'Heure très sévère de Boris Vildé," 329–41. On Vildé himself see *Boris Vildé: Journal et Lettres de Prison, 1941–42*, ed. François Bédarida and Dominique Veillon. The whole of vol. 7 (1988) of the *Cahiers de l'Institut d'Histoire du Temps Présent* is devoted to these documents. See Knobel, "De l'étude en France des types judaïques et négroïdes," 16.

Chamber of Deputies, the most bitter parliamentary opponents of Léon Blum's government. The road to this prominence began in 1903, when Marin joined the largest rightist political party, called then the Progressistes, to which Jules Méline and Raymond Poincaré also belonged.[55] When the incumbent of the parliamentary seat for Nancy died two years later, Marin put himself up as the Républicain-Progressiste candidate. His electoral statement assured the conservative voters of Nancy that a vote for him was a vote "against the candidates of the [left-liberal] Bloc, against disorder, and against social revolution."[56] In his electoral campaign and in his subsequent voting in the Chamber of Deputies he admirably performed the customary role of the local notable sent to the Chamber to advance local business interests. He championed the protectionist interests of the Lorraine distillers and brewers, as well as those of French wine and tobacco growers. He worked to obtain governmental aid for small business.[57] He also defended such principles as the value of family life and the integrity of the countryside, but above all a white-hot nationalism.

Marin gave his maiden speech in the Chamber in 1907 on the occasion of the embarrassed government's transfer of General Bailloud, who at a farewell dinner for a fellow officer had offered a toast in which he evoked the possibility of war with Germany and expressed the hope that should hostilities break out, the departing officer's regiment would make its contribution along with other units "to returning France's lost provinces." Marin, together with his friend and countryman Barrès, attacked the cowardly government for thus mistreating the patriotic soldier.[58] Marin soon earned a

55. The conservative republican Opportunists, who under Jules Méline controlled a commanding majority in the Chamber of Deputies, fell apart in the course of the Dreyfus affair. Its right regrouped as the Progressistes. In 1914 further Third Republic parliamentary cell division engendered the Groupe de l'Entente Démocratique. In 1924 Marin's group changed its name to L'Union Républicaine Démocratique. In 1925 Marin assumed its presidency. It soon took the name Fédération Républicaine, the name used throughout this chapter. See the anonymous report *Le 80e Anniversaire du Président Louis Marin* (Paris, 1954), 63.

56. Marin, *Louis Marin*, 151–55.

57. On Marin's local political-base building see Jean-François Eck, "Louis Marin et la Lorraine, 1905–14: Le Pouvoir local d'un parlementaire sous la IIIe République" (thèse de doctorat de troisième cycle, Institut d'Etudes Politiques de Paris, 1980).

58. Sanvoisin, "Le Parlement et la menace extérieure," 478.

reputation as "Deputy Revanche" for his frequent expressions of concern for the military reinforcement of the eastern frontier. The outbreak of war in 1914 confirmed Marin in his intense patriotism. And its conclusion unleashed his most revanchist sentiments. He opposed the armistice drafted in 1918 because, as written, it left Germany with an army. He voted against the Chamber's ratification of the Treaty of Versailles.[59] His nationalist extremism estranged him from his natural allies in the Bloc National for a time, but his political career nonetheless prospered. Poincaré invited him to serve in his government as minister of liberated regions in 1920.[60] In 1924 he took on the presidency of two right parliamentary groups: the Union Républicaine Démocratique and the Fédération Républicaine, which under him merged their political efforts. These activities mainly involved bringing down successive middle-of-the-road governments until late July 1926, when he agreed to take the portfolio for pensions in Poincaré's conservative ministry. He kept the post until 11 November 1928. Throughout the 1920s Marin opposed all diplomatic moves that in his opinion either reduced French sovereignty or rehabilitated Germany. Thus he attacked the Washington Accords, the Locarno Treaty, the Hague Agreements, the Dawes and Young plans, and the military evacuation of the Rhineland.[61]

In domestic politics under Marin's leadership the Fédération Républicaine became the ally of action groups on the radical right. In the late 1920s the party collaborated with the Action Française. Pierre Taittinger, leader of the Jeunesses Patriotes, served at the same time as a vice president of the Fédération. By 1934 three of the six vice presidents of the Jeunesses Patriotes—Xavier Vallat, Jean Ybarnegaray, and Marin's old friend François de Wendel (who financially subsidized the Jeunesse Patriotes)—had been elected as mem-

59. Ibid., 484.

60. He held the post for three months, and remained to serve in the cabinet of Premier François-Marsal after the resignation of Poincaré.

61. Sanvoisin, "Le Parlement et la menace extérieure," 488–92. Herriot once said of Marin, perhaps not without irony, "You appear in the Chamber as the incarnation of French patriotism"; repeated by Georges Mazerand in his banquet address honoring Louis Marin on his eightieth birthday. See Le 80ᵉ Anniversaire du Président Louis Marin, 66.

bers of parliament representing the Fédération Républicaine.[62] Marin blamed the right-wing riots of 6 February 1934, which followed the exposure of the Stavisky affair, not on its authors but on the "frightful and idiotic errors of incompetent governments." When in April 1937 Jacques Doriot of the Parti Populaire Français proposed a right united front, a "Front de la Liberté," to counter the Front Populaire that had been formed in 1935, Marin led the Fédération Républicaine into the alliance with Doriot and Taittinger's group. Together they went so far in opposing the leftward movement of the nation that some of the right nationalists in the alliance even dampened their hostility to the eternal German enemy because Hitler, too, was anti-Bolshevik. The diplomatic policy of appeasement, which they saw as assistance to domestic pacification, finally led many members of the Fédération to accept the new regime of Maréchal Pétain, who, like themselves, after all, had a vision of France with its old institutions restored and intact.[63]

Close to the Government and Yet Far from It

Marin was serving as a minister of state in the government of Paul Reynaud in the early summer of 1940 when the Germans invaded France. The Reynaud cabinet resigned, yielding power to Maréchal Pétain, but Marin stayed on in Vichy.[64] The new regime championed the values for which he himself had fought; the new government proclaimed its motto to be not "Liberty, Equality, Fraternity" but "Work, Family, Fatherland."

His friends and followers continued to view him as an active and influential political figure. In December a Republican Federation member from Grenoble wrote him to express his delight and that of

62. See Jean-Noël Jeanneney, *François de Wendel en république: L'Argent et le pouvoir, 1914–1940* (Paris, 1976), 485–86.

63. See Dieter Wolf, *Doriot, du communisme à la collaboration* (Paris, 1969), 168; Irvine, *French Conservatism in Crisis*, 107–19, 146, 159–203. A reading of Marin's journalism in *La Nation* for this period is as illuminating as the boxes of papers in the archives.

64. A.N. 317 AP, carton 75.

his friends that "morality and religion would once more be taught in our schools." Moreover, "the present government seems clearly on the way to instituting the reforms that you have always advocated, and of that you can be legitimately and extremely proud." Robert Péringuey, head of the Republican Federation in Algiers, wrote to consult on how to keep the natives of the colonial empire under control in those difficult times. People requested his support in their attempts to find jobs in the new regime and called on him to influence governmental personnel decisions. The Grenoble supporter wrote again to suggest that the moment was propitious officially to consecrate France to the Sacred Heart and to have its image added to the Tricolor. Unfortunately, we know neither Marin's replies nor the outcomes. He held no post in the new regime.

Marin's deep anti-German sentiments made it impossible to consider him for a post in a French regime dedicated to collaborating with the German conquerors, however much the people of the new French order may have admired and shared his domestic politics. As his friend André François-Poncet delicately expressed it after his death, "He was at the same time close to the government and very far from it."[65]

Two bodies over which he presided in the 1930s, the *Revue Anthropologique,* put out by his Ecole d'Anthropologie, and the Société de Géographie Commerciale, both supported the National Revolution. They supplied it with ideological underpinnings and received subsidies from the regime to continue the work, and their members accepted official posts. Politics and scholarship reached the high point of their partnership. The union of social science and policy was strengthened when the debate about French identity became almost as intense as it had been at the time of Dreyfus. In this conjuncture, however, scientifically based racism played a greater and more fatal role in the right's sorting out of who was French and who was not.

65. See in A.N. 317 AP, E. Romanet to Marin, 7 December 1940, carton 75, and 15 June 1940, carton 55; Robert Péringuey to Marin, 30 January 1941, carton 52. "Only the sons of France can now keep the flag of their *patrie* flying here; but they can do so only by force": André François-Poncet, "Notice sur la vie et les travaux de Louis Marin, 1871–1960," given at the session of 3 February 1964 of the Institut de France, Académie des Sciences Morales et Politiques, *Institut de France* (Paris, 1964), 31–32.

National Anthropology

From the early 1930s Georges Montandon, whom Marin had appointed to the faculty of the Ecole d'Anthropologie in 1933 and to the chair of ethnology in 1935, published ever more manifestly racist books and articles in what we would nominally call physical anthropology.[66] At first his colleagues at the school were slow to follow his lead.

Although the *Revue Anthropologique* carried articles on racial questions in the early 1930s, most contributors tended to be agnostic about attempts to explain ethnic group behavior in racial terms. Two communications on the Jews published in 1932, for example, agreed that the Jews were best understood as a religious group, not as a race. Racially, both authors argued, they were more like the group among whom they lived than like their coreligionists in other parts of the world.[67] Still, whatever good such views may have done to oppose the racist ideas being propagated across the border in Germany, they could not have been comforting to the Eastern European and North African Jews living in France at the time. In the course of the decade the tone of the journal's articles changed.

In 1939 Philibert Russo of Lyon agreed that there was no *zoological* Jewish race, although he saw the Jews as a "biological group." They might completely assimilate to the style of intellectual life (*pensées*) of a nation, but as a biological group they jealously maintain their own ethos (*sentimentalité*), which forever cuts them off from other peoples. And should the Jews as a group within a country grow sufficiently numerous, they could alter the fundamental ethos of the host nation.[68] In the same issue of the *Revue* Dr. A. Thooris warned of the danger of mixing races, because the mixture creates a mosaic that hides "a disorder that leads inevitably to racial reversion." The adversion of pure races for mixed blood is the result of historical

66. On the career and writings of Montandon, see Knobel, "De l'étude en France des types judaïques et négroïdes," and Schneider, *Quality and Quantity*, 257–60.

67. Nicholas Kossovitch and F. Benoit, "Contribution à l'étude anthropologique et sérologique (Groupes sanguins des juifs modernes)," *Revue Anthropologique*, 42 (1932), 99–125; Félix Regnault, "Il n'y a pas une race juive," ibid., 390–93.

68. Philibert Russo, "Essai sur le rôle social de la race zoologique et la race biologique," *Revue Anthropologique*, 49 (1939), 38–53. "We should remark . . . that the idea of the nation implies this community of sensibility" (51).

experience, "whereby *tradition* proves itself more powerful than science." Thus, he concluded, "there is a place for a moderate racism [*un racisme mesuré*] so that free men can father future free men." Finally, Thooris warned readers lest they misunderstand the direction of his analysis: "race does not mean class."[69]

Soon after the triumph of the National Revolution, Henri Briand, director of the *Revue* and professor of heredity at the Ecole d'Anthropologie, praised the plans of Pétain's government to introduce physical education and sports training to French schools "for the preservation of the race." Briand argued that a person who has a rudimentary education (*culture scientifique*) but a healthy body and a steady, honest character is a more useful member of the national community than one who, however gifted intellectually, is sickly. "This sentence is from *Mein Kampf*, it applies as well to France in 1941 as it did to Germany in 1926," he averred.[70]

Montandon, who in the late decade was devoting himself to demonstrating the identity of the Jewish and the Negroid ethnic types, and who in 1939 had called Léon Blum a "Nigger of the Nile" in an Italian racist publication, welcomed the freedom and opportunities the new order and the Germans gave him. In 1940 he agreed to head an anthropology review dedicated to support of the new French regime. *L'Ethnie Française*, the title of which can best be translated as "The French Volk," focused especially on ethno-racial problems. It was subsidized first by the Institut Allemand de Paris and then during the war by the Commissariat Général aux Questions Juives.

The SS wanted to place one of their experts on the Jewish race in Xavier Vallat's commissariat. But instead Vallat asked Montandon, who accepted, and thereby helped save another small bit of French sovereignty from German domination. In his capacity as investigator of Jewish questions he conducted physical examinations of persons suspected of being Jewish and drew conclusions as to their racial identity. In 1943 Montandon was named "technical director" of a

69. A. Thooris, "Réflexe de but et racisme," *Revue Anthropologique*, 49 (1939), 268–89; italics Thooris's. Going beyond even National Socialist practice, he praises Hitler's biological makeup (275).

70. H. Briand, "Education physique et sauvegarde de la race," *Revue Anthropologique*, 51 (1941), 8–15.

new Institut d'Etude des Questions Juives et Ethno-Raciales set up by the Commissariat Général aux Questions Juives. Apparently his lectures were not popular—typically only some two score people attended. During the war he continued his association with the Ecole d'Anthropologie, as did Louis Marin.[71]

Saving *Grande France*

Meanwhile, important members of Marin's Société de Géographie Commerciale were also eager to align themselves with the values of the new era. Marin's personal archives contain a copy of a letter to Maréchal Pétain dated at Carcassonne, 20 January 1941, from a Committee for the Study of the Imperial Economy of Greater France (*Grande France*), a body self-created in the zone still under French rule, made up of members of the geographic society, whose goals were those of the parent organization. They assured the *Chef de l'Etat Français* of their loyalty, of their willingness to serve, and of their resolve to continue the old organization's work in unoccupied France. It was signed not by Louis Marin but by the secretary general of the Société de Géographie, General Brissaud-Demaillet. Enclosed were typed by-laws that named Louis Marin to no post, although to that point he had served as president of the geographic society. In ink Marin had edited both the text and the format of the new membership form. He had also written his name in as *Président d'Honneur* on the printed list of officers.

The section of the by-laws headed "Doctrine and Program" was full of praise for the French of the National Revolution, but pro-

71. See Georges Montandon, "La Science française devant la question raciale aux XIXᵉ et XXᵉ siècles," *Deutschland-Frankreich*, 2 (1943), 104–20. The best work on Montandon is Marc Knobel, "L'Ethnologue à la dérive: Montandon et l'ethnoracisme," *Ethnologie Française*, 18 (1988), 107–13. After the war Marin tried to distance himself from Montandon and the Ecole d'Anthropologie of the war years, but the ambiguities of his writings on ethnicity and race make it difficult to accept his unsupported assertions as the whole truth. See Louis Marin, "Les Etudes portant sur l'homme et l'école d'anthropologie de 1926 à 1956," *Revue Anthropologique*, n.s. 2 (1956), 174. On racialist thought under Vichy, see Schneider, *Quality and Quantity*, 256–82.

posed that if it was to reach its full potential, it had to become an Imperial Revolution. Accordingly, employing such terms as "'Eurafrican collaboration,'" "mystique of great construction projects," and "renovation of the national economy by means of the Empire," the program focused on the retention of the colonies (at a moment when not only the British but the Germans might be suspected of looking covetously at French overseas possessions) and their continued development for the benefit of the French Empire.[72]

Another section, headed "Primacy of Education and Race in the Social Sphere," inscribed in the organization's principles the writings of an anthropologist and his definition of race. The by-laws defined the "French race" as a "resultant-race" in the sense of the "findings" (*données*) of Dr. René Martial, member of the new committee and prolific writer on questions of race and racial hygiene.[73]

The "Doctrine and Program" section concluded by calling upon all "Imperial Patriots from all regions of France and of the Empire"

72. On the intellectual pedigree of such colonial construction projects in the history of French imperialism I have found enlightening the unpublished paper by J. Malcolm Thompson, "French Technocracy and Colonial Expansion: The Trans-Saharan vs. the Kayes-Bamako Railroad Controversy, 1872–1892," Department of History, University of Minnesota.

73. René Martial (1873–1955), chargé du Cours d'Immigration at the Institut d'Hygiène at the Paris Faculty of Medicine, wrote extensively on questions of social medicine and race. He invented a discipline he called "anthropo-biology," which he believed bridged the intellectual gaps that divided the studies of peoples' history, psychology, and biology. Above all, he was interested in the consequences of racial mixtures, which he deemed largely negative in uncontrolled forms. His notion of a *race-résultat* was an attempt to align a racial doctrine with the evidence of a history of some racial mixing (in his sense) in France and an ultranationalism. For our discussion his most interesting work was *Les Métis* (Paris, 1942), subtitled "New Studies on Migrations, Racial Mixing, Mixed Breeds, the Reinvigoration of the French Race, and the Revision of Family Law," 10–11. On the definition of the *race-résultat*, see 94–118. His *Race française* (Paris, 1934) argues that the distinctive psychology of the French race is to be an agricultural people, and that the contemporary crisis of the race was a consequence of the flight from the land. The return to the land might best be accomplished by controlled racial mixing via immigration with other European agricultural people. He did not deem the Jews an appropriate population for this purpose. See 245–85. See further his *Race, hérédité, folie: Etude d'anthropo-sociologie appliquée à l'immigration* (Paris, 1938), the flavor of which may be understood from this sample sentence: "Selection in human racial mixture is just as rational a process as that followed in horse breeding" (102). There is also in this vein *Vie et constance des races* (Paris, 1939). See Schneider, *Quality and Quantity*, 233–55.

to join in the effort, to augment the phalanx, to begin the construction of a National Federation of Imperial France.

Like the old Paris-based geographic society, the new body periodically voted resolutions and transmitted them to the government for consideration. On 30 January 1941 its officers duly sent the *Chef de l'Etat* a copy of its "Doctrine and Program" along with a proposal for the "creation of a program of instruction for both elementary and higher education on the anthropo-biology of the races." Over the course of the year other resolutions dealing with economic, agricultural, and engineering questions, very much in the old interest-group style of advocacy of the Société de Géographie, were voted and sent off to the Maréchal. The warmth of their reception is hard to determine. Marin's files contain only a copy of a polite letter of acknowledgment of their receipt sent by one of Pétain's aides.

The Vichy regime welcomed the committee's devotion to the French colonial empire, and the Ministry of Colonies regularly subsidized it until the regime fell in 1944. The committee, as Maryse Demons, a member, reminded Marin from Paris, was "to propagandize for the empire by means of our studies, talks, traditional banquets, lectures in schools, prizes, etc."[74]

Marin remained a member of this successor to the Société de Géographie throughout the war years, or more exactly until 29 May 1944, when the society's minutes indicate that he, as well as a number of others, had been stripped of their membership. His hostility to Germany and things German finally prevailed over the principles that had put him in an orbit so close to the regime of Marshal Pétain. Although Marin's expulsion was surely connected to his departure for London on 10 April,[75] it cannot be said with any certainty whether the incumbent leadership acted out of motives of fear of implication in his defection or from a desire to punish him for his disloyalty to the committee's work. The latter explanation is more plausible in the light of the countercoup Marin carried out when he returned to France with the army of liberation.

74. Maryse Demons to Marin, 9 February and 20 February 1944 and n.d (1944), A.N. 317 AP, carton 58; Colonel Campet, in behalf of Maréchal Pétain, to Marin, 13 February 1941, A.N. 317 AP, carton 201.

75. François-Poncet, "Notice sur la vie," 32.

Living on Principal

Upon the liberation, the Conseil d'Administration of the old Société de Géographie was reconstituted, Marin was reelected president, and the Committee for the Study of the Imperial Economy of
Greater France was disbanded. With the resignation of the wartime
officers—including General Brissaud-Desmaillet—the Vichyite reorganization was reversed. Nevertheless, even with the record of its
wartime activities relegated to archives that remained closed until
the death of Marin in 1960, it was no longer a prominent colonial
society in the postwar years.[76] Marin also forgot his earlier acceptance of mixing physical anthropology with cultural studies, if his
tolerance for racism may be so expressed in the language of method.

In a meditation on method in the French cultural sciences written
in 1952, Marin affirmed the importance of the distinction that had
been drawn in the late nineteenth century between studies of human
physical development and the study of *mentalités*. Although he still
considered Paul Broca one of his progenitors, he was now not prepared to see the cultural reduced to the biological. He affirmed his
continued admiration, too, of Auguste Comte, for his positivism and
the distinction he had drawn between nature and the human, and of
Claude Bernard, for his belief that science could serve to improve
human life. He also, however, maintained his concern with values in
the social sciences. The realm in which these normative assessments
were made he now designated as "ethnodicy" (*l'ethnodicée*).[77]

Perhaps now out of disappointment with the uses of politics in
preserving tradition, Marin exhorted students to focus their studies
on the phenomenon of the decline of traditions. Moving from the
"salvage mode" (an old culture is passing) of his early years to the
"redemptive mode" (survivals despite change), he turned to writing
about the role of fairy tales in keeping alive the old ways of his native
Lorraine.[78] But even in this late work he struggled to synthesize his

76. A.N. 317 AP, carton 201.

77. Louis Marin, "Les Etudes ethniques en 1950: La Nature de leur objet et leur
propre relation avec les autres études portant sur l'homme: L'Etat de leurs méthodes," *L'Ethnographie*, n.s. 47 (1952), 3–70, esp. 11–18, 56.

78. For the distinction between these, finally, rhetorical styles of ethnographic
writing and a critique of the ahistoricity of both, see George E. Marcus, "Contemporary Problems of Ethnography in the Modern World System," in *Writing Culture: The*

ideas òn the role of anthropology and his political vision. In this study of the uses of children's stories he continued to hold to the idea that each nation had its special genius, a combination of the national psychology and historical circumstances, which imposed upon it a historic mission that had to be carried out even "at the most painful sacrifices."[79]

Neither Marin's anthropology nor the Fédération Républicaine survived the war. Called in the summer of 1945 to testify at the Pétain trial as a former minister in the Reynaud government, Marin, now seventy-four years old and once again deputy from Nancy, still bristled with pent-up nationalist rage at the humiliation France had experienced under Pétain.[80] Nevertheless, after an unsuccessful effort to renew his political party, it soon disbanded.[81] Marin threw himself into a campaign for a draconian peace with Germany, but the political atmosphere had changed as much as that of the social sciences.

In 1946, in a nicely self-serving meld of his near-pathological na-

---

Poetics and Politics of Ethnography, ed. James Clifford and George E. Marcus (Berkeley, 1986), 165–93, esp. 165n. For a meditation on the theme of the anthropologist as author and the possibilities of a new postcolonial anthropological discourse, see Clifford Geertz's Harry Camp Lectures at Stanford, *Works and Lives: The Anthropologist as Author* (Stanford, 1988), 1–24, 129–49.

79. Louis Marin, "La Naissance, la vie, la mort des traditions: Ce qu'il faut en savoir pour analyser leur crise mondiale au temps présent," *L'Ethnographie*, n.s. 44 (1946), 52. Although this issue of the journal is dated 1946, it appeared in 1950; the editors continued the numbering as if the journal had not stopped appearing during the war. This was one of the catch-up volumes. See also Louis Marin, "Enquête sur la crise des traditions: Disparition des institutions traditionnelles qui, en Lorraine, transmettaient et utilisaient les vieux contes populaires," *L'Ethnographie*, n.s. 40 (1942), 3–93 (another catch-up volume, actually published in 1948). The same article, somewhat expanded and with invidious references to Arabic peoples removed, was published posthumously as *Les Contes traditionnels en Lorraine: Institutions de transfert des valeurs morales et spirituelles* (Paris, 1964). The argument on national genius may be found on 166 of this text, and in his "Enquête sur la crise des traditions," 93.

80. Déposition de Louis Marin, Haute Cour de Justice, compte rendu in extensio des audiences, in *Procès du Maréchal Pétain* (Paris, 1945), 63–72. Marin argued that he and the majority of the government had been against asking for an armistice (there was no vote or *compte rendu* of the meeting), and that Pétain had taken advantage of ambiguities in the exchanges with the Germans to claim he had been authorized to conclude one.

81. On this end phase see A.N. 317 AP, esp. cartons 70 and 73, and Irvine, *French Conservatism in Crisis*, 107–19, 146, 159–203, and esp. 231–34.

tionalism and his anthropological concept that the deep substrata of societies change little, he lectured an audience at the Ecole d'Anthropologie on the elite across the Rhine:

> We hear a lot of talk about denazification, but it is of deprussianization that we ought to speak. For nazism was nothing other than a [recent] version of the Prussian spirit of aggression. In the eighteenth century it was the spirit of Frederick the Great, in the nineteenth the Bismarckian spirit, in the twentieth nazism. What form will it take in the future?[82]

But the voters of Lorraine were ready for a new political beginning and a real peace with Germany. In 1951 l'abbé Pierre defeated Marin in a contest for the parliamentary seat from Nancy to which he had been reelected after the war.

Although Marin resumed many of his posts of honor in the reconstituted scientific societies to which he had belonged, French social science, too, had now definitively turned away from prewar anthropology, in a sea-change that has not yet run its course. The Société des Océanistes, of which Marin had been a founder in 1937, was reconstituted under the pastor-ethnologist Maurice Leenhardt. Upon assuming its leadership Leenhardt immediately merged his organization with the Groupe d'Etudes Océaniennes of the Musée de l'Homme.[83] Under the leadership of socialists and left democrats such as Rivet, who had come home from Bogotá to resume his directorship of the Musée de l'Homme, and Claude Lévi-Strauss, who returned from the New School for Social Research in New York (and in a few years would assume a chair at the Collège de France), French anthropology began the difficult task of disengaging itself from the task of studying ways to maintain an old exclusive cultural

---

82. Louis Marin, "L'Elite rhénane," lecture given at the Ecole d'Anthropologie, 17 June 1946, and printed in his collection of radio talks from London upon his arrival there, occasional lectures, and the anti-German writings done after the war for his weekly *La Nation, La Sécurité de la France* (Paris, n.d. [1946]), 147.

83. For a fine nuanced appreciation of Leenhardt as anthropologist and missionary, see Paul Rabinow's review essay of Clifford's biography, *Person and Myth*, "'Facts Are a Word of God,'" in George W. Stocking, Jr., *Observers Observed: Essays in Ethnographic Field Work*, vol. 1 of his *History of Anthropology* (Madison, Wis., 1983), 196–207. Marin was kept on the largish council of the society but lost any leadership role. He did, however, regain the presidency of the Fédération Régionaliste Française, a conservative nonscholarly body. See A.N. 317 AP, carton 195.

heritage for its conservative values and seeking ways to theorize a new variegated world, and perhaps a nation, in which there were many ways of being French.[84]

Lévi-Strauss realized that the problem of identity inherited from conservative social science was insoluble, and he strove to lead French social theory away from questions of identity to an acceptance of cultural democracy within France and a genuine acceptance of pluralism—albeit in the peculiarly French way of positing one humanity indivisible. The death agony (perhaps) of the old ideas of exclusive identity and hierarchies of beings, or at least their contestation by democratically oriented social scientists, is at the heart of the present crisis in French anthropology, and in a good deal of Western social thought.[85]

Almost immediately upon Louis Marin's death in 1960 appeared the first issue (January 1961) of what quickly became France's leading journal in the field: L'Homme: Revue française d'anthropologie, under the editorship of Emile Benveniste, Pierre Gourou, and Lévi-Strauss. But this transformation of French anthropology was not simply a consequence of postwar decolonization, of the erosion of anthropology's special field of study.[86] Of more importance, as the history of the discipline seen through the career of Louis Marin reveals, is the death of the conservative system of social inquiry with

84. See, e.g., the introductory essay in P. Lucas and J. C. Vatin, L'Algérie des Anthropologues (Paris, 1982), and the meditation on larger questions of social theory by François Bourricaud, "Change and Theories of Change in France since 1945," in French Sociology: Rupture and Renewal since 1968, ed. Charles Lemert (New York, 1981), 396–427. On the "disarray" of contemporary high theory in anthropology see Marcus, "Contemporary Problems of Ethnography," 166.

85. See Georges Condominas, "Notes on the Present-Day State of Anthropology in the Third World," in The Politics of Anthropology, ed. Gerrit Huizer and Bruce Mannheim (The Hague and Paris, 1979), 187–99; Michel Leiris, "L'Ethnographie devant le colonialisme," Temps Modernes, 6 (1950), 357–74; Paul Mercier, Histoire de l'anthropologie (Paris, 1966), 21. More generally there are Clifford Geertz's new thoughts on the crisis and future of anthropology as the intermediary among peoples to promote better understanding, in his Works and Lives, 129–49.

86. See Talal Asad, ed., Anthropology and the Colonial Encounter (New York, 1973), esp. Asad's introductory essay, 9–19. An international colloquium on the present state and future of anthropology organized under the auspices of the Centre National de la Recherche Scientifique was published in 1979: Georges Condominas and Simone Dreyfus-Gamelon, eds., L'Anthropologie en France; Situation actuelle et avenir (Paris, 18–22 avril 1977) (Paris, 1979).

the death of the old right of the Third Republic in Vichy. Marin and the members of the scholarly societies he led were partisans of a small-town, traditional, Catholic, imperial society that in his lifetime came under increasing duress. It put up a last-ditch defense under Vichy, trying by authoritarian and violent means to renew the threatened values and relations of an authentic France. Marin and his school declined and passed on. He and his group had consumed in lost intellectual, cultural, and political causes, to use Pierre Bourdieu's concept, the remaining capital they retained in the field.[87] The values he championed, however—unified in the ontology of an authentic France—lived on after the death of his school. It remains his legacy to today's France.

Marin had drawn no rigorous distinction between anthropological theory as it applied to the regions of France and as it bore on cultures outside the country, although the fields themselves were professionally and theoretically distinct in the interwar years. His unit of analysis had been France as such, sometimes his own Lorraine, sometimes the parts overseas. He was a theorist of the *Grande France* that figured in his renamed colonial society of the Vichy years. With a better idea of the shape of conservative anthropology, we can now look at this idea of a *Grande France* and try to understand how it fitted into the creation of an identity for France.

87. Pierre Bourdieu, "Le Champ scientifique," *Actes de la recherche en sciences sociales*, 2/3 (1976), 88–104.

The Seductions of
the Picturesque
and the Irresistible
Magic of Art

A s France began to slide into the depression that had gripped the rest of the world for several years, the Paris Colonial International Exposition opened in the spring of 1931. The exposition offered visitors a magnificent celebration of the colonial achievement and the colonial future of France. Set tastefully on 110 hectares (272 acres) around Lac Daumesnil in the Bois de Vincennes, buildings representing all of France's colonial dependencies and trust territories, as well as pavilions celebrating the colonial achievements of the Netherlands, Belgium, Denmark, Portugal, Italy, and the United States, permitted French people and foreign tourists—transported around the grounds on a little train—a synoptic view of worldwide achievements. A large French metropolitan section displayed modern technology and *industries de luxe;* a Palais Permanente des Colonies, its imposing facade depicting the *mission civilisatrice* sculpted by Alfred Janniot, featured an aquarium; and a zoo for African fauna constructed by the firm of Carl Hagenbeck in the naturalistic style of the Hamburg zoo brought visitors even closer to the wonders of nature beyond Europe. Everywhere on the grounds the visitor encountered inhabitants of the colonies in their native dress. Fairgoers might take boat rides on the lake in a variety of native crafts, enjoy splendid light-and-water shows, dine at snack bars and restaurants offering typical dishes, and of course reward their culture-weary children with kiddy rides and amusements.

But lest the provisions for frivolous pleasures and the ambiance of exoticism mislead visitors as to the serious intentions of the organizers, André Demaison, well-known author in the new field of "colonial literature," put them on the right road to understanding in his "Word of Welcome to the Visitor" (Addresse au Visiteur) in the *Guide Officiel*: "It is evident that you took the trouble to come here to amuse yourselves, but not just for that alone." You are here out of curiosity, because "you have sensed that today this great human collectivity that is FRANCE has horizons wider than those you have been accustomed to see on the map of Europe. . . . You have understood, as well, that no one can remain indifferent to the colonial activities of our neighbors, be they friends or allies, linked as they are with our own destiny by the solidarity that the current economic difficulties impose on all of us." And, as if to quiet popular fears of another outbreak of international conflict over colonial possessions at that moment of world economic duress, the "Word of Welcome" admitted that "the colonies will therefore become the new battlefield," not in diplomatic rivalry and war, but—invoking the thought of Marshal Lyautey—"in works of peace and progress."

As you progress through the exposition, the *Guide* continued, you will "meet with one surprise after another. But you will not find us exploiting the low instincts of a vulgar public here." M. le maréchal Louis Hubert Lyautey, Commissaire général, his second in command, le gouverneur général Marcel Olivier, and we, their collaborators, "consider you, dear visitor, a person of good taste. You will see no blacks tastelessly throwing themselves about on stage [*bamboulas*], no belly dancers, no seamy sideshows, those vulgar displays that have brought discredit upon many another exhibition of the colonial sphere; but rather, reconstructions of tropical life with all its color and truly picturesque qualities."[1]

---

1. *Exposition coloniale internationale à Paris en 1931: Guide officiel*, text by André Demaison (Paris, 1931), 17–18. For a fine recent contribution to the *histoire des imaginaires* of French colonialism, see Jacques Marseille, *L'Age d'or de la France coloniale* (Paris, 1986). His text and the images of the 1931 exposition capture both the political goals and the lush exoticism of the colonial celebration (117–36). On the instructive history of belly dancing at universal expositions and its roles in the colonial discourse, see Zeynep Celik and Leila Kinney, "Ethnography and Exhibitionism at the Expositions Universelles," *Assemblage*, 13 (1990), 35–59, esp. 35–39.

People of a Greater France

He had agreed to head the Colonial Exposition, Marshal Lyautey explained, because he wanted to make the moment an opportunity to teach visitors not only the lesson of the union of the races in the French Empire but also the need for unity at home. Domestic peace, "union, finally, among us French," was key to the enterprise of empire, "because our colonial policy could not be continued and our empire maintained but by the unanimous support of metropolitan public opinion. . . . The French have to become more and more convinced to the marrow of their bones that the whole nation must line up behind its colonies, and that our future lies overseas."[2]

The organizers of the Exposition and their photojournalist helpers strove to take the mainly French visitors on "an around-the-world tour"; "if you actually took such a trip, it would cost you a fortune and take two years."[3] The 1889 Paris Exposition marked the centenary of the Revolution. Ideologically it celebrated the promise of liberal republicanism and the restoration of national equilibrium after the Prussian war and the Commune.[4] The centenary of French rule in Algeria was celebrated in 1931. But the fair's planners wished to accomplish something more than just to acclaim the successes of French colonialism. Their articulated intention—Lyautey's statement and many others like it were quite clear about the project—was to intensify the loyalty of the metropolitan population to the colonial empire so that the French visitors, and eventually the nation, would arrive at a deep realization that they lived in a new greater France with hometowns (*petites patries*) all over the globe.[5] In our era of

2. Interview in a special issue of the magazine *Monde & Voyage* dedicated to the exposition, Archives Nationales, sec. Outre-mer, Br 7700 D; for the goals and purposes of the Colonial Exposition, see Br 3590 D. See also Ministère des Colonies, Le Gouverneur-Général Marcel Olivier, Rapporteur Général, Délégué général à l'Exposition, *Rapport général: Exposition coloniale internationale de 1931*, 7 vols. (Paris, 1933), vol. 5, pt. 1, 30, and pt. 2; hereafter *Rapport général*.

3. *Guide officiel*, 20–21.

4. See Debora L. Silverman, "The 1889 Exhibition: The Crisis of Bourgeois Individualism," *Oppositions: A Journal for Ideas and Criticism in Architecture*, 8 (1977), 71–72, and *Art Nouveau in Fin-de-Siècle France: Politics, Psychology, and Style* (Berkeley, 1989).

5. Marcel Olivier, "Les Origines et les buts de l'exposition coloniale," *Revue des Deux Mondes*, 8th ser., 101 (1 May 1931), 46–57, and "Philosophie de l'exposition coloniale," ibid. (15 November 1931), 278–93. On late-nineteenth-century efforts see

decolonization we tend not to reflect much on the often herculean labors of imperialist campaigners to get the metropolitan population to go along with winning and ruling an empire, with accepting their destinies as an imperial people.[6] The building of domestic support for empire represented the most sustained domestic efforts of contemporary national leaders of expansionist lands in the arena of foreign relations, second only to the cultivation of xenophobic nationalism.

What new ideas did this simulacrum of the tropical part of the French Empire bring to the task of deepening colonial consciousness in the nation? Colonial sections had been features of earlier expositions. A colonial city had been built for the first time for the 1889 exhibition, both to give the French some sense of their new colonial realm and to impress the natives brought in to staff the section with the life of the metropole.[7] The Marseille expositions of 1900 and 1922 were entirely dedicated to colonialism. The Republic had been promoting a colonial consciousness at various expositions for over forty years. The strategies of representation had been refined by 1931; Sylviane Leprun has observed that by this point the genre had achieved "a certain classicism."[8] The exposition played upon the usual rampant exoticism and the inevitable Orientalism.[9] It exhibited elaborate pavilions made to represent completely unrelated cultures lining wide promenades at the edge of the city, like so many model homes of a mad suburban real estate developer. Having experienced the decolonialization of the European powers in the decades after World War II, our eyes spot the blatant techniques to seduce

William H. Schneider, *An Empire for the Masses: The French Popular Image of Africa, 1870–1900* (Westport, Conn., 1982), esp. 174–210. Actually, the centennial was 1930, but had the fair opened on schedule, it would have been too early. As we see, the celebration in the Bois de Vincennes was a year late.

6. Thomas G. August, *The Selling of the Empire: British and French Propaganda, 1890–1940* (Westport, Conn., 1985). One pioneering study (other than Lenin's) that does look into the works of persuasion is Bernard Semmel, *Imperialism and Social Reform in Great Britain, 1900–1914* (Cambridge, Mass., 1960).

7. Silverman, "1889 Exhibition," 81–82. In a nice example of form following ideology, the colonial section faced the medieval castle of the Ministry of War and the elaborate display dedicated to *l'économie sociale*, the welfare of industrial workers.

8. Sylviane Leprun, *Le Théâtre des colonies* (Paris, 1986), 12.

9. Edward Said, *Orientalism* (New York, 1978), might be consulted for this tradition of representation. We now need a critique of "Occidentalism."

the fairgoers to value what the empire had achieved. But the larger intention of the planners, and the novelty of *this* colonial exposition—to promote this grander conception of a new-style imperial France, a new definition of what it was to be French—requires closer analysis.[10]

Political Aesthetics

Here we come to a preliminary but difficult problem. We cannot experience the exposition as a literary critic can reread a book or a film critic can replay a film years after it was created. People who visited the exposition tell us how powerfully it worked on them. William Cohen reports, for example, that many colonial service officers remembered that their choice of career had been influenced by the powerful and lasting impression their visit to the exposition made on them.[11] How can we get an appreciation for what these people said they experienced? Useful written evidence exists, along with many visual images: paintings, drawings, photographs, picture postcards, lantern slides. We must keep in mind, however, that we are working at two removes from the life of the French colonial empire, or indeed of Paris in the spring, summer, and fall of 1931.

The exposition unveiled a radiant vision of the colonial empire. The beauty of the display transformed aesthetic appreciation into political ontology: the show became a token of the worth of the

10. This shift in colonial advocacy in the 1930s is not noted in Winfried Baumgart's otherwise useful review of new writings on the French colonial empire in the years 1880–1914. See his "'Grossere Frankreich': Neue Forschungen über den französischen Imperialismus, 1880–1914," *Vierteljahrsschrift für Sozial- und Wirtschaftsgeschichte*, 61 (1974), 185–98.

11. William Cohen, *Rulers of Empire: The French Colonial Service in Africa* (Stanford, 1971), 105–6. Charles-Robert Ageron, "L'Exposition coloniale de 1931: Mythe républicain ou mythe impérial," in *Les Lieux de mémoire*, ed. Pierre Nora, vol. 1, *La République* (Paris, 1984), 561–91, esp. 584, disputes Cohen on the exposition's success in gaining recruits for the colonial school. But admirers of the colonial empire keep its appeal and that of its expositions alive: to take just one recent act of witness, at a meeting of the French Colonial Historical Society in May 1987 Robert Cornevin of the Académie des Sciences d'Outre-mer told me that his visit to the exposition had greatly influenced his career choice.

colonial effort and of a new grander vision of what it was to be French. The photographs of the exposition imposed yet another layer of visual meaning; as we will see, they were well-wrought asethetic artifacts in their own right, which further validated the truth the exposition was designed to tell. They affirm, to follow Roland Barthes's idea of how photographs persuade, that their contents really existed as the viewer saw them.[12] But of what were visitors and viewers to be persuaded?

The Paris surrealists—those experts both on the images of bourgeois hegemony and on their subversion—gave their version of what was wanted and how it was being done. "Don't Visit the Colonial Exposition," urged Paul Eluard, André Breton, Louis Aragon, and Yves Tanguy (to name its most famous authors) in big type at the top of their leaflet. Boycott the fair not only to protest colonial massacres and exploitation, but above all as a way of rejecting the idea of "La Grande France," this "intellectual swindle" (*concept-escroquerie*) behind the exposition.

> What they are doing is giving the citizens of the metropole the sense of being proprietors, which they will need to believe to listen, at least without flinching, to the echoes of distant firing squads. What they are doing is adding to the fine landscape of France, already improved before the war by a song about a bamboo hut, a vision of minarets and pagodas.[13]

In ways both existential and symbolic the exposition did offer French visitors a sense of proprietorship over all these marvels. The fair was staged in the capital of the metropole; it was run by colonial

12. Roland Barthes, *Camera Lucida: Reflections on Photography*, trans. Richard Howard (New York, 1981), 82, 85–89, 96, 101–2, 118. See also Barthes's insightful description of how the photographic message works, in "The Photographic Message," in *Images, Music, Text*, trans. Stephen Heath (New York, 1977), 31. Patricia Mainardi's *Art and Politics of the Second Empire: The Universal Expositions of 1855 and 1867* (New Haven, 1987) is an especially rich contribution to a new art history with the politics of society left in. I have profited especially from her discussion of what is included and what is left out of Edouard Manet's "View of the Universal Exposition of Paris, 1867," 143–50.

13. Archives Nationales, sec. France d'Outre-mer, Aix-en-Provence, files of the Service de Liaison entre les Originaires des Territoires Français d'Outre-mer, ser. III, carton 5. Eluard and Breton had drafted the text; Breton gave it its final form. See also André Thirion, *Revolutionaries without Revolution*, trans. Joachim Neugroschel (New York, 1975), 283.

heroes and governors. The native participants were literally hired help, required to stay in their native dress while they were on the fairgrounds. But more important, it projected a vision of a greater France by wrapping native cultures within the high culture of European France. This enclosing worked in two ways. First, wrapping colonial cultures gave them legitimacy in the eyes of Europeans by relating them to European icons. Second, it set the aesthetic and political guidelines for the creation of an imperial culture, one neither purely metropolitan French nor devoid of nativeness, but dominated and circumscribed by the setting in the capital of Greater France.[14]

A visual example will clarify how this wrapping worked. The official guidebook's map situates Martinique, Algeria, French West Africa, and so forth in the park of an elegant neighborhood bordered by the avenues Daumesnil and Gravelle on the north and south, by the boulevard Poniatowski on the west, and by the Paris–Charenton road on the east (Figure 1). Visitors could reach it by trams, buses, a special boat service with connecting bus to the fairgrounds, and the extended Métro line no. 8 (which Marshal Lyautey demanded as a condition of accepting the post of *commissaire général*).[15] A non-Western civilization that can be approached by subway, picnic basket in hand, loses stature and awesomeness. Its glories seem easily appreciated and readily fathomed.[16]

14. See Fredric Jameson, "Spatial Equivalents: Post-Modern Architecture and the World Systems," paper presented at the State University of New York at Stony Brook, 1987. The idea of "wrapping" to incorporate and at the same time to give a new meaning is especially helpful for understanding the idea of Greater France. Jameson employed the notion to talk about the aesthetic and social commentary—the exchanges of meaning, the new meanings—created by the architect Frank Gehry's literally wrapping his bungalow in Santa Monica, California, with new walls, fences, and roofs of modern industrial materials and designs. The outer structure engulfs the older one, subordinating without entirely eliminating it. In the interaction of its differing forms, ages, walls, construction materials, and values the final nested building signs new levels of social and aesthetic significance. As a new-made building, moreover, it means something different from any of its component parts. This rich idea avoids a naive unhierarchical (and therefore unpolitical) vision of an intertextuality between the colonial rulers and the ruled. For more on wrapping see Jameson's *Politics of Post-Modernity; or, The Cultural Logic of Late Capitalism* (Durham, N.C., 1991), 101–29.

15. *Guide officiel*, 8–14; Olivier, "Origines et buts," 49.

16. In *One-Dimensional Man* (Boston, 1964) Herbert Marcuse regretted the sale of Plato and other great works of Western civilization on paperback racks in drugstores.

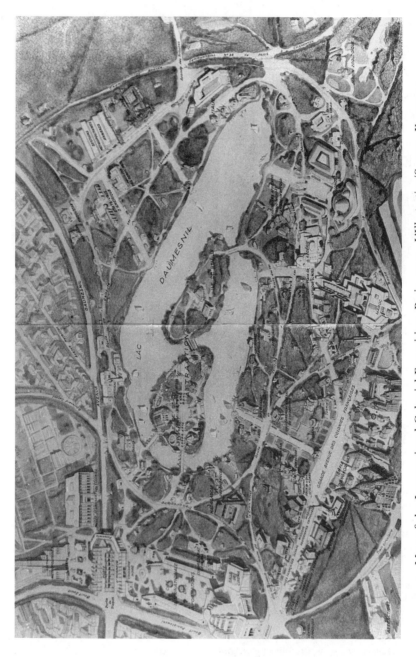

1. Map of the International Colonial Exposition, Paris, 1931. *L'Illustration*/Sygma, Keystone.

The scores of pictures in a special album published by the magazine *L'Illustration* glorify the architectural wonders of the pavilions.[17] The greatest of them, in both size and elaborateness, was the massive, *restored* reconstruction of the Khmer temple of Angkor Wat, the chief attraction on the fairground. One photograph, shot from the top, takes in the tower, bordering statues, and the hazy city beyond (Figure 2). On the left the massive (apparently) stone central tower of the temple ballasts the image. It signs strength, monumentality, a culture that honors religion. The ledge is flanked by evenly spaced stylized carved lions guarding the shrine. The rest of the temple structure is evident below; beyond lie the exposition grounds and the city over which the temple seems to watch.

The view seems curiously like the one in postcards we have sent or received of Notre Dame de Paris. It is one of the consecrated tourist images of the Paris cathedral: the wall of the heavily carved tower, a balcony, a gargoyle perched on the building's edge, and the city of Paris spread out in the hazy distance (Figure 3). Thus the visual equation of the picture editor of *L'Illustration:* Angkor Wat is their Notre Dame, their great monument of religious architecture, sacred and worthy of our respect. André Maurois, who wrote a breathless account of what he had seen in the Bois de Vincennes, read what the pavilion was signing the same way: "I also love Angkor as seen from the Tonkin pavilion, a confusion of towers, a riotous mass like Notre Dame viewed from the Île Saint-Louis.[18]

He was thinking of the loss of intellectual independence, elevation, and therefore power the classics suffered thereby.

17. Pierre Albert, "La Presse française de 1871 à 1940," in *Histoire générale de la presse française,* ed. Claude Bellanger et al., 3 vols. (Paris, 1972), vol. 3, *De 1871 à 1940,* describes *L'Illustration* variously as "sans concurrence, le magazine de qualité française, dont la lecture constituait une sorte de consécration sociale" (387) and as "devenu une sorte d'institution" (597–98). Its circulation mounted from 120,000 copies in 1926 to something like 200,000 by 1939. Its publishers, René Baschet and his sons, were rightist in their sympathies and vigorously opposed the Popular Front. The magazine promoted the cause of colonialism among its middle-class readers at the beginning of the 1930s, "et il n'est guère de numéro, autour des années 1930, qui n'évoque les paysages, les hommes ou les événements de l'outre-mer," writes Raoul Girardet in *L'Idée coloniale en France de 1871 à 1962* (Paris, 1972), 122.

18. André Maurois, *"Sur le vif": L'Exposition coloniale, Paris, 1931* (Paris, 1931), 17. Maurois liked also the friezes on the buildings on the Togo and Cameroon exhibit, "ces frises rouges, noires, blanches, qui semblent courir sur un vase grec archaïque" (7). The idea that Angkor Wat was faithfully represented in 1931 in Paris and the "this

2. View from a tower of Angkor Wat. *L'Illustration*/Sygma, Keystone.

Quoting from sacred monuments to legitimate a style or a new value was already part of the practice of the exposition mode. Debora Silverman has pointed out that the layout of the 1889 exhibition

---

is their Notre Dame" figure seem both to have become part of art-historical folklore. In *Le Monde*'s review of Claude Jacques's *Angkor*, the reviewer comments that the

3. View from a tower of Notre Dame de Paris; picture postcard sold at tourist shops near the Paris cathedral. Abeille-Cartes.

tion grounds took the form of a cathedral: the Eiffel Tower, with which Alexandre Gustave Eiffel specifically quoted the spire of Notre Dame; the central nave made by the Champs de Mars; at the opposite end from the spire, the Central Dome, and flanking it the Palace of Machines effecting a transept.[19] In 1889 the liberal capitalism of the newborn secular republic was the object of veneration.

Now it cannot be denied that the temple built at the edge of the city was clearly magnificent; casts of portions of it, saved after the exposition's close and still to be seen in the Musée Guimet in Paris, attest to the artistry of its construction and decoration. The issue here is not its misrepresentation but, on the contrary, its representa-

exposition's "réplique partielle" of the complex of temples of which Angkor Wat is just one structure was "fidèle" to the original, but the grandness of the ensemble can be properly appreciated only when we realize that "une bonne demi-douzaine [of the other buildings] sont, comme Angkor-Vat, grands comme nos cathédrales": Y. R., "Angkor, toujours," Le Monde, 8 December 1990, 33.

19. Silverman, "1889 Exhibition," 74–75.

tion. The photo validates the beauty and the worth of the fair's Cambodian temple—the original was in ruins—by linking it with high Western religious art. This art and these artistic and devout people are worthy to take their place alongside the Bretons, Alsatians, Gascons, Niçoises, and all the other populations of the regions of France, with their native customs and patois, and with their loyalty to the great cultural and political force radiating out of Paris. They shall be part of our new Greater France. We should welcome them in as we did the others, especially now during the current depression, when France needs their consumption and the raw materials from their beautiful *pays*.[20]

The Inauguration

The Exposition was not planned to counteract the Great Depression of the 1930s. The extraordinary number of tourists in Paris during half of 1931 was a serendipitous result of the delay in opening. In 1914 President Poincaré had laid the first stone of a colonial exposition planned to open in Marseille in 1916. The coming of war halted the planning. At the end of the hostilities, in the course of which the full worth of the colonies and especially of troops from the colonies became evident to all, the Parisians tried to move the venue to the capital.[21] The parliamentary commission on the colonies, whose decision it was, suffered the cross-fire of the contending cities. The solution the government hit upon was that the Marseillais should have an *exposition nationale* in 1922 and Paris would host an *exposition interalliée* in 1925. When the opening of the long-planned

20. *Exposition coloniale internationale de Paris, 1931: Album de 154 pages comprenant les matières parues dans les numéros de "L'Illustration" des 23 mai, 27 juin, 25 juillet, 22 août et 28 novembre 1931* (Paris, 1931), 30; hereafter cited as *L'Illustration*. The pages are not numbered. I arrived at my own page numbers by counting from the beginning; the reader should use them as an approximate guide.

21. Nearly a million natives of the colonies and external regions of France fought in World War I; 205,000 died for France. See Raoul Girardet, "L'Apothéose de la 'plus grande France': L'Idée coloniale devant l'opinion française (1930–1935)," *Revue Française de Science Politique*, 18 (1968), 1086.

Exposition des Arts Decoratifs conflicted with this schedule, the Paris colonial fair was postponed till 1928.

Meanwhile, the planners realized that major colonial powers—Portugal and Holland, for example—would be excluded if the exposition remained restricted to war partners. Major allies, too, would not take part. The British, committed to their British Empire Exhibition to be held at Wembley in 1924—too close to the scheduled opening date of the French fair—chose not to participate in the celebration of France's imperial destiny.[22] The adjective was changed from *interalliée* to *internationale,* the other interested nations were given time to catch up, and, with additional construction delays, the opening was finally set for the spring of 1931. "If we focus on the present economic fortunes of our country, we might be tempted to exclaim, 'lucky delay,'" judged Governor General Olivier, putting a good face on the misadventures in the timing.[23]

The exposition opened on 6 May 1931. Departing from protocol, which normally placed the premier at the side of the president of the Republic in ceremonies, Gaston Doumergue was driven from his residence to the main gate of the exposition with Marshal Lyautey seated beside him for the elaborate inauguration ceremonies. After reviewing the troops of the 23d colonial battalion, he and his entourage circled the grounds in a motorcade escorted by a squadron of colonial cavalry (*spahis*). The reverberations of a 100-gun salute filled the air; the dignitaries accepted the salutes of the native troops lined up before the pavilions of their *pays.* At the Indochinese section President Doumergue had the car stopped so that he could pause for a moment of meditation before the temple of Angkor Wat, the ruins of which he had first seen many years before while serving as a young magistrate in Indochina.

An honored guest, pictured during the opening festivities accompanied by Albert Sarraut, leading spirit of the colonial movement in the 1920s, and Indochinese Governor General Pierre Pasquier, was

22. August, *Selling of the Empire,* 125–53. Bernard Semmel suggested to me that perhaps, with Labour in power during much of the planning period and many of the Conservatives open to the idea of cutting the colonial empire loose, it was all the British fair planners could do to get their own exposition launched, without the added expense and trouble of celebrating another nation's empire.

23. Olivier, "Origines et buts," 48–49, 54.

the emperor of Annam, Bao Dai, newly restored to his throne and about to be sent back to Vietnam to take part in the cultural pacification after the recent uprisings (Figure 4). In weighty regal clothing that contrasted with his young innocent face, he seemed a miscast extra in the imperial performance. The statue of a warrior France guarding the entrance of the Musée des Colonies towered over him.

A motorcade through the fairgrounds finally brought the dignitaries to the Musée Permanent, in whose auditorium the inauguration ceremony would conclude (Figure 5). There, with Premier Pierre Laval, Minister of Colonies Paul Reynaud, the cabinet, the presidents of both chambers, members of the Municipal Council of Paris and the Council General of the Seine, as well as many other important dignitaries in attendance, the audience heard four speakers.

Marshal Lyautey reviewed the history of the creation of the exposition since the first stone was ceremonially laid on 8 November 1928 and concluded "with a few magisterial words" on the ethos of French colonialism. Jean de Castellane, president of the Paris Municipal Council, expressed his delight at the benefits the city would reap from hosting the exposition. The doyen of the representatives of the other governments with pavilions, Prince Lanza di Scalea, minister of colonies of Fascist Italy, thanked France for its hospitality on behalf of the foreign commissioners and reflected proudly on "the Homeric Odyssey of the white race, which, having now reached every corner of the world, has transformed, or is in the process of transforming, barbaric continents into civilized regions."

Finally, it was for Paul Reynaud to present the two key new governmental ideas of the decade on the relation of France and the colonies. After glorifying France's role in "the discovery of the world" (sic) and declaring that the prime goal of the exposition was "to make the empire a part of French consciousness," he emphasized the great importance of "each of us coming to understand himself as a citizen of Greater France [*Grande France*]." In 1928 Léon Archimbaud, Radical Socialist reporter of the colonial budget in the Chamber of Deputies, had written in *La Plus Grande France* of an empire of many *pays*. The memory of the book and its agenda was still fresh in people's minds. Reynaud, in comparing the size of metropolitan France with that of its colonies (the area of the colonies was twenty-three times greater than that of European France), spoke of "*l'Em-*

4. Emperor Bao Dai of Annam leaving the Colonial Museum flanked by
Albert Sarraut and Governor General Pierre Pasquier (in uniform). *L'Illustration*/Sygma, Keystone.

5. Motorcade passing before honor guards at pavilions of their native lands.
L'Illustration/Sygma, Keystone.

pire français." These were relatively novel visions of France's colonial enterprise. In subsequent years these terms—"Greater France" and "French Empire"—appeared ever more commonly in the media and in public discourse.[24] President Doumergue declared the exposition opened (Figure 6).

The Simulacrum of Greater France

Before we begin an imaginary tour by passing through the entrance used for the inauguration and follow the itinerary a visitor might take, let us look carefully at the rendering of the approach to the main gate done by its architect, Henry Bazin (Figure 7). The organization of the painting poses no subtleties: all the lines of perspective—marked by the columns, the trees, and the visitors—direct the eye to the entrance gate. Everything else is strange. Palm trees do not flourish in the Bois de Vincennes, but large palms did indeed flank the entranceway during the six months of the exposition. The stark modern columns with slabs as capitals suggest the ruins of an earlier, greater civilization in a Middle Eastern setting, an idea reinforced by the Middle Eastern and African pilgrims streaming toward the new—Occidental—Mecca. And all is under a bright blue sky such as one sees in North Africa, but rarely in Paris, and even more rarely during the dismal rainy spring of 1931.[25]

24. Girardet, *L'Idée coloniale en France,* 124–25. The first systematic use of the word and elaboration of the concept I have found was by Henri Vast in *La Plus Grande France: Bilan de la France coloniale* (Paris, 1909). A liberal republican—he quoted John Stuart Mill—Vast acknowledged his vocabulary debt to the British "Greater Britain," and asserted that the days of exploitation and colonial abuse were over: "La France traite maternellement ses nouveau enfants" (5). He associated modernity and the future of France with the colonies: "*La plus grande France,* c'est la France nouvelle" (7). The book contains a chapter on each colony, giving area, resources, population, languages, and other such data. Charles-Robert Ageron, *France coloniale ou parti colonial?* (Paris, 1978), 253, discusses Léon Archimbaud, author in June 1928 of *La Plus Grande France,* in which he tried to foster an imperial consciousness among the French on the order of the Englishman's sense of imperial calling.
25. Paul Morand evoked the same sense of the interpenetration of metropolitan and overseas France in his word picture of the exposition, "Rien que la terre à l'Exposition coloniale: Les Tropiques à Vincennes," *Revue des Deux Mondes,* 8th ser.,

6. Inaguration of the exposition in the Great Hall of the Colonial Museum. *L'Illustration*/Sygma, Keystone

7. La Porte de Picpus, main entrance to the exposition grounds. *L'Illustra-tion*/Sygma, Keystone.

We have here an illusion that evokes still another illusion: blue sky and palm trees in Paris; Arab and African visitors come to admire European representations of their homelands, when we know that the visitors were overwhelmingly Europeans. Everything is conflated and turned upside down. The line between here and there, between metropolitan France and the colonies, is erased; it is a pictorial representation of an ethnically diverse but politically unified and centralized French empire.[26] Bazin's painting of his architec-

---

101 (15 July 1931), 329. Moreover, he affirmed the worth of offering "aux Parisiens sédentaires des Tropiques sans moustiques ni venins, sans soif ni fièvres," etc., because "il est bon que l'homme soit trompé; les grandes choses sont à ce prix."

26. I have to admit puzzlement over the distinction between assimilation and association in French colonial policy. August, *Selling of the Empire*, 146, suggests that the values of the exposition were those of association and yet the ideology of *La Grande France* seems certainly assimilationist in intent.

tural design conveys the message that the exposition's planners attempted to convey to visitors: that despite differences, we are all interconnected, we are all part of a new Grander France. We see here Bazin's vision of the peoples coming like the Magi to celebrate the birth of a new life.[27]

Before we look at the pavilions it might be useful to distinguish the two faces of the fair. The Bazin painting, many exhibits, and photographs of exhibits presented the empire romantically, as fable, as wonder, as curiosity. But other representations of France and the colonies emphasized what was valuable, useful, beneficial to both the French of the metropole and those overseas. The persuasive quality of the spectacle lay, I believe, in the dialectic it established of a wondrous verisimilitude, of the alternation of fable and utility from display to display and within exhibits. The wondrous constructions confirmed for the visitor the truthfulness of the statistics and graphs precisely because the data on the achievements of French colonialism were so very different from the visual images. By their juxtaposition the imaginative made plausible the factual. Keeping in mind, then, that we are dealing not with aesthetic imagination and "the facts" but with two aspects of simulation, let us call the one dimension the fabulous exposition, the other, the improving exposition.[28]

When we enter the Porte de Picpus and follow the itinerary rec-

27. In what follows I understand Baudrillard's claim that the simulacrum dissimulates that there is nothing to mean in the last instance that the vision of the powerful eclipsed the vision of the weak. Accordingly, Baudrillard's deep pessimism about living in a world of self-referential simulation is an assertion that the weak have been silenced by the controllers of images—in effect the power-political terms he refuses. That was not the case of the Vietnamese rebels of 1930–31, or of the disruptive native students in Paris, or finally of the anticolonial forces of much of what was the French colonial empire in 1931. So here, too, I have attempted to historicize a compelling perspective and to replace Baudrillard's conception of the tyranny of the signmakers with a social and colonial world of dissenters and rebels. See Jean Baudrillard, "The Precession of Simulacra," in *Simulations,* trans. Paul Foss, Paul Patten, and Philip Beitchman (New York, 1983), 2, 5, 11–12, and *In the Shadow of the Silent Majorities* (1978; New York, 1983). See further Mike Cater, "From Red Centre to Black Hole," 63–81, and R. Gibson, "Custom and Excise," 45–57, both in André Frankovits, *Seduced and Abandoned* (Glebe, N.S.W., Australia, 1984).

28. See Baudrillard, *Simulations,* 23–26; Leprun, *Théâtre des colonies,* 17. See also Sandy Petrie, "The Reality of Representation: Between Marx and Balzac," *Critical Inquiry,* 14 (1988), 448–67, esp. 461.

ommended by the guidebook, we are directed in a long loop around the central lake starting with the Cité des Informations, a large modern building containing displays of orientation materials, statistical compilations, production data—in short, important facts about the French colonial empire to start us on our world tour. This section clearly partakes of the serious and mind-improving exposition. The guide then directs us to look in on the pavilion of colonial wood products, the only pavilion in the colonial section dedicated exclusively inside and out to the economic value of colonial raw materials, in contrast to the metropolitan section at the end of the itinerary, which focuses on highly wrought industrial products.

Only with the Madagascar pavilion (Figure 8) do we reach the fabulous exposition. The reproduction of the Tour des Bucrânes rises 50 meters (160 feet) into the Paris sky; at the top are four horned heads of the Ox God (Dieu Boeuf), which honor the principal industry on the island. Like Bazin's painting of the Porte de Picpus—it was not just the quirk of one artist—the sepia print of André Maire shows a column and the adjoining "enlarged and stylized copy" of the dwelling of an important former king in a tropical setting. On the ground floor of the striking and strange pavilion the colonial authorities erected exhibits on improvements in hygiene and on local ethnography, history, and education. The other three floors offered visitors evidence of the economic potential of the island—forests, mines, precious stones—and of French-inspired development since 1895. The guidebook comments that "it is a *pays* especially suited to recreate the atmosphere of France."[29]

Quite different is the nearby group of pavilions representing the Indochinese Union: Cochin China, Tonkin, Annam, Cambodia, and Laos. Here is the splendid Far East of great civilizations in their own right. The guidebook does not speak of their early assimilation of metropolitan culture, but rather describes the pavilions as an initiation into the life of Indochina before the visitor goes on to view the glories of the great temple farther along the promenade.

After passing a typical fisherman's home on St. Pierre and Miquelon, the two French islands off the coast of Canada, France's only bit of territory left in North America and still completely inhabited

29. *Guide officiel*, 31–35.

8. The Madagascar pavilion. *L'Illustration*/Sygma, Keystone.

by descendants of the original French settlers, we come to the large pavilions dedicated to both Protestant and Catholic French missionary work abroad. The Protestant structure maintains the simplicity of presentation associated with reformed Christianity in France. The Catholic building is more majestic and elaborate. The tiled facade is decorated with flowers, figures, and symbols celebrating the diversity and universality of the faith. Inside, the visitor looks up into an azure sky filled with gold stars. Jesus is portrayed (as a European) in an immense glass window behind the altar. Below, under representations of Mary and the Apostles, is inscribed the Gospel admonition to take up the evangelical mission: "Go teach all the nations, baptize them in the name of the Father, the Son, and the Holy Ghost."[30] "The simple and noble words of Christ," noted Maurice Larrouy, "seem addressed as much to missionary efforts at home as to work with the inhabitants of our colonies." When a European in the tropics sees a bell tower rising "in the burning sky, a bell tower built by workers whose faith gives them their skill, it is a French vision he sees and which moves him emotionally regardless of his politics or his religious persuasion."[31] The guidebook evokes here not only a new definition of what it is to be French but also (accurately) the absence of anticlerical sentiments and a heightened patriotism that link settlers of all religious and political persuasions in the colonies.[32]

Next, according to the guidebook, we should visit the buildings of French Guinea, French India, Somalia, and France's possessions in the Pacific, chief among them Tahiti. With the exhibits for this island the fabulous exposition now comes to the fore. After a perfunctory sentence about the valuable food products (vanilla) and resources

30. *Rapport général*, vol. 5, pt. 1, 315.

31. Maurice Larrouy, "Les Possessions océaniques," *L'Illustration*, 42.

32. *Guide officiel*, 40–41. This ethos of reconciliation in the colonies was important in creating the sense of trust required if conservatives and republicans in the period 1880–1900 were to unite to create the new ruling order of the Republic, its second foundation. Throughout the sometimes anticlerical Third Republic, missionary work in the colonies was always tolerated and often aided by the most convinced laic republicans. See my *Alliance of Iron and Wheat in the Third French Republic, 1860–1914: Origins of the New Conservatism* (Baton Rouge, 1988), chap. 6. For a meditation on the martyrdom of colonial missionary life, see André Bellessort, "Nos Missionaires tels que les ai vus," *Revue des Deux Mondes*, 8th ser., 101 (15 July 1931), 346–65.

(phosphates, pearls), the guidebook immerses us in the world of Pierre Loti and Gauguin. A painting and a line cut picture the now consecrated images of topless dusky women in sarongs (Figure 9).[33]

We now go on to New Caledonia, the New Hebrides, Martinique, Réunion, Guadeloupe. In the New Caledonian pavilion André Maurois saw walls covered with "paintings done in browns and whites which are primitive, and because of that, modern"; and the women looked as though they had stepped out of a Gauguin: "Gauguin's women exist; I saw them in the New Caledonian pavilion."[34] When contemporary conservatives here and in France speak of preserving our intellectual and aesthetic traditions, unfortunately, that voyeuristic appropriation of women in the tropics, not just the paintings of Fragonard and David, must be reckoned as part of the Western heritage.

But after the languid titillations of island life we come to sacred beauty set in the six hectares (fifteen acres) of the Indochina exhibits, dominated by Angkor Wat, flower of Khmer architectural style, dedicated in the twelfth century to Vishnu but soon after also made a Buddhist holy place by King Jahyavarman VII, "the Khmer Louis XIV," as Robert de La Sizeranne characterized him to help the readers of the *Revue des Deux Mondes* grasp the Asian ruler's importance.[35] The very form of this square structure, measuring 70 meters (230 feet) on each side, can teach us about the achievements of French rule. Are not the five towers on the structure, reaching a height of 45 meters (the grand tower in the center measured 55 meters), all resting on carved and decorated rock bases, the guidebook asks, "the representation [*l'image*] of the five *pays* of the Indochinese Union, now brought together and consolidated by us?"[36] Cochin China, Cambodia, Annam, Tonkin, and Laos, once separated by high mountains, political barriers, and ethnic differences, had been united under "French protection" to form a powerful French confederation in the Pacific.

33. See Linda Nochlin, "The Imaginary Orient," in *The Politics of Vision: Essays on Nineteenth-Century Art and Society* (New York, 1989), 33–59.

34. Maurois, *"Sur le vif,"* 13.

35. Robert de La Sizeranne, "L'Art à l'Exposition coloniale: Les Dieux d'Angkor et leurs cortèges," *Revue des Deux Mondes*, 8th ser., 101 (1 July 1931), 121–22.

36. *Guide officiel*, 53.

9. Two representations of women in the colonies. *L'Illustration/Sygma, Keystone; Exposition coloniale internationale à Paris en 1931: Guide officiel*, 47.

The remarkable photo reproduced here (Figure 10)—the temple, the artist, the policemen watching—manifests a return of the politically repressed, a tableau of colonialism. Had the semiology of the photograph been expressed in unadorned language, such as "Profound Oriental spiritualism captured in great (Western) art under the surveillance of the police," the readers of *L'Illustration* might well have been shocked and offended, but also perhaps rendered more thoughtful.

The exhibits inside the shrine inform us via tables of statistics, displays, and exhibitions of products and resources that Indochina has been much improved under French protection. The *résident supérieur,* Pierre Guesde, and the technical director of the section, Henri Gourdon, wanted to show the visitor a modern Indochina. "To draw visitors and to hold them, it was indispensable to have recourse to all the seductions of the picturesque and to the irresistible magic of art."[37] (See Figure 11.)

Governor General Pasquier saw the enterprise of Greater France as the task of making ancient civilizations worthy parts of a modern state:

> The Indochina of pagodas, but also of schools, factories, mines, plantations, spacious harbors; the Indochina of litter chairs [*palanquins*] and of elephants, but also of extensive rail lines, of mighty radio towers and airlines; a traditionalist Indochina, deeply moving, but also a young Indochina, stirring, awakening under the watchful eyes of France, eager for progress, an Indochina ready for action, [a land] from which the vital force of a marvelous renewal pours forth.

And to conclude with the beautiful, Demaison urged visitors to return at sunset to see the sun sink behind the five towers.[38]

A territory nine times the area of France, French West Africa, comprising then Senegal, French Guinea, the Ivory Coast, Dahomey, Mauritania, Sudan, Upper Volta, and Niger, is represented by a magnificent red mud palace capped by a 45-meter (150-foot) tower built in what the guidebook characterizes as the Sudanese manner (Figure 12). The towers and walls bristle with embedded poles, as

37. Robert de Beauplan, "Les Palais de l'Indochine," *L'Illustration,* 109.
38. *Guide officiel,* 61.

10. Policemen watch an artist painting the Angkor Wat under construction at the edge of Paris. *L'Illustration*/Sygma, Keystone.

11. Interior courtyard of Angkor Wat. *L'Illustration*/Sygma, Keystone.

would be the case in West Africa, placed there to allow masons to climb about to repair the damage of the rainy season. The inside is given over to exhibits of improving didacticism: the economic, social, and administrative evolution of the parts and the whole of French West Africa. But once outside the area of four hectares around the palace, the visitor may participate in the varied and colorful life of black Africa. We can shop for jewelry, leather goods, fabrics, pottery, baskets, and wood carvings made by traditional craftworkers in the seemingly transplanted narrow streets of Djenné, the major Sudanese commercial town (Figure 13). We can watch the young women weave rugs, a new art taught them by the Soeurs Blanches (White Sisters). But there is also a "'fetishist'" village nearby, where 200 native inhabitants go through the daily routines of their lives before our eyes. In addition the commissioners offer the public for their entertainment and wonder four African dance troupes (from the upper Ivory Coast, Sudan, Dahomey, and the upper Niger).

12. The French West Africa pavilion. *L'Illustration*/Sygma, Keystone.

Yes, these are people with unfamiliar names from *pays* with names that sound bizarre to our ears, acknowledges the official guide. But just wait until French West African possessions are linked by rail to those in North Africa, wait for the development of aviation in Africa, wait a few decades. "These names will be more familiar to our ears than Provençal or Gascon names became to Parisians in the seventeenth century." Then "our Africa, tightly bound to us now for both its defense and its prosperity, will become a magnificent and direct extension of our French humanity."[39]

The governing ideal here recognizes the wrapping of cultures around a French core as a kind of mutual apprenticeship in citizenship: on the one side natives learning to be French while of course retaining their local customs; on the other European French, recalling their own apprenticeships as Gascons or Bretons, learning to welcome the new French. The new French were exposed to an

39. Ibid., 68.

13. Tourists crowd into a boutique on a typical Sudanese street. *L'Illustration*/Sygma, Keystone.

array of persuasions to accept French rule in their native lands; it was the task of the exposition to offer the already assimilated French of Europe insight into the identity that they would henceforth share with their brethren of Greater France.[40] As the correspondent of

40. See Ageron, *France coloniale ou parti colonial?* 189–90. Ageron's history of policy is as follows: Assimilation was ascendant between 1880 and 1895, out of fashion around the turn of the century, and at its apogee under the Popular Front. In between

The Times of London remarked with some surprise in his report of the exposition, "No attempt is made to prevent [the colonial people working at the fair] from getting to know their European visitors. . . . The French do not regard the natives at Vincennes as a sort of raree show!"[41]

Next we come to French Equatorial Africa, where not so long ago the explorer Pierre-Paul Brazza won his fame, but whose native art was now captivating avant-garde French artists. Rays of light were beginning to penetrate to the forest house of these recently benighted and barbarous people, we learn. Not far from this African area lies the installation of the Forces d'Outre-mer, a tower topped by an observation platform and beacon before which native troops from various regions of the empire take their turn each evening honoring the colors.

Farther along we see the pavilions of North Africa, Morocco, Tunisia, Algeria, and North African tourism.[42] The editors of *L'Illustration* chose a painting of the replica of the Moroccan palace of Maghzen—with North African plants, native people, and Mediterranean blue sky—for the cover of their commemorative volume. The Algerian building, Demaison admits, represents nothing that exists in the colony, but is rather a "stylized synthesis of Algerian architecture." Not only are the French rulers able to create native cultural traditions when they must, but they can invent characteristic architecture. The North African pavilions feature the now-customary array of native houses, local crafts and craftspeople in souks, dioramas, religious buildings (minarets), and authentic cafés,

policy shifted from maintaining protectorates with little interference in native life and institutions (e.g., Lyautey in Morocco) to association (Albert Sarraut in both his writings and his term as governor general of Indochina). But clearly Ageron is dealing with degrees of emphasis, not clear-cut turns, for the ideology of the exposition contained elements of both the assimilationist and the associationist views. See ibid., 194–232.

41. *Times*, 23 July 1931, 13, cited in Burton Benedict, *The Anthropology of World's Fairs: San Francisco's Panama Pacific Exposition of 1915* (Berkeley, 1983), 48.

42. See Pierre Benoît's reverie on his visit to the Tunisian pavilion, "La Tunisie," *Revue des Deux Mondes*, 8th ser., 4 (1 July 1931), 110–19. An old *colon*, he did not help advance the exposition's theme of progress under French rule with his variation on the old song of the "eternal Orient": "En dépit du Dar-Zarrouk et du photographe, des dancings et du golf à neuf trous, rien n'a changé, vraiment, mon Dieu! rien n'a changé" (118).

14. Members of the Senegalese Rifles take French lessons in their off-duty hours. *L'Illustration*/Sygma, Keystone.

as well as edifying exhibits on local resources and the French-created or-improved infrastructure.[43]

Just behind the Moroccan pavilion in a quiet courtyard we come upon a small structure open on one side, containing rows of benches and a blackboard. Sitting on the benches, we observe, depending on the time of day, Senegalese soldiers, Arab vendors, Vietnamese rickshaw pullers, or other peoples of the colonies brought to France to play their part in the Vincennes show and now united in struggle with the complexities of written French (Figure 14). The Ligue pour l'Instruction des Illettrés has set up a branch of its Ecole Française pour Indigènes for the duration of the exposition. A fresco by a French artist, Mme Loyau, shows tropical plants and animals in cheerful profusion. Here and there on the wall short texts encourage students and visitors: "Illiterate people are blind people," "To belong to our league is to do the work of the nation." In thirty or forty lessons during their off-duty hours, natives of Asia and Africa

43. *Guide officiel,* 77–104; Benoit, "La Tunisie," 111.

could learn the basics of spoken and written French, claimed Mme Morel-Chailly, the league's founder. Spreading knowledge of the French language throughout the empire, comments *L'Illustration*, is, "for us, the surest means of penetration there is, and for them, no less certain a way both to understand us better and to love us more each day."[44]

Finally we come to the last French colonial exhibit, Togo and Cameroon, territories approximating the area of metropolitan France. Demaison is clear in his own mind that these areas, taken from their German rulers in the war and mandated to France by the League of Nations, should be seen simply as new French colonies. A large hall with uplifting exhibits about how much the French have accomplished in a short time is bordered by native huts of the northern Cameroon region, "naturally, the huts quite stylized by the French architect." In the building devoted to the hunt in Africa, dioramas portray jungle scenes into which are integrated memorabilia of the life of the explorer Bruneau de Laborie, who unfortunately was killed by a lion the year before.[45] One wonders whether this reminder of the dangers of Darkest Africa weakened the message of the exhibit in the eyes of those as yet unpersuaded of the *projet* of Greater France.

The New Holy Alliance

Seven countries decided to accept the French invitation to set up exhibits in the Bois de Vincennes: Belgium, Brazil, Denmark, the United States, Italy, the Netherlands, and Portugal. In puzzling out why France needed the help of other nations to celebrate its colonial achievements we must take account of two distinct epochs in the history of European colonialism.

First, during the exposition's planning period, the haunting accusation that the recent war had had something to do with imperialist rivalries (recall the invocation of Lyautey on this theme in the guide-

44. L. R.-M., "Une Ecole française pour indigènes," *L'Illustration*, 132.
45. *Guide officiel*, 105; Jean Gallotti, "Somalis—A.O.F.—Togo—Cameroun," *L'Illustration*, 25.

book's welcoming statement) had to be laid to rest. Then, too, the Germans, stripped of their colonies, might begin to contemplate their own revanche. As French diplomacy organized structures of alliances to contain future German aggression, so the planners of the exposition sought architectural tokens of solidarity among the colonial powers. To be sure, the British did not come; in the interwar years the British were not interested in becoming entangled once again with the French.[46] But other nations with empires accepted the agenda of the French, at least aesthetically.

Second, there was the idea Charles-Robert Ageron aptly called the "colonial holy alliance." Much as in the aftermath of the Napoleonic wars, when the tsar invited rulers with something to lose by the spread of nationalism to join him in putting down revolution, Albert Sarraut wanted to unify imperialist nations to stem the new tide of nationalism and Bolshevism. The anticolonial thrust of Bolshevism-in-power had been there from the start, and the turn of the Comintern to colonial liberation in the interwar years was further cause for concern. The year before the fair opened, the nationalist Yen-Bay insurrection followed by the communist-led jacquerie in North Annam announced the beginnings of the challenge to French colonial rule. Therefore, the sight of pavilions of other nations in Paris gave hope that international communism might be contained and driven back by a newly wrought international fraternity of imperialist countries.[47]

Two of the foreign pavilions are worth a visit. First, that of the United States, which refused to sign the treaty of Versailles— France's hoped-for American commitment to European security— but joined the international celebration of empire. The semiology of the American exhibit is wonderfully revelatory. The United States chose to build a replica of George Washington's home, Mount Vernon, as the center of its offering. Washington had been the friend of

46. In his *Grandeur et servitude coloniales* (Paris, 1931), whose appearance coincided with the exposition, Albert Sarraut emphasized the common colonial heritage of European nations and called upon them to build on this tradition to overcome lingering past rivalries and animosities. See Girardet, *L'Idée coloniale en France*, 130–32.

47. See Ageron, *France coloniale ou parti colonial?* 230–31. On the change from colonial apotheosis to the beginnings of "colonial restiveness," see Girardet, "L'Apothéose de la 'plus grande France,'" 1085–1114.

Lafayette; America remained France's friend. The room in which Lafayette stayed on his visit in 1793 is on view, with a copy of the bronzed key to the Bastille which Lafayette gave the hero of the American war for independence exhibited on a table. Visitors could also see a reproduction of the dove of peace which Washington had given his guest. Somewhat tactlessly, the Americans placed on a floor of the west room of Mount Vernon a reproduction of the carpet Louis XVI had had specially woven for the president of the American republic.[48] But there was another message the Americans wanted to convey in focusing on the first American president: Washington was also the president who warned against foreign entanglements.

The American pavilion omitted a third possible take on Washington at a colonial exposition: Washington as the leader of the first successful anticolonial uprising in the New World. On the contrary, the wings of Mount Vernon and adjoining structures housed exhibits on Alaska, Panama, the Philippines, Samoa, the Virgin Isles, Hawaii, and Puerto Rico. So much had reality and illusion interpenetrated that one cannot tell from the organizers' reports or from the articles in *L'Illustration* whether the "dusky beauties" (*filles brunes*) from the Philippines, the Hawaiians who danced on hot coals, and American Indians were real people or diorama figures. It seemed not to matter. It is a fact, however, that the United States sent no individuals to act out the life of Mount Vernon, neither Virginian patricians nor black slaves.[49]

The Italian heritage of empire, actively linked to the empire of the Caesars in the imagery of the Fascist state, was celebrated by the erection of a restored rendering of the basilica of Leptis Magna, built by the second-century emperor Septimus Severus. The emperor, who was born in what became the Italian colony of Libya, celebrated his hometown with this monument of Roman grandeur, a combination of force and beauty, as Lyautey characterized it. The grandest memorial to the expansionist civilization of Rome in the North African desert, put on display in Europe three years before

48. *Le Livre d'or de l'Exposition coloniale internationale de Paris, 1931* (Paris, 1931), 293.
49. *Guide officiel*, 143–46; Raymond Lécuyer, "La Participation étrangère à l'exposition," *L'Illustration*, 70–71; Paul Morand, "Rien que la terre à l'Exposition coloniale," *Revue des Deux Mondes*, 8th ser., 101 (15 July 1931), 342–43.

the Italian invasion of Ethiopia, was a most fitting contribution. The Fascist government's choice of a classical basilica in Africa made no pretense that the Italians were being solicitous about the persistence of contemporary indigenous cultures in their colonial empire. In the Bois de Vincennes the Italian kingdom was signaling its intention of reclaiming its ancient imperial legacy.[50]

Technology in Command

Lest the reader think that the fabulous exposition clouded visitors' understanding of the improving one, we must make a last stop at the metropolitan display. Here we see exhibits of the finely made luxury goods that have made French crafts world-famous. The visitor can also see the achievements of modern French industrial technology, not just in agricultural and forestry implements but also in aeronautics, automobile production, and electricity. To appreciate the politics of these representations we must be attuned less to the images themselves than to the contexts and juxtapositions. To present ancient Asian temples and primitive African huts cheek by jowl with displays of closely machined electric turbine blades is to school the viewer in a dialectic of ancient stability and modern dynamism, of magnificent but backward cultures that need modern metropolitan France to find their way to a common future. The strange modern columns emulating ancient ruins which mark the main entrance to the exposition grounds make the same point. The coexistence of scenes of contemporary tropical life and of modern European civilization at the Bois de Vincennes instruct metropolitan visitors about what capitalist economic modernization is doing for tropical Greater France, while at the same time reminding them of what it has done for their ancestors' lives and how fortunate they are to be citizens of a modern European state.

Two kinds of representations make this point. An examination of the layout of the *Guide officiel* reveals an interesting pattern of im-

50. *Guide officiel,* 129–32; Pierre Deloncle, "La Participation italienne à l'exposition," *L'Illustration,* 97–100.

ages. Throughout, on facing pages, the editors have systematically juxtaposed pictures of technological modernity and of primitive native life: a gleaming dynamo opposite burdened camels framed by the buildings of a primitive town (Figure 15); an African residential compound, pavilions at the exposition, pictured above an advertisement for construction equipment shown working in the streets of Paris (Figure 16); the New Hebrides "Place des Tabous" sandwiched between ads for banks (Figure 17).[51]

A picture of visitors gazing in wonderment at the display of machinery in the metropolitan hall (Figure 18) presents the vision of Greater France perhaps better than any other image in L'Illustration. Standing, perhaps intimidated, certainly dwarfed by large machines, are three visitors, a man and two women, apparently French. But they are not Parisians. The man's black suit, white shirt, and short-brimmed felt hat tell us he is probably a peasant. The women's black formal clothes of an unusual cut and white lace caps tell us they are Bretons. Breton peasants, from a unique tradition with its own patois, costumes, and culture, have come to admire the mechanical marvels of what has now also become their greater French culture. This is what La Grande France has in store for its tropical inhabitants: their local ways will survive while they are aided and at the same time overawed—wrapped around—by the capitalist technology created and controlled at the capital.

Seduction and Magic

We have grown a bit more sophisticated since 1931 about the domination of political communication by the visual, by the image. Thus it may be hard for us to imagine the powerful impact on French visitors of the ensemble of exotic temples, mosques, primi-

51. An ad for Schneider & Cie opposite a drawing of hungry-looking alligators; a European mother embracing her healthy child, selling Nestlé cocoa, facing a missionary priest surrounded by barefoot African children of uncertain health; an advertisement for a grocery chain's automatic food dispenser facing a water carrier on a donkey; an ad for modern photographic equipment with a romantic painting of yet another dusky tropical beauty with a flower over her ear, etc.

15. The confrontation of the dynamo and camel power. *Exposition coloniale internationale à Paris en 1931: Guide officiel*, 81 and facing page.

Les Pavillons CAMEROUN et TOGO. — M. Boileau, arch.
Cl. Sartony-Laffite.

Aux Colonies employez aussi le matériel à air comprimé de

Flottmann

I bis, Bd. de Magenta, Paris (X°)

16. Building the city: the Cameroons and Togo and a Paris scene.
Exposition coloniale internationale à Paris en 1931: Guide officiel, 173.

BANQUE COMMERCIALE AFRICAINE

SOCIÉTÉ ANONYME - CAPITAL : 40.000.000 de francs

Siège Social : **52, rue Laffitte, PARIS** ———— R. C. Seine 215-757 B.

Agence de Bordeaux : 27, rue Esprit-des-Lois

Adresse Télégraphique : COMAFRIC, Paris 09

AGENCES EN AFRIQUE

Dakar, Rufisque, Kaolack, Ziguinchor (Sénégal) ; Bamako (Soudan) ;
Grand-Bassam, Abidjan (Côte-d'Ivoire) ; Lomé (Togo) ; Cotonou, Porto-
Novo (Dahomey) ; Douala (Cameroun) ; Libreville, Port-Gentil (Gabon) ;
Brazzaville et Pointe-Noire (Moyen Congo) ; Bangui (Oubangui-Chari).

Correspondants sur les autres places de
L'AFRIQUE OCCIDENTALE & ÉQUATORIALE
Toutes Opérations de Banque

NOUVELLES HÉBRIDES. — Place des Tabous.

**AGENCE CENTRALE des
BANQUES COLONIALES**

63 *bis*, *Rue Jouffroy, PARIS (17 ème)*

DIRECTEUR:
M. HELLIER

Tél. Carnot 16-16
R. C. Seine 232.033

REPRÉSENTANT LÉGAL EN FRANCE DES
BANQUES DE LA MARTINIQUE,
DE LA GUADELOUPE, DE LA GUYANE ET DE LA RÉUNION.

COLONIAUX... **Pour votre santé**
**LE FILTRE CHAMBERLAND
SYSTÈME PASTEUR**
vous est nécessaire

IL CONSERVE A L'EAU TOUTES SES QUALITÉS DIGESTIVES
ET TOUS LES SELS NUTRITIFS NÉCESSAIRES A L'ORGANISME
L'EAU AINSI FILTRÉE EST ABSOLUMENT PURE ET EXEMPTE
DE TOUS MICROBES PATHOGÈNES.

Téléphone
Vaug. 26-53

**Filtres à pression et sans pression
Filtres Colonial et de Voyage
Bougies graduées de Laboratoire**

Adr. Télégr.
Filtran-Paris

SIÈGE SOCIAL : 80 BIS, RUE DUTOT, PARIS

17. Money fetishism and the New Hebrides style. *Exposition coloniale internationale à Paris en 1931: Guide officiel*, 199.

18. Visitors stand before the machines in the pavilion of metropolitan France. *L'Illustration*/Sygma, Keystone.

tive huts, strange peoples in strange dress performing curious dances and ceremonies, parading colonial soldiers, and wonders of modern French technology brought together for the colonial show at the edge of the capital of Greater France. The French government extended itself as never before to win the people to what Robert W. Rydell, writing about American expositions, has called "an enduring vision of empire."[52] Using Paul Reynaud's term from his address at the inauguration, Raoul Girardet called the moment of the exposition an "apotheosis." "Never, in the course of our national history, in any case never since the beginnings of the Third Republic, have so many voices been raised so loudly, with so much force and with such

52. Robert W. Rydell, *All the World's a Fair: Visions of Empire at American International Expositions, 1876–1916* (Chicago, 1984), 237. Rydell is also interested in the domestic workings of empire in a bourgeois republic. He sees the expositions as deeply significant for American life: "The influence of America's international expositions permeated the nation's arts, political system, and economic structure. Far from simply reflecting American culture, the expositions were intended to shape that culture. They left an enduring vision of empire" (ibid.).

self-assurance, to celebrate the grandeur of overseas expansion."[53] Reynaud, writing in the handsome commemorative *Livre d'or* of the exposition, was certain that every French visitor who had seen the glory, beauty, and resources of the colonies displayed at Vincennes must henceforth "feel himself a citizen of Greater France."[54]

Can we measure the success of such an event? What would "success" mean? In calculable ways the exposition achieved a great triumph. In less than six months in the midst of an economic depression, the early months dreary and overcast, more people visited the Bois de Vincennes than had seen the Universal Exposition of 1889 (33.5 million vs. 32.3 million). The fair made a profit; income (admissions, subscriptions, and the popular zoo) exceeded expenses by 30 to 35 million francs.[55]

In many other ways—in displays on the colonies in subsequent expositions in the 1930s, in education, the press, and films—the supporters of the growing idea of Overseas France went about promoting imperial consciousness and a new sense of national identity at home.[56] Charles-Robert Ageron reports that such articulate intellectuals as Paul Valéry liked the exposition, but "as for the spontaneous reactions of the little people, we have to admit we just do not know."[57] Just beginning at that moment to articulate the idea of *négritude,* Léopold Senghor remembers that he and his student friends—perhaps following the lead of the surrealists, some of whom Senghor knew and whose leaflet urging people to boycott the exposition he had probably seen—dismissed the exposition as simply a colonialist celebration, and did not go.[58] It is hard to imagine

53. Girardet, "L'Apothéose de la 'plus grande France,'" 1085–86.

54. *Livre d'or,* 9.

55. General A. Messimy, "Le Bilan financier de l'Exposition coloniale," *L'Illustration,* 151–53. Subsidies of 80 million francs from the state and 15 million francs from the city of Paris had to be paid back on a prorated basis from that profit. People bought multiple-entry tickets, so attendance does not equal the sum of individual visitors, but at least 8 million individuals passed through the turnstile.

56. See August, *Selling of the Empire,* esp. 125–53. See further Rémy Pithon, "Opinions publiques et représentations culturelles face aux problèmes de la puissance: Le Témoignage du cinéma français (1938–1939)," *Relations Internationales,* 33 (1933), 91–102.

57. Ageron, "L'Exposition coloniale de 1931," 579.

58. Léopold Sédar Senghor, personal correspondence, 13 February 1988.

what light a measure equivalent to market share, say, might throw on the outcomes of this effort.

The exposition probably might better be understood as a ceremony of self-validation for the pro-imperialists and of initiation to La Plus Grande France for French visitors than as an act of merchandising.[59] But as we have seen, it was above all an important early exercise in twentieth-century cultural ontology: an effort to promote a French identity as a colonial people, a people whose genius lay in assimilating peoples so that they both kept their *petit pays* and yet partook of the universal identity of a French-defined and French-administered humanity.

A few years after the exposition, Robert Delavignette, the thoughtful colonial administrator who succeeded Georges Hardy as head of the Ecole Coloniale, urged young Frenchmen who wished to reform France to "use the Sudan to remake the polity in France." He urged his young countrymen to bring together in their consciousness, without attempting to create a hierarchy of valuation, ideas of the colonies, the capital, and the provinces; for all were truly part of the same project, "the work of the new Occident."[60]

Success in political aesthetics takes the form of an ideological loop: certain signs—good attendance, vocal support in the right circles, smooth execution, the political conjuncture—encourage the organizers to carry on; their belief in their own simulacrum becomes stronger. Attendance, good press, and the like are signs that the course the organizers believe they must take is right. Such victories might better be understood as triumphs of the will of their organizers to believe their own fables than as plebescites measuring popular sentiment. And yet as late as 1949, on the eve of decolonization, 84 percent of *lycée* students believed that France had an interest in continuing the union with its overseas territories; 77 percent held this opinion strongly.[61]

---

59. Ageron insists that the 1931 exposition "failed to create a colonial mentality": "L'Exposition coloniale de 1931," 590. However, what would be the Baudrillardian view, that everything at issue was fiction, might be the right one. In any case, the public was not consulted on the details of colonial policy, only summoned to celebrate it and to make it theirs.

60. Robert Dalavignette, *Soudan–Paris–Bourgogne* (Paris, 1935), 253.

61. Marseille, *L'Age d'or de la France coloniale*, 137.

If we compare the budgets, grandeur, number of visitors, and magic of the exposition with those of its communist counterexposition (about which more in Chapter 3), there can be no doubt which was the better one. Yet if we compare the results of the two projects both on the maps of Africa and Asia and in French popular sentiment, we recall with some embarrassment this unabashed celebration of colonialism, as does Charles-Robert Ageron, and try to see decolonization as an opportunity for the economic and perhaps spiritual renewal of metropolitan France, as Jacques Marseille proposes.[62]

A final insight into the culture of the West in the interwar years is to be gained from our imaginary visit to the exposition. Cultural modernism in those two decades demonstrated a remarkable affinity for the things of the colonial world. Certainly this was the case in the arts, as James Clifford has pointed out in his critique of the ahistoricity of the 1984 primitivism exhibition at the Museum of Modern Art in New York.[63] Picasso, Léger, and Apollinaire, he remarks, discovered the "'magical'" in African art at a moment of French *négrophilie*. This rage of French intellectuals and artists for the exotic primitive, together with the encouragement of African-American intellectuals then in Paris, created a climate for the emergence of *négritude* among African and Caribbean students in Paris in the days of the colonial exposition.

To be modern in France was to seek a colonial vision of the world in the fine arts and in literature. Even in the realm of technological innovation—cross-desert auto races, aircraft safely carrying travelers over trackless regions, wireless radio instantly connecting metropolitan centers to people living in the most remote jungles—modernity and colonial life meshed.

Moreover, this movement differed from the taking up of foreign cultures which has periodically swept European elites since at least Tacitus's *Germania*. This was no eighteenth-century *chinoiserie*. The *projet* of Greater France in its broadest cultural implications proposed to carry out the last move in the triumph of modernity: to link

---

62. See Ageron, "L'Exposition coloniale de 1931"; Jacques Marseille, *Empire colonial et capitalisme français: Histoire d'un divorce* (Paris, 1984).

63. James Clifford, *The Predicament of Culture: Twentieth-Century Ethnography, Literature, and Art* (Cambridge, Mass., 1988), 196–97.

19. The Fountain of Totems. *L'Illustration*/Sygma, Keystone.

20. Angkor Wat illuminated by colored lights. *L'Illustration*/Sygma, Keystone.

21. The ruins of Angkor Wat, Cambodia. Ecole Française d'Extrême-Orient.

the innovative in European culture with the primitive, the anciently new (non-European) ways of seeing with the permanently exotic extra-European, and perhaps to move toward a French world culture.[64] The ideological construction of European hegemony in the world by the creation of European definitions of colonial cultures necessarily dialectically changed those cultures. They could not be both exotic and part of a European, a French future. Sylviane Leprun points out that, aside from small sections in expositions dedicated to other things, there were no more colonial expositions in the world after 1931. The genre had been exhausted that fall in the Bois de Vincennes.[65]

64. Girardet, *L'Idée coloniale en France*, 132, points out that *L'Illustration*, so pro-colonial, was at the same time full of images of fast highways, automobiles, aviation, and modern urban construction projects. In this sense it might be intriguing to follow up Clifford's affirmation of the belief held by both Edward Said and Stanley Diamond that "Western culture can conceive itself critically only with reference to fictions of the primitive": *Predicament of Culture*, 272.

65. Leprun, *Théâtre des colonies*, 208.

The 1931 exposition used electricity in magnificent and dramatic ways for light shows and to illuminate ancient temples and ceremonial art. As the intense colored lights lifted the darkness and enabled us to see the Fountain of Totems, representing fetishes from many of the colonial cultures on display in the Bois de Vincennes (Figure 19), or dramatically enveloped Angkor Wat (Figure 20), we saw the transubstantiation of ancient independent cultures into adornments of modern European civilization. Taken out of darkness, enlightened by the electric power generated in the metropole, the European identity wrapping and transcending the non-European one (Figure 21), we can better see what the price of glorification as part of Grande France was. In this light we can observe most clearly, finally, that the organizers of the exposition and the policy makers in the government meant the simulations in the Bois de Vincennes to become the new reality of the peoples of the colonial empire, a metropolitan-focused reality.[66]

But what of the sentiments of the objects of the show, the people of the colonies? If the metropolitan French were to become a colonial people, how must the souls of the peoples of Overseas France be transformed? How were they to become French? Were they prepared to undergo the metamorphosis and to take on a new wrapped identity? In seeking answers to these questions we may discover another facet of the politics of identity.

66. Jean Baudrillard, "La Précession des simulacres," in *Simulacres et simulation* (Paris, 1981), 9–68.

Frenchmen into Peasants: Rerooting the Vietnamese in Their Villages

On 19 April 1931, on the eve of the opening of the Colonial Exposition, the Paris police detained thirty-three Vietnamese (*Annamites*) leaving a meeting held in the basement of the Café à la Petite Source in the Latin Quarter. All but two were students. They had gathered to listen to a talk by Nguyen Van Tao, a member of the Central Committee of the newly formed Indochinese Communist Party, who, according to the police report, had attempted to incite the students to create incidents at the exposition, so that "the world would know of the discontent of the workers and peasants in the French colonies." He had urged the students to set up action committees (*comités de lutte*), to encourage friends from other ethnic groups to do the same, and to plan both demonstrations and actions against the upcoming celebration of colonialism.

Nguyen Van Tao had entered France illicitly in 1926 to continue studies interrupted when he had been expelled for political activities from the Lycée Chasseloup-Laubat in Saigon. He soon joined the French Communist Party (PCF), worked actively in the party's colonial commission, and wrote on colonial questions for the party press. He propagandized among the colonial students of Paris beginning in 1929, directing his strongest attacks against the poor quality of colonial education.

Soon, however, he began to resent the lukewarmness of the party on colonial struggles. In 1930, in private correspondence with the

PCF leadership, he expressed strongly critical views of the inadequacy of the party's anticolonial work.[1] This was just a reproach. As we shall see, the PCF's ambivalence about anticolonial struggles—and domestic cultural ones—stemmed from an acceptance of the validity of the European essentialist high cultural paradigm.

Accordingly, the young Vietnamese militant welcomed the creation of the Indochinese Communist Party, founded in Hong Kong the same year; its headquarters were moved in 1931 to Vietnam.[2] The new party immediately took up the just-formulated initiative of the Communist International to spread revolutionary ideas throughout the colonial world, especially in Asia.[3]

A group with a very different view of the role of colonies in French life also had decided to hold its meeting to coincide with the exposition. The annual congress of the Société de Géographie Commerciale de Paris, one of France's most powerful colonial societies, opened on 16 September.[4]

Marshal Lyautey had entrusted the Institut International d'Anthropologie, whose offices were housed in the Ecole d'Anthropologie—both societies were presided over by his friend Louis Marin—with organizing the scientific educational section of the exposition. From the Ecole d'Anthropologie Georges Papillault,

1. See Scott McConnell, *Leftward Journey: The Education of Vietnamese Students in France, 1919–1939* (New Brunswick, N.J., 1989), 115–17.

2. It is interesting to note the insensitivity or ignorance of the leaders of the Communist International in insisting on the French colonial label for the party. "Indochina" was a French administrative fiction that covered five distinct cultural or national traditions. The politically most active group, and the one we will be concerned with here, was the Vietnamese.

3. Lenin had presented his "Preliminary Draft Theses on the National and Colonial Question" in 1920 at the Second Congress of the Communist International. He called for an alliance between the communist working class of the West and the revolutionary peasantry of the East. Although the text did not mention Indochina, it was very influential among young Vietnamese radicals. In 1924 the Fifth Congress of the International, meeting in Moscow, created an Eastern Bureau, of which the Vietnamese founding member of the French Communist Party, known under his party name, Ho Chi Minh, became an important member. In 1928 the Sixth Congress, held in the wake of the Canton commune in China, foretold new initiatives and new heights of revolutionary struggle in the Far East. See Alexander B. Woodside, *Community and Revolution in Modern Vietnam* (Boston, 1976), 165–73.

4. A report of the activities and participants at the congress may be found in *L'Ethnographie*, n.s. 24 (1931), 11–14.

holder of a degree in medicine and author of a questionnaire to guide the investigations of colonial officials and scholarly tourists, took charge of the section of the physical anthropology of the indigenous races of the French colonial empire. Bernard Le Pontois concerned himself with prehistory. Marin supervised the selection and installation of the ethnographic displays.[5] Accordingly, the scheduling of the meeting of the colonial society once the fair had opened was highly appropriate for these partisans of Greater France. Marin, since 1925 also president of this society, opened the congress with a speech of welcome.[6]

Again linking scholarly with colonial pursuits, he praised the marvelous research work of the major societies concerned with the colonial empire. He named, among many other bodies, the Académie des Sciences Coloniales, the Institut de Géographie, Sciences Coloniales, and the Union Coloniale Française, and held them up as models to be emulated. "Just a glance at the pages of *Le Temps Colonial* and *La Dépêche Coloniale* gives one a sense of the enormously useful information furnished by these research bodies."[7]

At the end of the congress, as was the society's practice, the president capped the year's work by proposing several resolutions for the members' ratification. One called for the creation of a Ministry of France Overseas; a second called upon the French government to supply additional credits to the colonies in that period of world depression. The members of the society called on the metropolitan government to build more railroads in France's African possessions, to diffuse more information on the colonies, and to work to improve diplomatic and commercial relations with China.

Finally, the topic of education in the colonies, an issue then undergoing serious reconsideration, was addressed. This recommendation—formally, in two resolutions—urged the reorientation of edu-

5. Unfortunately, I have not found any record of the specific tasks or accomplishments of Marin and his associates at the exposition.

6. A trail of street addresses frequently facilitated the tracing of connections and influences in French intellectual history. Just as Marin's national anthropological society and the international society shared space provided by the faculty of medicine, before 1923 his ethnographic society was housed in the building of the Commercial Geography Society. It then moved to new quarters at La Librairie Orientale et Américaine, the leading commercial publisher of works in anthropology.

7. Marin Papers, Archives Nationales (A.N.), 317 AP, carton 201.

cation, especially higher education, among the indigenous peoples of the empire in ways more suitable to their circumstances and more in line with their cultural heritages. These last resolutions bear generally on the history of French anthropological science, to be sure, and directly on our interest in the politics of the struggle over the definition of French identity and its offer to the peoples of the colonial empire. They mark an important new departure in French thinking about the place of indigenous culture under colonial rule, and as such call into question the assimilation-association dualism that has occupied the center of discussions on the relations of the cultures.[8] Historically, the resolutions on education in the colonies expressed and furthered a new cultural policy just in its infancy, a policy involving the French invention of a new native cultural tradition for the people of Indochina to don.[9]

If, as we saw in our tour of the Colonial Exposition, the population of the metropole was being asked to accept an imperial identity while retaining their loyalty to their several *petites patries,* how did the peoples of the empire have to be transformed to become part of the creation of a Greater France? What was the hegemonic project of the Colonial Ministry and its allies?[10]

One must be wary of pitfalls in employing the concept of identity to theorize the struggles of oppressed populations. The story of the Vietnamese students in Paris raises questions about approaches in contemporary scholarship which seek to focus narrowly on the otherness of subject peoples, on difference, or on the role of the moral

8. See Raymond F. Betts, *Assimilation and Association in French Colonial Theory, 1890–1914* (New York, 1961). In his last chapter, "Ideal and Reality," Betts attempts to sort out the contradictions between France's professed intentions to foster association while it often followed policies better understood as assimilative. My argument accepts the sincerity of both intentions after World War I, provided that neither policy nor any confused mixture threatened the continuation of French political and cultural hegemony.

9. Eric Hobsbawm, "Introduction: Inventing Traditions," in *The Invention of Tradition,* ed. Hobsbawm and Terence Ranger (Cambridge, 1984), 1–14.

10. The formulation of the question of cultural domination by the state as a "hegemonic project" has been fruitfully employed by Ian Lustick. Currently available is his *State-Building Failure in British Ireland and French Algeria,* Institute of International Studies, University of California, Berkeley, Research Series no. 63 (Berkeley, 1985). David Laitin of Wilder House, University of Chicago, also makes good use of the formulation in his *Hegemony and Culture: Politics and Religious Change among the Yoruba* (Chicago, 1986), esp. 1–20, 171–83.

economy of the subject population to understand colonialized peoples' resistance to or rebellion against colonial rule.[11]

Outside Agitators

A few days after his arrest, out on the street again, Nguyen Van Tao was observed in a *brasserie* urging "two Indochinese, a Japanese, a Korean, and a Negro" to organize demonstrations and incidents at the exposition. Together the Association Indochinoise d'Enseignement Mutuel and the Ligue de Défense de la Race Nègre undertook to agitate among the individuals brought in from the colonies to staff the various exhibits and services. Officers of the Colonial Ministry unit in Marseille charged with the surveillance of natives of the empire residing in France, the Service de Contrôle et d'Assistance en France des Indigènes des Colonies (CAI), uncovered and thwarted a planned anti-imperialist demonstration on the occasion of the arrival of a passenger liner bringing a large number of Indochinese to work at the fair.[12] On 10 April in Toulouse radical Indochinese published leaflets attacking the exposition as a celebration of colonialism. The literature reminded the reader of the recent execution of

11. The most successful studies employing this line of argument are James C. Scott, *The Moral Economy of the Peasant: Rebellion and Subsistence in Southeast Asia* (New Haven, 1977) and his *Weapons of the Weak: Everyday Forms of Peasant Resistance* (New Haven, 1985). Scott starts out from the seminal article by E. P. Thompson, "The Moral Economy of the English Crowd in the Eighteenth Century," *Past and Present*, 50 (1971), 76–136, and the theoretical vision of Barrington Moore, Jr., *The Social Origins of Dictatorship and Democracy: Lord and Peasant in the Making of Modern Society* (Boston, 1966) and his *Injustice: The Social Basis of Obedience and Revolt* (White Plains, N.Y., 1978).

12. CAI Marseille Report to the Directeur d'Affaires Politiques of the Colonial Ministry, 13 April 1931, A.N., Service de Liaison entre les Originaires des Territoires d'Outre-mer (SLOTFOM), III, carton 5. The CAI reported to the director of political affairs while keeping in permanent liaison with the Sûreté. After World War II the functions of the CAI were taken over by SLOTFOM. All CAI police reports may be found indexed under SLOTFOM entries in A.N., sec. France d'Outre-mer, Aix-en-Provence. For a useful guide to the history of this little-known agency—whose existence was not admitted to and whose budget was disguised in the colonial appropriation—see J. Dion, "Historique de SLOTFOM," introduction to the index volume of the SLOTFOM collection at the Aix archives.

Indochinese insurgents in Tonkin and denounced the cultural humiliation that accompanied the representation of non-European cultures at such expositions.[13] Surveillance agents found copies of this literature distributed to radical student groups in Marseille, Paris, Lyon, and Limoges. Soon after the exposition opened, the Toulouse section of the Communist Party held a large protest meeting. French and Vietnamese speakers assailed colonialism; André Marty gave what the informant in attendance reported to have been a moving talk.[14]

Once the exposition opened, radical students tried to disrupt its operations. Before the opening day the CAI uncovered the plan of the Comité de Lutte contre l'Exposition to blanket the fairgrounds with anti-imperialist stickers and to release balloons carrying red flags and streamers bearing slogans. They managed to prevent this potential embarrassment to the celebration. The students contested the servile image of Asians projected by the pedicabs that had been brought from Indochina to convey visitors around the fair; however, they did not manage to get them removed. But the CAI and police could not stop what probably was the politically inspired departure of twenty-three North African musicians of the total of forty-two. Indochinese students in Paris persuaded the Vietnamese at the ex-

13. See the descriptions of the poorly done colonial section of the Paris exposition of 1900 and the attempts to portray the empire in a better light at the colonial exposition held at Marseille in 1906 in William H. Schneider, *An Empire for the Masses: The French Popular Image of Africa, 1870–1900* (Westport, Conn., 1982), 177–99. A sordid but not untypical practice connected with the exposition was the contracting of colonial peoples to commercial exhibitors. When Maurice Leenhardt, missionary-anthropologist of New Caledonia, tried to visit some old friends on the exposition grounds, security personnel prevented him from doing so and the Melanesians were then taken away to fulfill an agreement concluded by the exposition's organizers for them to perform in an itinerant circus as a cannibal-dancers act. Leenhardt needed the strenuous help of the Ligue des Droits de l'Homme to free them from the contract. On this incident see James Clifford, *Person and Myth: Maurice Leenhardt in the Melanesian World* (Berkeley, 1982), 159, and specifically on the sequestering of the *Canaques* in the Bois de Vincennes see R. Dousset, *Colonialisme et contradictions* (Paris, 1970), 16. On the practice of putting colonial peoples on exhibit in France and in traveling shows see Schneider, *Empire for the Masses*, 125–51.

14. Gaston Joseph of the CAI to Governor General Pierre Pasquier, with copies to the police and the Sûreté Générale, SLOTFOM, ser. III, carton 5. The Communist Party also published its own *True Guide to the Colonial Exposition*, accusing the French imperialists of crimes and exploitations: A.N., sec. Outre-mer, Agence France Outre-mer, dossier 2700.

position not to carry the giant Oriental dragon around the fair-grounds, and the administration had to ask Africans to do it. The police arrested several students on Saturday, 1 August, before they could start demonstrations before the temple of Angkor Wat and the fair's headquarters building. In September early intelligence allowed the authorities to block the plan of other Indochinese students to knock over and smash the statue of His Majesty Khai Dinh, emperor of Annam, which stood before the Annamite pavilion.[15]

The Uprooted

Many of the students who had demonstrated in support of the colonial insurrectionists in 1930 had been deported. The agitation around the fair brought down a new wave of exclusions. On 22 May 1931 the hero of CAI reports, Nguyen Van Tao, was arrested at a demonstration in front of the Elysée Palace and sent back to his *pays* with other Indochinese undesirables. Gaston Joseph, head of the CAI, revealed a talent for political shamanism with his assessment that "in their own interest it is good that they be reintegrated into their natural environment, where family life and the influence of ancestral traditions can help them recover from a crisis we have often found to be short-lived."[16]

The good information and quick reaction of the authorities thwarted the radical students' attempts to "cause trouble and sow disorder" on the fairgrounds and in the residences for natives of the colonies at the fair. The "Final Report on the Indochinese Participation at the Exposition," for example, dwelt on both the indifference with which the troublemakers were met and the effectiveness of the police in blocking their activities.[17] However, the report contained

15. Various secret reports from CAI agents "Joe" (operating in the Ligue de Défense de la Race Nègre inside the exposition), "Désiré" (assigned to undercover work outside the fairgrounds), and "Guillaume" (competence not given), SLOTFOM, ser. III, carton 5.

16. Directeur des Affaires Politiques, SLOTFOM, ser. III, carton 2.

17. "Rapport sur la Participation de l'Indochine à l'Exposition Coloniale Internationale de Paris, 1931," A.N., sec. Outre-mer, carton 533, dossier 53, 121.

nothing to suggest that the authorities would not face further trouble from radical Vietnamese students in France and in Indochina.[18]

These incidents, or more accurately these intentions to foment incidents, would not merit our attention if the representatives of the Colonial Ministry and the organizers of the fair themselves had not shown the serious concern they did.[19] Here the microcosm of the small battles of position on the grounds of the Colonial Exposition guides our understanding of the macrocosm of the larger wars of position within the French colonial empire. As Scott McConnell concludes, from 1925 to 1931 a handful of radical students brought about a change in "the very language in which French-educated Vietnamese talked about the liberation of their country."[20] Especially after the destruction of the nonleft nationalist movement in the failed uprising, the claims of Vietnamese political and cultural liberty were wrapped up with socialist revolution. Wrong-thinking young Vietnamese, with the encouragement of the Comintern and some side-line cheering from the PCF, were disrupting the creation of a greater French consciousness. At the opening of the exposition this probable coalition was joined by the improbable surrealists around André Breton.

The Antiexposition

In late April agents of the Service de Contrôle et d'Assistance en France des Indigènes des Colonies began to come upon raffle-ticket-

18. A good history—from a policeman's point of view—of the implantation of communism in Indochina may be found in "Associations antifrançaises en Indochine et propagande communiste, no. 1: Historique," SLOTFOM, ser. III, carton 48.

19. See the copies of messages marked "Secret" reporting the activities of the subversives and the official responses in A.N., Outre-mer, Agence France Outre-mer, dossier 2700.

20. McConnell, *Leftward Journey*, 117. McConnell attributes this ideological shift to French Communists rather than to the destruction of the nationalist movement by the French and the efforts of young Vietnamese of the left to work out their destinies. The PCF deserves, I think, neither such credit nor such reproach. On language, translation, and power, see Vincente L. Rafael, *Contracting Colonialism: Translation and Christian Conversion in Tagalog Society under Early Spanish Rule* (Ithaca, N.Y., 1988), 210–19.

size cards marked "1 fr," which asked people to "support the Anti-imperialist Exposition." The card named no place and no date. They soon learned that this was the work of a newly created organization called the Ligue Anti-impérialiste. The league's efforts to put on exhibit "the truth about the colonies" were not very impressive. Yet it was the first anticolonial exposition in French history, and it was organized not by politicians but by artists and poets.

The idea for the counterexposition came from Alfred Kurella, a Comintern representative in France and world head of the Anti-imperialist League. A German by origin, Kurella was a friend to Bertolt Brecht and to the French left-wing avant-garde. He was disappointed by the French Communist Party's failure to take any serious initiatives either directly against the exposition or in support of the colonial protesters, and came to the surrealists, who had already spoken out strongly in their leaflet against the event, to encourage their efforts. Through André Thirion he offered them the league's patronage, including a venue, but left them to plan and organize the antifair on their own. André Breton and his friends seized the opportunity to speak out on behalf of oppressed peoples, whose artistic cultures fascinated them.

But only on 24 September did the league manage to open its antiexposition in three rooms of the former Soviet pavilion, one of the most modern structures built for the Exposition of Decorative Arts in 1925, designed by the constructivist architects the Vesnin brothers. Moved after the closing of the exposition to a lot on Avenue Mathurin-Moreau, it had been used as the annex of the adjoining Maison des Syndicats of the Confédération Générale du Travail Unitaire in Paris. Thirion asked Louis Aragon to present the cultural issues and Georges Sadoul to do the propaganda and publicity.

The main floor, organized by Thirion, contained about twenty display panels of posters, photographs cut out of magazines, and maps—many of the items just thumbtacked up. On display were sketches of generals notorious for their colonial exploits (Mangin and Gouraud, one of Lyautey's chief collaborators in the 1913 campaign to pacify Morocco), as well as twenty photos of Lyautey. There were pictures of forest workers in Africa and scenes of the construction of the Brazzaville-Ocean railroad, with an accompanying text about the 18,000 deaths the project cost. Pictures illustrating the work of the Secours-Rouge were also shown.

The rest of the exhibit was more imaginative but equally amateurish. Yves Tanguy designed the larger of two rooms on the second floor, which Eluard and Aragon filled with objects of colonial art, most of them from their apartments: wooden statues, masks, and musical instruments, as well as "two snake skins and a leopard pelt," in the dry just-the-facts language of the police report, in its own way a modest contribution to surrealist writing. The surrealist sensibility came through in the little display of "European fetishes" (Figure 22), a kind of rejoinder to the fetishist village at the fair (and the European high culture's dismissal of African religions as magical mumbo-jumbo), which featured kitschy plaster Jesuses and Marys and votive statues. The other room exhibited photographs of Soviet achievements and pronouncements of Karl Marx (Figure 23). Recorded music—Polynesian and Asian songs chosen by Aragon, some current hits and the newly fashionable rumba, selected by his wife, Elsa—played on loudspeakers directed to the street. Perhaps passers-by on their way to the nearby Buttes-Chaumont might be incited by the music or broadcast political messages to look in.

On opening day, the CAI informant who attended between 3:00 and 4:30 counted only fourteen visitors. By the time of the 31 October meeting of the Ligue Anti-impérialiste, where the poor quality of the antiexposition was much criticized, the organizers could point to 2,380 admissions with 32,000 francs in receipts and subventions. No members of the Political Bureau of the PCF visited; surrealists and Communists were apparently not always united in struggle against a common enemy.[21]

21. SLOTFOM, ser. III, carton 5; André Thirion, Revolutionaries without Revolution, trans. Joachim Neugroschel (New York, 1975), 288–90. Jacques Marseille gives a total attendance of 5,000 visitors, including group visits organized by trade unions, to closing day in February 1932: L'Âge d'or de la France coloniale (Paris, 1986), 135. On the surrealist project of unmasking aestheticism, especially the idea of the autonomy of art, see Jack J. Spector, "The Avant-Garde Object: Form and Fetish between World War I and World War II," Res, 12 (1986), 125–43, and his review of the exhibition and publication, "Fashion and Surrealism," in Art Journal, 47 (1988), 372–75. See also the acute development of this argument by Peter Berger, Theory of the Avant-Garde (Minneapolis, 1984). Walter Benjamin, "Surrealism: The Last Snapshot of the European Intelligentsia," in Reflections, trans. Edmund Jephcott (New York, 1978), 177–92, accused left-wing French intellectuals and "their Russian counterparts" of feeling an obligation not to the revolution "but to traditional culture" (186). Moreover, he suggested, the Satanism cultivated by some of the surrealists, once closely looked at, was "a political device, however romantic, to disinfect and isolate against all moralizing dilettantism" (187).

22. The surrealists' display of "European fetishes." *Le Surréalisme au service de la révolution* (Paris, 1931), 40.

Le Véritable Guide de l'exposition coloniale (The True Guide to the Colonial Exposition) was also the work of beginners in anti-imperialist struggles. A guide neither to the Vincennes display nor

23. A display at the surrealists' antiexposition: "A people that oppresses others will never know how to be free." *Le Surréalisme au service de la révolution* (Paris, 1931), 40.

to the antiexposition, *Le Véritable Guide* was an eight-page pamphlet with sections on Madagascar, Guadeloupe, French Equatorial Africa, Syria, North Africa, Indochina, and Guyana. In short, direct sentences it reported the low wages of Guadeloupe cane cutters, the profits of the sugar companies, the murderous railroad construction in Africa, the plundered raw materials and profits made by French capitalists in Syria, acts of repression committed and profits made in the North African possessions, and, under the headline "Our Most Energetically Civilized Colony," two pages on the poverty of Indochina and the brutality with which the French military suppressed uprisings there. In the margins of the text were drawings of the African continent held in a cage; an overseer, whip in hand, brutalizing a bearer; an ugly marine officer, drawn pistol at the ready; and a drawing of Governor Pasquier bearing a tray of severed and bloody Vietnamese heads. The pamphlet asked workers to hand it on to others, and ended with "Vive la révolution mondiale prolétarienne!" (Long live the world proletarian revolution!). The files of the colonial archives contain a fair number of copies; the CAI agents had been diligent.[22] Yet, however disruptive the Vietnamese students and their supporters in metropolitan France, it was in Vietnam that the French had to attempt to master this cultural conflict. There the new, Greater French identity had to be forged.

Creating a New *Petit Pays*

The 1930 nationalist uprising and the Communist-organized troubles later that year menaced the peace of French Indochina as it had threatened the peace of the celebration of colonial achievement.[23] The agents of disruption were easy enough to identify in the ranks of the young Communist movement and among the nationalists, both in France and in Indochina. French administrators and police knew that they were intellectuals and students, historically the bearers of Vietnamese high culture and now seeking facili-

22. *Le Véritable Guide de l'exposition coloniale: L'Oeuvre civilisatrice de la France magnifée en quelques pages* (n.p. [Paris], n.d. [1931]).

23. See Joseph Buttinger, *Vietnam: A Dragon Embattled*, vol. 1, *From Colonialism to the Vietminh* (New York, 1967), 208–20; Albert de Pouvourville, *Griffes rouges sur l'Asie* (Paris, 1933); Donald Lancaster, *The Emancipation of French Indochina* (London, 1961), 78–83; Woodside, *Community and Revolution in Modern Vietnam*, 173–78. Jean Dorsenne expressed alarm for the future of France's Asian possessions because "Soviet Russia has launched in Asia a great offensive against Europe—that of the entire Asiatic world": "Le Péril rouge en Indochine," *Revue des Deux Mondes*, 1 April 1932, 519–56. Ironically, by so effectively crushing the nationalist movement in its infancy in 1930, the French left the field open to the Communists, now able freely to use the appeals of nationalism to press for popular liberation.

ty with French intellectual culture. Unfortunately, these young Indochinese seemed not to understand the incapacity of their peoples to rule themselves, nor did they appreciate the positive achievements of French efforts. Despite what at one time had been the most extensive schooling system in Asia, and probably the best one among the French possessions, they were ill educated.

Before the French arrived in Indochina there had existed a rather well-functioning educational system in the part they called Annam, well adapted to local conditions and concerned to carry on indigenous culture. In higher education a system of examinations based on Confucian classics supplied bureaucrat-scholars for the monarchy's civil service. Applicants who failed could sit for the examinations several times. While preparing for the next opportunity, and to employ their literary skills, the candidates for the mandarinate often turned to teaching in local schools. As a result, in the early 1860s the French came upon a widely literate population educated within the context of a vital local culture roughly framed on a Chinese model, but not subordinate to it.[24] Under King Tu Duc the scholar-gentry and many village schoolmasters refused to collaborate with the French authorities, and in the south irregular forces put up active resistance.[25]

Minimally, the French naval officers who governed the new colonies needed educated lower clerical employees and translators drawn from the native population. Initially there were enough graduates of the mission schools to fill these posts.[26] In the last decades of the nineteenth century first the military authorities and then the civilian administration, which replaced the navy, undertook various halfhearted measures to create a wider French-controlled school system.[27]

---

24. Buttinger, *Vietnam*, 1:46–48. Buttinger, without crediting a source, suggests an improbable 80% literacy rate on the arrival of the French.

25. Gail Paradise Kelly, "Colonial Schools in Vietnam: Policy and Practice," in *Education and Colonialism*, ed. Philip G. Altbach and Gail P. Kelly (London and New York, 1978), 96; David G. Marr, *Vietnamese Anticolonialism, 1885–1925* (Berkeley, 1971), 22–43.

26. Henri Gourdon, "L'Education des indigènes dans l'Indochine française," *L'Asie Française*, 31 May 1931, 162.

27. William J. Duiker, *The Rise of Nationalism in Vietnam, 1900–1941* (Ithaca, N.Y., 1976), 107–8; Milton E. Osborne, *The French Presence in Cochinchina and Cambodia: Rule and Response, 1859–1905* (Ithaca, N.Y., 1969).

Not until the educational law of 1917, however, can we discern a vision of a school system articulated for all levels of learning. The system of Franco-Vietnamese schools established by that law was the response of the Council for the Improvement of Native Education both to the continued existence of independent Vietnamese village schools and to the new Western-model free schools accessible to the native intelligentsia. The colonial authorities wished to transcend the old precolonial schooling and at the same time to cut short inappropriate experiments in adapting modern Western education to the needs of the Westernizers among the native intelligentsia. The timing of the proclamation of a major new approach to native schooling, just a few years after the overthrow of the Manchu dynasty on the borders of Indochina and a month after the Bolshevik Revolution, was probably more fortuitous than planned, but the pacifying function of this now exclusive system for native education was not.

Henceforth Vietnamese children were to be tracked in a mandatory educational system that approximated those French primary and secondary schools that did not prepare students for university study. These Franco-Vietnamese schools conveyed to the schoolchildren of the colony a certain idea both of France and of Vietnamese civilization which tended to enforce metropolitan hegemony, to pervert the locally created contents and development of the indigenous culture, and above all to inhibit the formation of an independent indigenous educated stratum capable of becoming the organic intellectuals of an anti-French movement.[28]

Louis Vignon, a professor at the Ecole Coloniale and, like Louis Marin, an admirer of Le Bon on social theory and Lyautey on colonial administration, had been strongly urging a move away from a policy that would turn colonial natives into Frenchmen. In 1919 he published *Un Programme de politique coloniale*, in which he argued for

28. Gail Paradise Kelly, "Franco-Vietnamese Schools, 1918–1933" (Ph.D. diss., University of Wisconsin–Madison, 1975), 376; Daniel Hémery, "Aux origines des guerres d'independence vietnamiennes: Pouvoir colonial et phénomène communiste en Indochine avant la Seconde Guerre mondiale," *Mouvement social*, 101 (1977), 3–35. This was not far from the thinking of the socialist colonial specialist Alexandre Varenne, but he was interested in breeding a future ruling class for an Indochina with dominion status (Hémery, 9).

leaving the colonies' institutions, leadership, and values intact as the best means to avoid instilling in indigenous peoples "a permanent state of fever and disequilibrium." His conservative appeals for the revalidation of indigenous cultures under French rule described what would be French colonial educational policy in the interwar years. Moreover, two knowledgeable colonial administrators, Henri Gourdon, for a time inspector general of public instruction in Indochina, and Henri Delétie, an Asian specialist in the administration, both championed the restoration of the old Vietnamese traditions. Albert Sarraut, returned from serving as governor general of Indochina and named colonial minister in 1920, was also close to Vignon's position on colonial education.[29]

The French educational reformers in the interwar years, sensitized by the new conservative ethnography, turned away from simply replicating the educational system of the metropole. The Franco-Vietnamese school system that took shape between 1917 and 1924 purveyed a French-defined version of the indigenous culture, albeit in the French language. "Local" languages were offered to replace past options of European classical and modern languages. Secondary school students began to study Indochinese geography and history instead of these subjects oriented toward France. Nowhere in the system could students engage in serious study of any natural science. The manual arts were emphasized for all, and the gifted were encouraged to take up the artistic crafts that the French so prized in Indochinese cultures.[30] The colonial administration un-

---

29. See Louis Vignon, *Un Programme de politique coloniale: Les Questions indigènes* (Paris, 1919), 466–508; Rudolf von Albertini, *Decolonization: The Administration and Future of the Colonies, 1919–1960* (Garden City, N.Y., 1971), 293–95; McConnell, *Leftward Journey,* 17–20, 84–85; Henri Delétie, "Le Problème universitaire indochinois," *Académie des sciences coloniales,* 8 (1926–27); "De l'adaptation de nos programmes d'enseignement au milieu annamite," *Académie des sciences coloniales,* 14. In the 1920s and again in the 1950s, South African doctors and administrators strongly encouraged the removal of urban natives to "'healthy reserves'" where they could leave the maladies of the cities behind and revert to their natural state. See Frederick Cooper and Ann L. Stoler, introduction to the special section Tensions of Empire, "Colonial Control and Visions of Rule," *American Ethnologist,* 16 (1989), 609–20, esp. 612.

30. The French did little to encourage vocational schools for the Vietnamese in the 1920s and 1930s other than those dedicated to traditional arts. In 1923, 820 Vietnamese attended eight vocational schools. Of this number 500 were studying paint-

dertook to implant a system the Vietnamese would come to see and accept as their own.[31]

The new system undercut the remnants of the old local village schools at one end of the educational process and prepared students to be unsuitable for admission into French higher education at the other. In 1921 the colonial administration had decreed that Vietnamese students had to obtain the authorization of the governor general in their *livret universitaire* (school transcript) in order to study in France. By 1924 the candidate for study abroad had to assemble a total of eleven valid official documents for successful application for European study. From the mid-1920s onward, once the reform was in place, the Office of Public Instruction began slowly to squeeze out the young Vietnamese who had managed to enter the French schools intended for *colons* and leading to a high school diploma and therefore access to French higher education.[32] André Malraux, then in Vietnam with Paul Monin, a local attorney, editing a pro-Vietnamese newspaper, *L'Indochine,* attacked the administration's policy in the last issue to appear before Governor General Cognacq suppressed it, warning that excluding the young students from pursuing their studies in France "would immediately mobilize *against us* a coalition of Vietnamese of the highest character and the most tenacious energies."[33]

Nor did the inferiority of the Indochinese educational system escape aware Vietnamese; they assessed it as a trap of intellectual

---

ing, pottery, and weaving. To that date no higher education in the beaux arts was available to Vietnamese. Here too, in part simply by omission, the French attempted to make their ideological aspirations for Vietnam the reality: simple family farmers practicing traditional arts and handicrafts. See Kelly, "Franco-Vietnamese Schools," 66, 79. On the passionate promotion of the Vietnamese language by the nationalists from the 1920s on—in opposition to Chinese and French—see David G. Marr, *Vietnamese Tradition on Trial, 1920–1945* (Berkeley, 1981), 136–39.

31. Kelly, "Colonial Schools in Vietnam," 102, and "Franco-Vietnamese Schools," 62.

32. To 1930 young Vietnamese could still sit for the French baccalaureate examination in the version given in Indochina. The test was harder than that administered in France; in 1934–35 only 29.62% of the Indochinese candidates passed. To 1929 only two *lycées,* one in Hanoi and the other in Saigon, prepared students for the examinations. See Kelly, "Franco-Vietnamese Schools," 64.

33. André Malraux, "Sélection d'énergies," *L'Indochine,* August 1925, cited in Jean Lacouture, *Malraux: Une Vie dans le siècle* (Paris, 1975), 85–86 (Malraux's italics).

second-ratedness. Determined parents with adequate means sought to send their children abroad for secondary and university education—to China, to Japan, and above all to metropolitan France. The ones who could get out, Malraux predicted, "would return to Vietnam educated *against us;* they would become the allies, if not the leaders, of all the revolts."[34]

Students who had been allowed to travel to France for their education, however, were subject to police background investigations both at home and in France from 1929 on.[35] The Indochinese rebellions, we can appreciate, energized the French administrators who were institutionalizing these ideas on educational streaming in the 1930s.[36]

Marin's resolution on education in the colonies at the 1931 congress of the Société de Géographie Commerciale encouraged this new project, giving it a manifestly anticommunist twist that was new. Because so many young colonials come to the metropole in pursuit of higher education, read the final resolution of the 1931 congress, "they are readily recruited onto the general staff of the enterprise of social disruption emanating from the Third International. These uprooted young men, intoxicated by Moscow's doctrines, return home to become agents of nationalist agitation or revolution." The resolution commended Governor General Pierre Pasquier for declaring himself opposed to continuing to send young Vietnamese to

34. Ibid. (Malraux's italics). See also Kelly, "Franco-Vietnamese Schools," 66; Hémery, "Aux origines des guerres d'indépendance vietnamiennes."

35. SLOTFOM, ser. III, carton 118, contains background checks filed by "Guillaume" and "Désiré" between 1929 and March 1931. See Daniel Hémery, "Du Patriotisme au marxisme: L'Immigration vietnamienne en France de 1926 à 1930," *Mouvement Social,* 90 (1975), 21–23. McConnell's judgment that "no serious barrier stopped the Vietnamese from coming to France" is puzzling in view of this series of obstacles: *Leftward Journey,* 37.

36. Even while the French authorities visited brutal repression on participants in the two uprisings, there was contemporary awareness of the depth and persistence of the ideas and values that had informed the leaders of the insurgencies. See Pierre Varet, *Au pays d'Annam: Les Dieux qui meurent* (Paris, 1932), 271. See further Louis Roubaud's report of a conversation with Phan Boi Chau, an old and respected Vietnamese patriot, who in 1931 centered his criticism of French rule on the French educational system, which to date, he believed, had only destroyed traditional values and thereby uprooted the people. See Roubaud, *Vietnam: La Tragédie indochinoise* (Paris, 1931), 232ff. Andrée Viollis's equally well-known account of the nationalist uprising relates a similar conversation with Phan: *Indochine S.O.S.* (Paris, 1935), 96.

France for higher education. He wanted them educated at home in the context of their culture and away from the corrupting intellectual and political evils of the metropole. The resolution further urged such a policy as the wisest course for Madagascar and the other large colonies. If in the future students were sent to France for study trips, it ought to be to see evidence of France's economic achievements, "so that they might understand the beauty of the goals pursued by the leaders of colonial France." But above all, higher education in the colonies ought to be adapted "to the *mentalité* and the habitat of each of the great colonies, to their resources, needs, and special conditions."[37]

And so it was, in a remarkable intensification of the trend to Vietnamize Vietnamese education in the 1930s. At the time of the insurrection and exposition about 1,500 Indochinese students were studying in France. The number was not large, to be sure, but it represented a powerful increase over a total of just a few hundred Vietnamese university graduates during the previous sixty years.[38]

Pierre Pasquier, who had bloodily put down the insurrections of 1930, had in that year had his Office of Public Instruction publish a bilingual pamphlet urging Vietnamese parents not to send their children to France for their education. He assured them that in Indochina students could obtain an education equal in quality to that of the metropole and that the schools in the colony were beginning to provide more instruction in Vietnamese language and literature, history, and Indochinese and Asian geography.[39]

37. A.N. 317 AP, carton 198. An interesting Vietnamese thinker who shared many of Marin's ideas was Pham Quynh, editor of an important journal that sought to promote a synthesis of Western science and Eastern philosophy, with emphasis on keeping alive Vietnamese values and traditions. To this end he found the ideas of Maurras and Barrès, among others, useful. On Pham Quynh see Duiker, *Rise of Nationalism in Vietnam*, 116–27.

38. A study by the Sûreté Générale of 13 March 1930 counted 2,924 Vietnamese, of whom 1,556 were students, in the nine largest French cities. Most of the students studied in Paris; the rest were clustered in the south. The next biggest group, about 890 sailors, caused the Sûreté concern, too, as they were believed to be open to revolutionary propaganda. See Hémery, "Du patriotisme au marxisme," 5n; Kelly, "Franco-Vietnamese Schools," 108n; McConnell, *Leftward Journey*, xiii.

39. Pierre Pasquier, *Circulaire aux familles au sujet de l'envoi des étudiants indochinois en France* (Hanoi, 1930). Pasquier, a career colonial official, had replaced the socialist Alexandre Varenne in the office of governor general in 1928. Pasquier's training in

In 1933 the Office of Public Instruction normalized the unwritten policy by formally decreeing the exclusion of Vietnamese from the French schools of the colony, forcing them into the reformed colonial system. Gail Paradise Kelly's careful review of educational directives in these schools, teaching materials circulated as guides, material used, and interviews with former students supports the argument that the French were inventing a cultural tradition for their Vietnamese pupils.[40] First, and most important practically, French elements in the curriculum were drastically reduced. In the elementary grades French classes were limited to five hours per week and the time saved was used to provide more instruction in the Vietnamese language, geography, hygiene, nature studies, and manual labor. By 1936 French was no longer taught in the primary grades.

But even in more advanced schooling, where French figured importantly, texts in French classes evoked and honored old Vietnam and its good old ways: family, religious piety, and, above all, the inevitability of simple agricultural life. Neither the *colons* who dominated the colony's extractive industries nor the protected and inefficient industrialists at home wanted to see industrialization in Indochina. Such ideas could be readily recoded in cultural terms. "There are moments in the life of a people when progress consists in returning to the past," philosophized Pierre Pasquier in 1935.[41]

Most remarkably, contemporary France was portrayed in a like manner. As Kelly found, "when Vietnamese life was the subject, it

---

the Ecole Coloniale and his long service in Indochina made him ideally suited to lead the reinterpretation of the indigenous culture. His political master stroke—other than putting down the insurrections—was the recall of the last emperor's son, Bao-Dai, from Paris in May 1932. Upon assuming the throne the young emperor managed to attract numbers of young Vietnamese to his work of Westernizing progress within viable native traditions. See Thomas E. Ennis, *French Policy and Development in Indochina* (Chicago, 1936), 106–8; Buttinger, *Vietnam*, 1:107–10.

40. See Kelly, "Franco-Vietnamese Schools," chaps. 3–4.

41. The statement of 19 August 1935 is from Pasquier's response to a written question addressed to him in connection with a legal action against the Vietnamese newspaper *La Lutte*. See Hémery, "Aux origines des guerres d'independence vietnamiennes," 15. McConnell devotes a section to the nonindustrialization of Vietnam by the French and the bitterness this lack caused among indigenous intellectuals, for reasons of both nationalism and employment possibilities. See McConnell, *Leftward Journey*, 94–99.

tended to become a compendium of life as it was hundreds of years ago seen by Frenchmen, anthropological accounts of peasant life, or the French family and its values presented as Vietnamese."[42]

From 1931 teachers found that the teaching guides issued to them contained many more readings than in the past praising Vietnamese family and village life, ritual, and folkways. Trains and airplanes were depicted as awesome and often frightening, like the metropolitan exhibitions at the Colonial Exposition, irresistible as the civilization that produced them. In the authorized readings industry was usually presented as local and traditional. Manual skills were highly prized, but rice farming was more important. The texts praised science but generally by lionizing such men as Louis Pasteur, not by explaining biological concepts; in any case, the French vocabulary for scientific expression was not taught. In the history and geography teachers' guides neighboring China appeared as currently chaotic and badly governed and, in the past, oppressive of the Vietnamese and contemptuous of their culture, whereas the French were pictured as having brought order to Vietnam and as respectful of the people's traditions.[43]

Finally, the one Indochinese university that this training prepared an elite to attend increased its admissions after 1931, but, because of the depression, reduced its faculty and programs of study. By 1932 the schools of commerce, education, agriculture, and applied science were closed. What survived were the schools of law, medicine, and the newly founded beaux arts. In 1937 the university counted 631 students: 378 in law, 202 in medicine, and 51 in the beaux arts.

To be sure, the university's programs were inferior in quality to those offered in metropolitan institutions. Vietnamese-trained doctors, for example, could not practice in France. Law graduates were trained to work in the local administration, not in Paris. French

---

42. Kelly, "Franco-Vietnamese Schools," 134.

43. Ibid., 140–85. As an example of the ideological project of the teaching material given French teachers, Kelly quotes a poem in French by Crayssac, an official in the education bureaucracy of mixed French-Vietnamese ancestry, titled "Ode to the Nha-Que" (143):

> Push your humble plough in the rice grass,
> O nha-que, under the sparkling azure which you stand,
> From dawn to evening, from one year to the next,
> As will your son, as did your father.

educational authorities deemed this education adequate to serve local needs.[44] But the low level of higher education the French offered
was not the main fault with the system. After all, simply the establishment of an institution of higher learning for natives was a distinction enjoyed by none of the other French possessions, and only
by British India and South Africa among other nations' colonies.[45]
Rather, here too the issue was locking Vietnamese intellectuals into a
colonized culture dominated, indeed created, by the French colonial
administration. After decrying the loss of older Indochinese art traditions, or worse, their "mongrelization" (*un métis d'art détestable*), a
circular of the Direction Générale de l'Instruction Publique of Indochina reported that, "as a result, we are inclined to consider the
possibility of creating a school of *authentic* Annamite art intended to
bring about the renaissance of a tradition that is endangered, without diverting it from its natural level."[46]

Room at the Top

Of course it was impossible, even unwise, to exclude Indochinese
from all metropolitan higher education. The colonial administration
seemed willing to allow a trickle of colonials to attend French universities. But in the first half of the 1930s the authorities were troubled
by the question of their admission to the elite schools of higher
education called collectively the *grandes écoles*. The vestiges of republican egalitarianism, strengthened by the new ideology that saw
colonials as apprentice Frenchmen, prohibited any across-the-board
exclusion. The difficult entrance requirements were adequate barriers in general. But was not some of the knowledge that might be
taught the young *indigènes* who managed to gain admission dan-

44. Ibid., 70–79.
45. By way of contrast it should be noted that, with the exception of South Africa,
very little *secondary* schooling was open to the native inhabitants of Europe's African
colonies in the 1930s. See Altbach and Kelly, "Introduction," in *Education and Colonialism,* 7.
46. Indochine Française, Direction Générale de l'Instruction Publique, *Trois Ecoles
d'art de l'Indochine* (Hanoi, 1931), 8ff., quoted in Charles La Mache, "Le Trouble
croissant," *L'Ethnographie,* n.s. 23 (1931), 170–71; my italics.

gerous for them to know? The CAI considered admission of natives of the colonies into the purely military academies unthinkable. "There is no need to demonstrate the serious drawbacks our authority in the colonies would suffer if thoughtlessly we created a seedbed of officers with the same prerogatives as French officers and capable of exerting effective command over troops of their own race." It took the same position with respect to non-Europeans' admission to the Ecole Coloniale, "the only function of which is to prepare its students for positions of authority [in the colonies]."

What of *indigènes* in the Ecole Polytechnique, a science, engineering, and military school all in one? In August 1932 Pierre Pasquier wrote the minister of colonies expressing his support for allowing *indigènes* into all the elite academic institutions except the Colonial School and institutions in which military training was given. In a position paper of 2 November 1933, stamped "Secret," Gaston Joseph, the CAI chief, repeated his organization's concerns about maintaining French authority in the colonies. He added that "what we need to do, above all, is to supply our colonies with the native technicians required for their economic development." But a systematic policy had not yet been worked out on the admission of qualified natives of the colonies to the schools that trained people with the skills needed for economic development.

After an internal conference of all the pertinent directorates of the Colonial Ministry failed to hammer out a unified policy on the admission of *indigènes* to the *grandes écoles* in 1933, in March 1934 the directors of both the Military Services and Political Affairs of the ministry agreed formally to sanction their admission, but only to the nonsensitive schools. But the concession was offensive to the ministers of war and agriculture in Gaston Doumergue's coalition government, which had been formed in the wake of the Stavisky riots. These ministries did not wish to allow any colonials to sit for the entrance examinations to any of the *grandes écoles*. After some politicking that led to an agreement circumscribing such admissions, the *Journal Officiel* for 21 March 1935 carried a notice by Minister of War G. Maurin, accepted and signed by the president of the Republic, permitting foreigners, nonnaturalized natives of the empire, and residents of places under French protection admission into the Ecole Polytechnique. They had to pay all or part of the fees, unlike

French students, and were obliged to study science courses exclusively.

Although colonials had now gained the right to elite higher education, it was very much a case of repressive tolerance. Their attendance at the *grandes écoles*—even the Polytechnique—was regularized as long as they did not study two topics that might have interested them: colonial administration and military science. Moreover, since colonial graduates could not easily find jobs appropriate to their schooling and skills, the door opened by education was slammed shut by the discriminatory employment policies. Only graduates who were very well connected could find suitable positions in potentially sensitive or prestigious places. It could even happen that a young candidate for the most ordinary of posts needed to seek the intervention of a sometime colonial minister, a governor general, and the emperor of Annam just to get his foot in the door.

In August 1932 Albert Sarraut, the most powerful politician concerned with colonial issues in the interwar years, wrote Governor General Pasquier on behalf of a young graduate of the Polytechnique, Hoang Xuan Han. The young man was a candidate for a position with the Corps des Ponts et Chaussées in Indochina—the publics works department. Sarraut mentioned that Emperor Bao Dai had asked for his good offices in the matter. Usually graduates of the Polytechnique had little difficulty finding places at Ponts et Chausées in the colonies, if they cared to accept such a post. But Sarraut was not even lobbying Pasquier for a proper appointment. He proposed rather that the young *indigène* be given a contract and the title of "acting engineer" (*ingénieur adjoint*). That way, Sarraut wrote, there was no danger "of . . . creating a precedent." Presumably with such support, the young *polytechnicien* got to serve as an assistant engineer in the colony. But there could not have been many others like him; the colonial administration of Indochina, at least in the interwar years, had few natives in responsible positions.[47]

---

47. In the folder of projects under consideration marked "Pièces non expédiées," containing many texts and letters in fact sent off, see Pierre Pasquier to Minister of Colonies, 15 August 1932; the unsigned CAI memo dated Paris, 22 September 1933; the secret note of the director of the CAI to the governor general of Indochina (n.d. [late 1932, early 1933?]); the secret review of the question by the head of the CAI dated Paris, 2 November 1933; and Sarraut to Pasquier, 27 August 1932, all in

Identity Crises

The commitment of the French colonial administration to a certain kind of education in Vietnam requires comment not to arrive at some score of the relative benevolence or destructiveness visited on the native culture by the colonial authorities but rather to draw more nuanced conclusions about the nature of colonial-metropolitan interplay in the confection of native identities under colonialism.[48] At least as regards the interwar years, the distinction between association and assimilation, the customary categories employed in discussions of France's agenda for the colonies, in a metropolitan *cultural* policy toward Indochina makes no sense. Moreover, it is clear that we must now go beyond the world systems approach, with its sharp demarcation of center and periphery. Although that approach has helped us speak of economic and political power relations, it does little to increase our understanding of the complexities and sophistication of the pretensions of Europeans (here the supporters of French colonialism) to dominate their colonial possessions culturally.[49]

Specifically, we need to gain a better grasp on how the project of metropolitan cultural hegemony in the colonies was constructed, and, as in the case of Vietnam, why, finally, it failed. When, for example, in the Jonnart reforms of 1919 the French administration offered enfranchisement to Algerians who would give up their Muslim personal status—their religion and the recognition of their marriage(s) and property rights under Koranic law—very few took up the offer.[50] The *colons*, too, often manifested little dedication to

SLOTFOM, ser. III, carton 118. For a critical evaluation of the colonial policy and achievements of the Popular Front government, see William B. Cohen, "Colonial Policy of the Popular Front," *French Historical Studies*, 7 (1972), 368–93.

48. The British followed a not dissimilar policy in India.

49. Current theory in this realm builds, of course, on Antonio Gramsci's idea of hegemony, as developed in his *Prison Notebooks*. See further passages from an editorial in *L'Ordine Nuovo*, "The Colonial Populations," in *Selections from Political Writings, 1910–1920*, ed. Quintin Hoare (New York, 1977), 303. See also the polemical but insightful account of Gramsci's thought in Lesek Kolakowski, *Main Currents of Marxism: Its Origins, Growth, and Dissolution*, vol. 3, *The Breakdown* (Oxford, 1981), 220–52, esp. 240–44.

50. Charles-Robert Ageron reports that between 1919 and 1923, 317 Algerians residing in Algeria applied for French naturalization; 256 were accepted: *Les Algériens*

building a Greater France. When in 1936 the Popular Front introduced a more liberal measure that would not require apostasy for
the Muslims of Algeria to become eligible for naturalization, the
European mayors of Algerian towns resigned as a body. The proposal was dropped. In colonies that had significant numbers of European settlers, the role these *colons* could play in thwarting metropolitan projects of colonial hegemony may have been the most
decisive cause of their failure.[51] But Indochina had relatively few
Europeans, so the *colons*, although important, could not so easily
thwart the project of creating Greater France in Vietnam. As for the
Vietnamese themselves, their struggles, however crucial for the
overthrow of French rule—and, for that matter, of American domination—cannot be at the center of attention here. In tracing the
construction of True France, we must focus on the weapons of the
creators of hegemony rather than those of the weak.

As a conceptual brush-clearing tool, the theory of invented traditions has value in suggesting ways to look at the manner in which
metropolitan hegemony was put together in the colonies.[52] We are
now in a position to identify some of the cultural-political issues that
still need to be probed. They can be expressed as five connected
theses and the questions they imply. First, the radical (essentially
metaphysical) separation of the identities of oppressor and oppressed is neither good theory nor good history. Traditions, even
top-down invented ones, can become battlefields in culture wars.
Once implanted, they change, perhaps even becoming weapons of
the colonized against the metropole. Moreover, the resisters often
also invent some of their own traditions, which may bear little rela-

musulmans et la France (1870–1919), 2 vols. (Paris, 1968), 2:1190–1227, esp. 1221–23.
See also David Prochaska, *Making Algeria French: Colonialism in Bône, 1870–1920*
(Cambridge, 1990), 236.

51. Charles-Robert Ageron, *Histoire de l'Algerie contemporaine,* 2 vols. (Paris, 1979),
2:450–51; Lustick, *State-Building Failure;* Prochaska, *Making Algeria French,* 237.

52. See the essays in Hobsbawm and Ranger, *Invention of Tradition,* esp. Ranger,
"The Invention of Tradition in Colonial Africa," 211–62, and the excellent piece by
Bernard S. Cohn, "Representing Authority in Victorian India," 165–209. I have
found no one symbol for the complex phenomenon of the invention of traditions by a
colonial power for a subject people more evocative than the Prince of Wales's present
of Max Müller's English translation of the Vedas to the British subjects of India in
thanks for the gifts they gave him during his tour of 1875–76: ibid., 182.

tion to history. Nor is it useful to see the struggle as one between the little identity defending itself against the grand one. Serious penalties are attached to the heedless pursuit of difference and diversity as *the* key to liberation or autonomy. Second, there is the issue of cultural power to clarify. Third, we have to look at what or whom to study so that we can pose better questions about how cultural power works. Fourth, in response to arguments that focus on the moral economy of the subjected, we have to think in better ways about leadership in cultural struggles. Finally, what role did the construction of True France in Vietnam play in metropolitan France?

First, the problem of identity. The Sartrean model employed by Frantz Fanon (and Simone de Beauvoir, for that matter) of oppressor and oppressed (as the theory conceptualized it at its most abstract level, the Subject and the Other) fits badly into most contemporary discussions of resistance struggles. Rather, as in the Vietnamese cultural resistance, we see an interpenetration of the two forces, on one side French colonial administrators who admired the civilizations of Indochina and tried to revive them, and on the other, Westernized native radical intellectuals seeking European knowledge.

It is time to transcend the Sartrean perspective for at least four reasons. First, the oppressed use the hegemonic ideology for their own ends in the struggle; the students invoked the values of the French Revolution and of republicanism in their combats with the French Republic.

The second reason we cannot treat empire and colony as ontologically distinct is that the subjugated regularly demand to be free—that is, to be left alone—and at the same time want the resources and aid of the dominant power to facilitate their emancipation. The Vietnamese students wanted high-quality French education for their own purposes. In particular, study at elite institutions such as the Ecole Polytechnique would have been valuable for goals quite contrary to those set for Indochina by the Colonial Ministry.[53]

Third, the oppressed often also invent some of their own traditions, which may or may not bear a relation to their own history, but are adapted from the culture of the hegemonic country. Here too

53. Peter Sahlins made me aware of the importance of this point in a discussion of Native American cultural resistance while we were visiting Kwakiutl friends in Fort Ruppert, British Columbia, 27 March 1991.

the values of egalitarian republicanism and socialism, as employed by the Paris students, instance the point. And we know that the traditions and definitions of identity of both the rulers and the ruled change with time and circumstance.[54]

A fourth problem with a Sartrean philosophical anthropology of the subject is that analyses of hegemonic relations are dangerous when they focus primarily on *differences and the right to differences* of the dominated in emancipation struggles. We saw how French imperialists were quite willing to recognize the uniqueness of Vietnamese culture and to encourage its revival. Today, for example, Jean-Marie Le Pen and other French racists use the ways immigrants are different and the uniqueness of their cultures to argue for their exclusion, since they can never become part of French national life. Nor can they conceive of an ancient French civilization changing to accommodate the cultural peculiarities of the new French.[55]

What justification is there, then, for making sharply drawn attributions of cultural identity? It is a project nationalist intellectuals undertake at moments of great cultural-political contestation; and it is just at those conjunctures that the interpenetration of cultures is most evident. The Sartre theory gives us hard balls in collision, which make a satisfying revolutionary bang, to be sure, but what we need is an understanding of fluids in many states of mixture and agitation, including violent reaction.

Cultural Politics

It is still necessary to formulate—now in cultural-political terms— Lenin's famous "Who, whom?" question, the question of power. Simply stated, the premise of cultural determinism is inadequate as a basis for understanding—or carrying out, I suggest—cultural strug-

---

54. See Cooper and Stoler, "Colonial Control," 610.

55. Michel de Certeau, *L'Invention du quotidien: Arts de faire* (Paris, 1980), 31–94. Zeynep Celik and Leila Kinney, "Ethnography and Exhibitionism at the Expositions Universelles," *Assemblage*, 13 (1990), 54–56, develop an incisive critique of Sartre's adaptation from Hegel of his analysis of power and domination founded upon "squaring two pairs of oppositions."

gles. Political power in an imperial setting must be counted as a paramount source of invention in the areas of culture and values.[56] But I am not concerned here with the political power of the old political history, a story only of ministries, officials, and decrees. Our inquiry into the enterprise of colonial education in Vietnam makes it manifest that political authority is quite as much constructed as is cultural policy. Accordingly, we need to continue refining theoretical tools, such as the idea of a hegemonic project, for looking at the role of institutional power in the process of diffusion of values across the membrane of culture.

Further, these same tools, as we will see, should help us understand in what ways the diffusion of culture within the metropolitan nation—both down the class system and from Paris to provinces— serves as the model for the phenomenon in the colonies. How were the processes similar? How did they differ? Certainly the use of the school system to make peasants into Frenchmen had been extensively tested in provincial France before it was tried with reverse intentions in Vietnam.[57] The idea of hegemony is a tool capable of taking the different cutting edges for different applications; so we should not automatically assume that the growth of Parisian power in the provinces should be understood as the same process as the ascendancy of France over distant colonies.

Accordingly, we have to know the circumstances and the ideologies of the European rulers of the colonies, as well as the influence of European rule on both the material circumstances of all strata of the population and the well-educated section of the colonial population. Social historians have shown us ways to learn about the lives of people not before acknowledged by historians. Their work has been an important corrective to histories of the mighty in Europe and of famous events and administrators in colonial studies.

56. Abdou Mounmouni, *Education in Africa* (New York, 1968), argues along these lines, but Remi Clignet, "Damned if You Do and Damned if You Don't: The Dilemmas of Colonizer-Colonized Relations," in Altbach and Kelly, *Education and Colonialism*, 122–45, sees Mounmouni's position, among other versions of it, as psychologically reductionist.

57. Altbach and Kelly argue that British charity schools, the American schools for former slaves after the Civil War, and the elementary education provided French working-class children after the 1880s served as models for the training of various colonial elites to the needed level of learning: *Education and Colonialism*, 19.

But we have learned very little from it about how the politically powerful arrayed and exercised cultural power. In this realm history exclusively from the bottom up may well have bottomed out.

The new cultural history tries to remedy this methodological blind spot. And the best of it, such as the work of Roger Chartier on the ancien régime, Lynn Hunt on the French Revolution, Pascal Ory on the culture of the Popular Front, the group associated with Jean-Pierre Rioux on the interactions of culture and politics in contemporary history, and Jean Jamin, working the veins marked out by Michel Leiris and Michel Foucault on the history of the twentieth-century *sciences humaines* and—specifically on the issue of colonialism—the workers in subaltern studies, does not fall into simplifying cultural determinism. Ethnic groups, little traditions, communities of peasants or workers are and always were too interconnected with the powerful both near and far, the mighty of the great house on the hill or those at desks in far-off offices in the capital, to be treated any longer, as George Marcus put it, "as an integral spatio-temporal isolate," with internal tensions, to be sure, "but at least with its own integrity against the world, so to speak."[58] The Vietnamese colonial administrators understood very well that they could not just by education expect to reorient the colonials' consciousness.

In the wake of the rebellions of 1930, the colonial authorities tried to introduce more security and stability to peasant life. They made credit available to peasant proprietors, introduced a bit more juridical protection for small owners, improved sanitation, and in the north and center improved flood control and water management. Moreover, in the life of the villages they attempted to carry through the logic that informed their educational policy: they tried

58. Renato Rosaldo's extended analysis of Emmanuel Le Roy Ladurie's *Montaillou* is a good critique of some of the problems of the *Annales* style of social history. See his "From the Door of the Tent: The Fieldworker and the Inquisitor," in *Writing Culture: The Poetics and Politics of Ethnography,* ed. James Clifford and George E. Marcus (Berkeley, 1986), 77–87, 96–97. For an appreciation and at the same time an excellent methodological critique of the English genre of history from the bottom up—in this case of Paul Willis's study of working-class English youth, *Learning to Labour: How Working-Class Kids Get Working-Class Jobs* (New York, 1981)—see Marcus, "Contemporary Problems of Ethnography in the Modern World System," in *Writing Culture,* 173–93. For an attempt to do justice to the idea both of class and of culture, see Gerald M. Sider, *Culture and Class in Anthropology and History: A Newfoundland Illustration* (Cambridge, 1986).

to restore the frayed net of mutual constraints and obligations on which the communal hierarchies rested. Using modern methods to teach old ways, the colonial administrators tried to revitalize the old order their presence was unraveling.[59] Down to the village level, then, they hoped ultimately to implant their own dependent Vietnamese mandarin-teachers to frustrate the development of rebellious organic intellectuals.

The Sûreté Notes a Psychological Error

This brings us to a fourth point, the question of leadership. James C. Scott, writing of the myriad ways the weak of the countryside resist the domination of the strong, has critiqued the idea of hegemony in the sense in which I am using it, the sense of ideological and cultural domination. His five objections to the uses of the concept of hegemony by Althusser, Miliband, Poulantzas, Habermas, Marcuse, and people who follow them may be summarized as follows. He argues (1) that dominated classes can penetrate the ideological mystifications of the rulers, (2) that they are not so naive as to credit the inevitable class constraints of their lives as just (as Barrington Moore, Jr., says they do), (3) that the hegemonic system contains its own explosive inner contradictions, so that an elaborate intellectually strong counterideology of the weak is unnecessary, (4) that small demands for everyday improvements can sometimes lead to revolution, and (5) that the dominant ideology is often broken not by peasants or workers but by those who introduce a new mode of production (such as the capitalists who overthrow an older economic order).[60]

One can agree with these points—as on the whole I do—and still ask Scott how what he calls "the tenacity of self-preservation" might lead the oppressed to consider the implementation of a new—or at least better—life for themselves. He adduces no case of social-revolutionary transformation—however deep the resentments of

59. Hémery, "Aux origines des guerres d'indépendance vietnamiennes," 16.
60. Scott, *Weapons of the Weak,* 314–50.

peasants or workers may have been—in which organic intellectuals did not lead the resistance to the cultural hegemony of the powerful. Antonio Gramsci termed this kind of resistance a "war of position," and the idea has value for cultural history. He saw the war of position, in the largest sense, as an educational struggle: "Every relation of hegemony is necessarily a pedagogic relationship."

The term "organic intellectual," Gramsci's key concept of the intellectual, political, and, yes, moral connection between leaders and disaffected in combats over cultural control, is not in Scott's analysis. When he addresses the issue of leadership in the struggle to seize power from rulers, he refers to "outside leadership in some form— for example, a political party, an intelligentsia—" as perhaps necessary. He misses Gramsci's point that potentially victorious struggles can be thought out and organized only in the dialectic of communication and trust between strategists and disaffected group. The strategists cannot be seen, as Scott seems to suggest, as somehow ethnographically outside agitators.[61]

Oppressed populations are not leaderless tribes. Within the community or group there are fissures and hierarchies and many different projects. And there are also spokespersons for subgroups or human projects who interpret the meaning and workings of the

61. Employing a military metaphor that perhaps the dynamics of World War I suggested to him, Gramsci distinguished in his *Prison Notebooks* between the strategies of wars and revolutions of movement and those of position. The Germans' attempt to take Paris in a great military sweep in 1914 and the Bolsheviks' seizure of the Winter Palace on 7 November 1917 are examples of the movement mode. But when a quick decisive victory is not possible—as it was not for the German army—then warfare and revolution must be conducted piecemeal, over time, by capture of one and then another strongpoint. In the modern class struggle in Italy, Gramsci believed, the time for storming ruling-class strongholds was over. The victory of the working class had to be cumulative, institution by institution, until the hegemony of the ruling classes had been broken. Hegemony here meant cultural domination, the ability of the rulers to impose their vision of reality or "common sense." To become ascendant the oppressed had to respond with their own vision of the world and fight for it in the media, in the educational system, in what the members of the society took to be self-evident and mere common sense. See Antonio Gramsci, *Selections from the Prison Notebooks of Antonio Gramsci*, ed. and trans. Quintin Hoare and Geoffrey Newell Smith (London, 1971), 243, 356; Christian Reichers, *Antonio Gramsci: Marxismus in Italien* (Frankfurt am Main, 1970), 211–23, esp. 213–14; James Joll, *Antonio Gramsci* (London, 1977), 127–34; John Cammett, *Antonio Gramsci and the Origins of Italian Communism* (Stanford, 1967), 201–12.

outside authority's power upon the group and who take the lead in negotiating or contesting with that power as well. Thus Gramsci's idea of an organic intellectual—now to be understood in the sense of a go-between *on behalf* of the community with an ability to operate in several cultural contexts—continues to be useful to us even in the case of societies far different from Italy in the interwar years.

It is true, to resist in the everyday and over the seasons the Vietnamese did not need intellectual vanguards to infuse them with revolutionary consciousness and sophisticated ideologies. Staying on this level of cultural resistance—within the culture as symbolic anthropology might define it—Scott cannot be optimistic about revolution coming from the weak in the future; he is being honest about the limits of his claims for the efficacy of a resistance model.[62] But as less of a pessimist, as less a believer in the seamless web of culture, as well as a historian of past struggles—such as the one conducted by the student-vandals at the Paris Colonial Exposition, which led finally to successful overthrow of colonial rule in Vietnam—I would rather encourage us to follow the open-ended utopianism of Ernst Bloch's principle of hope.[63]

My point about writing about the culture of resistance in the case of French Indochina, in brief, is that revolutionary armies must have soldiers, to be sure, but they must also have strategists. And from the point of view of method, neither the motives nor the grievances of either component are deducible from those of the other. Nor are the historical outcomes necessarily understandable completely from the bottom up, especially not in struggles, as here, for decolonization.[64]

The members of the Sûreté Générale of Indochina were by profession not inept theorists of resistance and, in the nature of the

62. Gramsci, *Selections*, 345, 350.

63. Scott expresses pessimism about the fruits of revolution for workers and peasants. His concluding meditation on peasant resistance under capitalism or communism is therefore truly dismal: "the steady, grinding efforts to hold one's own against overwhelming odds—a spirit and practice that prevent the worst and promises something better" (350). He gives us no reason to believe that they will hold their own, except in very small ways, or to theorize what the promise of something better is for them in the villages or as they leave for the cities, or for us now living in the cities. For another critical perspective on Scott's argument see Samuel L. Popkin, *The Rational Peasant: The Political Economy of Rural Society in Vietnam* (Berkeley, 1979); Popkin makes a case for the role of political entrepreneurs in Vietnamese peasant society.

64. In the late 1970s in polemics with Maoists, Michel Foucault attacked the conception of "leading intellectuals." In his "On Popular Justice," he rejected any need

case, of cultural resistance. As part of its duties in Indochina the Sûreté filed monthly reviews of the political situation for the information of the governor general. Here in very detailed and thorough fashion it chronicled political incidents and strikes, reproduced seized revolutionary documents and leaflets, and provided the governor general with its appreciation of the major trends in movements of subversion in the colony. In the report for May 1931— therefore in the aftermath of the suppression of the uprisings—an introductory overview reported serious problems in the Indochinese Communist Party. The party organization was in disorder, funds were short, and the leadership had made some bad moves. In particular, "there is a growing tendency in the Indochinese Communist Party to remove intellectuals from leadership positions and to replace them with manual workers. This is evidently the new line [of the Comintern], but in this country it commits a psychological error that can only benefit us."[65]

The Empire at Home

A final issue in this history, which began with an incident at the 1931 Colonial Exposition and led to a consideration of colonial

---

for organic intellectuals to guide the people, holding "that an act of popular justice cannot achieve its full significance unless it is clarified politically under the supervision of *the masses* themselves": *Power/Knowledge* (New York, 1980), 1–36 (the quotation, 3). Paul A. Bové, *Intellectuals in Power: A Genealogy of Critical Humanism* (New York, 1986), 227, endorses Foucault's position, supporting it by accusing the state and leading intellectuals (everywhere and always?) of wishing "to deny to *the people* the power of self-regulation and self-imagination" (my italics in both quotes). I suspect that to some degree Foucault was putting the young *gauchistes* on by taking up this ultraradical populist (and silly) position. I cannot explain Bové's unmediated devotion to 1960s hopes in the mid-1980s. Let me add as a historian that both authors' use of such words as "the masses" and "the people" in social analysis cause me despair. I cannot understand how such a vocabulary can be compatible with ideas of liberation, empowerment, and creation by the humans who must live in a real social world. It is not a trivial historical fact that General Giap, military leader of the Vietnamese struggle against first the French and then the Americans, like many of the leaders of what we came to call the Viet Cong, had first studied to be a schoolteacher.

65. These reports were filed in bound volumes and subtitled by date. See "Les Faits du mois mai 1931," in "Les Associations antifrançaises et la propagande communiste en Indochine," SLOTFOM, ser. III, carton 49.

hegemony, should be seen as an incitement to historians of culture to take a more dialectical view of the relation of colonial cultural policy to the efforts of the metropolitan ruling class to consolidate its cultural hegemony at home.

To the dictum that all history is present history we might usefully add that in the end, all our inquiries into the way power and cultural influence work in colonial settings are concerns about our own lives in metropolitan centers. It is muddled to claim that the efforts of a European state to secure cultural hegemony over its colonies are the same as those of its capital to assimilate its provinces. However, there are parallels between the means French rulers employed to gain the loyalty of a subject population abroad and the cultural apparatus of induced loyalty at home. In particular, conservative ethnography, and those who accepted its ways and truths, called the attention of colonial and domestic authorities to the need to preserve or revive the politically inhibiting aspects of colonial and regional cultures.

But the way the project of colonial hegemony works back in the metropole is also important, in general, and key for our interest in the workings of the ideology of True France. Ian Lustick has pointed out the important legitimating function exercised by the systematic pairing of the Republic with the colonial empire in the 1930s in the propagation of the idea of a Greater France.[66]

Charles La Mache's support of the return of Indochinese education to the Indochinese and the revitalization of their traditions under French supervision in 1931 is a case in point.[67] Like Louis Marin, he was a man of the right. He valued the old traditions of Indochina as the best protection of its social stability and the best crutch for the social hierarchy. Secular education that shakes old beliefs and calls all into question—foreign (i.e., French) ideas, rural exodus, even interest in the French Revolution—contributed to what he termed "the growing disorder" in Asia. But it is clear from the context that, like Marin, he believed these same factors were at the heart of metropolitan troubles in the early 1930s. In this new

---

66. See Ian Lustick's draft chapter "Where and What Is France?: Three Failures of Hegemonic Construction" (1991), 6–9. D. Bruce Marshall, *The French Colonial Myth and Constitution-Making in the Fourth Republic* (New Haven, 1973), shares Lustick's view of the ideological role of the empire in modern France.

67. La Mache, "Trouble croissant," 158, 160, 167.

manifestation of respect for Indochinese culture, the French right employed *its* noble savage—here the pious, learned Annamite—to pummel a secular, irreligious, and radicalizing metropolitan society.[68]

Pierre Taittinger, head of the fascistic Jeunesses Patriotes and a political collaborator of Louis Marin in the Chamber, also wanted the Vietnamese returned to their authentic culture. Rather than making Annamites alienated intellectuals and philosophers, he argued in June 1930, during the Chamber debate on the Yen-Bay uprising and the agitation of the Indochinese students living in France who supported it, their education should reconnect them to their native cultural and artistic heritage, as perhaps artisans, carvers, artists.[69]

Conservatives' fears for the loss of traditions, and with them of a certain essential identity—and not just the right had these concerns, we have seen—fueled the anxieties and projects of Frenchmen concerned with Indochina. If bad imitations of Frenchmen could be turned once more into good Vietnamese peasants, the disorder of the world would subside. To be sure, we see here the not uncommon prejudice of the colonial official—Lyautey, for example—who preferred the primitives and bush natives to their assimilated brethren; the primitives were so much more authentic, and easier to rule. And if such a project was feasible for far-off Vietnam, could it not benefit a strife-torn metropolitan France, which also had become unanchored from its rural and peasant heritage?

French folklorists began to discover the passing of a fabled rural France at the same time, just after World War I, as colonial administrators began to assess the dangers of Europeanization of the native cultures. For our last probing of the manner of the conservative construction of True France, let us look at the genesis and development of French folklore as an intellectually symbiotic process with that of the colonial rerooting project.

When the Colonial Exposition closed, one of the structures built

68. Pascal Bruckner, *The Tears of the White Man: Compassion as Contempt,* trans. William R. Beer (New York, 1986), is an often mean-spirited attack on contemporary Western Third Worldism by a man of the right who has given up his illusions about what the West may do to benefit the underdeveloped parts of the world.

69. Chamber of Deputies, *Journal officiel,* 6 June 1930.

for it—the building containing exhibition halls and an aquarium—
was left in place and rededicated as the Musée des Colonies et de
l'Aquarium. The decree creating it named members of the committee for the exposition as directors, most of them officials of the
Colonial Ministry.[70] Thereafter, in the innocent semiology of the
days before decolonization, Parisians could go to the Bois de Vincennes to admire the exotic fish in their tanks and the fruits of
colonial culture and industry in their cases.[71] Here too, as at the
exposition, a lesson was suggested to visitors, if only by implication:
the world was full of wondrous species and their arts; but a French
structure was needed to contain, validate, and interpret them.[72]

70. The decrees and a number of other official documents related to the creation
of the new museum are found in A.N. F[21] 4916.

71. In its first years the Musée put on rather dull shows illustrating the economic
utility of the colonies. From 18 October to 4 December 1933 it presented an exhibition of the uses of colonial woods in the making of French furniture. From 6 May to
20 November 1936 it offered an exposition on tea and coffee. When he served as
minister of culture under Charles de Gaulle, André Malraux made of it a museum
dedicated to the art/artifacts of the French possessions of Africa and Oceania. See
A.N. F[21] 4731, folder 5.

72. On French decolonization see the relevant sections of the excellent summing
up by Jacques Marseille, *Empire colonial et capitalisme français: Histoire d'un divorce*
(Paris, 1984), and for an excellent critique of the moral economy school from a
judicious adherent, see Brooke Larson, *Exploitation and Moral Economy in the Southern
Andes: A Critical Reconsideration*, Columbia–New York University Latin American, Caribbean, and Iberian Occasional Papers no. 8 (New York, 1989).

Identity Conflicts:
Folklore and the
National Heritage

Having examined the politics of heritage in anthropological theory and in the attempts to assimilate the population of the country to the colonial empire and the indigenous peoples of the colonies to the mother country, we may now finally look at the play of theories of national cultural identity in metropolitan France.

It might be clarifying to begin by presenting two contrasting pictures of French cultural identity, both created just after the collapse of the Third Republic and at the start of the Pétain regime. The first image captures the essentialism of Vichy cultural politics. In the beginning of Vichy rule the new state made serious efforts to win over the French young people to the old truths it was refurbishing. In a collection of pictures for children done under Vichy there is a marvelous drawing depicting the marshal shaking the hand of a peasant at his plow with a tricolor flag waving behind them and the spire of a village church in the distance. Above the picture was the often-used Vichy motto "The earth does not lie" (La terre, elle ne ment pas). The text beneath directs children to color in appropriate hues the marshal's suit, the horses, and the peasant's clothes. When folded along the dotted lines, the drawing made a pretty tableau of eternally patient draft animals, forever respectful farmers, a flag ever waving, a church tower faithfully guiding us to our village, and an old soldier who would always be there when we needed him.[1]

Now a second, a different kind of picture. In June 1941, under the German occupation of Paris, for an exposition at the Grand Palais with—at that moment—the highly ambiguous title "La France Européenne," Georges-Henri Rivière, head of the national folklore museum, curated the interior of a Norman farmhouse, the principal attraction at the show. He furnished the main room with a beautiful old cupboard, a chest carved with ancient geometric forms, and a splendid *panetière* (a suspended wooden bread cage). But he also placed a modern desk among the old pieces, and on an antique bureau visitors saw a telephone and a radio. Country classics such as the *Almanac des bergers* sat on the shelves alongside modern works on agricultural techniques and management.

A political and cultural civil war raged in interwar France over which of the two pictures—and a third one, offered by the Popular Front but looking very much like the first, with the figure of a worker awkwardly painted in as an afterthought—portrayed the culture of France. In the interwar years, folklore studies, the prime field of the pursuit of cultural identity, emerged and took disciplinary form. And from the Popular Front to the era of Vichy, in arguably the most crucial few years of French national debate about the national essence since the French Revolution, folklore was a major battleground of what Henry Rousso has termed the great "Franco-French civil war" over what was the authentic France.[2]

As the 1930s drew to a close, the central debate in France's politicized intellectual milieu, as well as in the politics of the streets, had moved beyond the one launched by Charles Maurras in the era of the Dreyfus affair and of Louis Marin's apprenticeship, that of the *pays réel* versus the *pays légal*, the True France and the France that for

1. A reproduction may be found in the catalogue for the exhibition "La Propagande sous Vichy, 1940–1944," held by the Musée d'Histoire Contemporaine de la Bibliothèque de Documentation Internationale Contemporaine, at the Hôtel des Invalides, 17 May–21 July 1990. The catalogue has the same title and was edited by Laurent Gervereau and Denis Peschanski (Paris, 1990), 115.

2. See Henry Rousso, *Le Syndrome de Vichy, 1944–198 . . .* (Paris, 1987), 18, 38–43. For more on the idea of the recurrent civil wars in French history, see his "Guerres franco-françaises," *Vingtième Siècle*, 5 (1985).

the moment was controlled by republicans.[3] In posing that duality Maurras appropriated to himself and to the new conservatism the right to articulate the unique vision of the true and eternal France. The Maurrasian image of an essential France had successfully challenged republican essentialism, with its roots in the great revolution. Its diffusion helped to bring on the cultural death of the Third Republic well before its political demise in 1940.[4] Thus in the last years of the Republic the dispute in politics, in literature, and most pervasively in the *sciences humaines* of the epoc was no longer over the validity of the disjunction, but only over what constituted, or might constitute, the *pays réel* itself. That it was not merely the concern of antiquarians, seekers after the quaint, and diehard localists becomes evident when we follow the struggle over French culture from the era of the Popular Front to that of the Etat Français of Vichy.

The first version of the cultural-political polemic fought out so acrimoniously in the *sciences humaines* and in politics in the 1930s was whether workers counted as part of the popular culture studied by folklore, or whether peasants alone represented the True France. If finally the culture of urban workers might be blended into that of the rest of the nation, supporters of the *Rassemblement* in the social sciences believed, the Popular Front would have modified to the good a new expanded identity for old France.

But if workers were excluded, if only rural France partook of the national essence, the reactionary agenda that was Charles Maurras's and would be that of Vichy would become the norm. Christian Faure has suggested that the discipline of folklore studies, by privileging the rural over the urban and by its ahistoricity in the interwar years, lent itself to political and intellectual appropriation by Marshal Pétain's new state.[5] Doubtless the state that glorified the peasant, the soil, and the fixity of tradition, that proclaimed the return to region-

---

3. The distinction goes back to the new Orléanist monarchy, established in 1830, which divided the few legal voters from the rest of the (disfranchised) nation.

4. Daniel Lindenberg, *Les Années souterraines, 1937–1947* (Paris, 1990), 15, 54.

5. Christian Faure, "Folklore et révolution nationale: Doctrine et action sous Vichy (1940–44)," 2 vols. (thèse doctorat, Université de Lyon II, 1986), 71, 226. Together with the valuable studies of Marc Knobel on racialist social science, Faure's is one of the first sustained efforts to approach the development of an important *science humaine* from Republic to Etat Français, and certainly the most finished piece of work we have. See Marc Knobel, "Un Ethnologue à la dérive, Georges Montadon et l'eth-

al organization in France for the first time since the Revolution,[6] could be expected to welcome research studies of French artisan industry, rural furnishing, and styles of architecture, for example. For urban researchers without much previous formal training in anthropology, these topics permitted insight into important and relatively accessible peculiarities of the *pays* that made up France.

But there is another dimension, a third path among the *problématiques* of the discipline of the ethnography of France, as contemporary French anthropologists would now designate the field that played a key role in French cultural conflicts in general and in the passage from republican democracy to Vichy dictatorship specifically. Like the other positions, it lives on today. For the wars between the proponents of an antique France and of a France with workers at its heart obscured a more fundamental question, which some contemporaries were just then struggling to formulate: Why should we speak in terms of a French identity or essence at all?

In Search of the Real France

The search for the *pays réel* was launched in its early-twentieth-century cultural and political incarnations by Charles Maurras, Maurice Barrès, his friend, and Frédéric Mistral, to name just the most prominent. Their opponents among the left republicans would not allow themselves to be defined out of national life by allegations of their foreignness framed both in the language of social science theory and in that of an aesthetic mystique. This was perhaps the greatest contribution of Jean Jaurès to the culture of modern French

noracisme," *Ethnologie Française*, 18 (1988), 107–13, and "L'Ethnologie à la dérive," *Le Monde Juif: Revue du Centre de Documentation Juive Contemporaine*, 132 (1988), 179–92. Since 1985 Knobel has been working with an international task force dedicated to the study of anthropology and the variety of fascisms. A volume of their work is nearing completion.

6. J. Charles-Brun, "La France et ses provinces," in *France 1941: La Révolution constructive—un bilan et un programme* (Paris, 1941), 126–46; Pierre Barral, "Idéal et pratique du régionalisme dans le régime de Vichy," *Revue française de science politique*, 24 (1974), 911–39; Maurice Agulhon, "Conscience nationale et conscience régionale en France de 1815 à nos jours," in *Histoire vagabonde: Idéologies et politique dans la France du XIXe siècle*, 2 vols. (Paris, 1988), 2:144–74.

politics: in the setting of the new republic, he formulated—although he could not make them a part of the common sense of his day—ideas and the myths that made plausible socialist claims that workers, too, partook of the national heritage.

The origins of both the French regionalist movement and a new interest in the ethnography of France in the last years of the previous century, at the height of the campaign of the republican bloc to consolidate their leadership of the Third Republic (what I have called elsewhere the refounding of the Republic) and their apotheosis *in state policy* in the Vichy period, suggests that we may better understand the development of culture studies in France by looking at the places where field of culture incorporated the political.[7] Accordingly, I think it more useful intellectually to begin with the idea that French folklore studies was the field—in the sense advanced by Pierre Bourdieu[8]—in which conflicting paradigms coexisted and within which the political struggles over the *pays réel* were fought, rather than to credit the old tale about the political destruction of the democratic cultural paradigm of the 1930s by the peasantist conservative one of the early 1940s.

In the first half of this century, then, there were two conflicts about the identity of French culture. The first was the long-burning dispute inherited from the era of the French Revolution, and perennially disputed since then, as to what was the French *patrimoine* and who had the right to speak for it. By the 1920s and 1930s the candidates of the right and of the left, respectively, were peasants alone and both workers and peasants. This was, to put it schematically, a kind of Franco-French *Kulturkampf*.

The second and in the long run more important issue, one that most historians took for granted until recently rather than understood as a problem, was whether, for all its regional diversity, France was an essential whole that had been created over time but that by

---

7. On the argument for a second, sociopolitical founding of the Republic in the period 1880–1900, see my *Alliance of Iron and Wheat in the Third French Republic, 1860–1914: Origins of the New Conservatism* (Baton Rouge, 1988).

8. Pierre Bourdieu, "Le Champ scientifique," *Actes de la Recherche en Sciences Sociales*, 2/3 (1976), 88–104. See further the exchange between David Laitin and Aaron Wildavsky in "Political Culture and Political Preferences," *American Political Science Review*, 82 (1988), 589–96.

the twentieth century embodied a fixed identity, as the conservative paradigm had it. Was the fact that Louis Marin and the Gallo-Roman chieftain dug up in front of his apartment building had the same cephalic indices, for example, a meaningful link between the ancient and latter-day Frenchmen? Did the values of Saint Louis and of Joan of Arc still have meaning—still inspire the contemporary nation, among whose founders Marin and the right believed the two saints must be counted? Or, as Georges-Henri Rivière believed, was French civilization a cosmopolitan, multicultural, syncretic, and ever-changing product of the lives of diverse populations, a world not usefully understood under the rubric of a single French "identity" or "essence"?

In what follows I shall argue three points: (1) that a search for the essence of France was at the heart of the founding *problématique* of folklore studies, so that cultural studies became an ontological matter; (2) that this approach was itself rooted in new conservative discourses from the beginning years of the Third Republic; and (3) because of the high stakes in this chase after essences—the very soul of France—the forces of the Popular Front yielded to the temptation to fight to *include* the urban working class in this conservatively theorized metaphysic of national identity.[9]

The Dying Land

Students of French rural society have focused on the nineteenth century as the great watershed of irreversible cultural change. Maurice Agulhon saw in the earlier part of the century the beginnings of a self-redefinition of southern localisms into identification with the national republican state. Eugen Weber puts the decisive decades of the transformation of peasants into Frenchmen in the years between the beginnings of the Third Republic and the war.

9. See Pascal Ory, "La Politique culturelle de Vichy: Ruptures et continuités," in *Politiques et pratiques culturelles dans la France de Vichy,* ed. Jean-Pierre Rioux, Cahiers de l'Institut d'Histoire du Temps Present, no. 8 (Paris, 1988), 147–48.

Peter Sahlins proposes, contrary to Weber's argument, that identity with the nation grew out of local struggles over local issues rather than from the center. The local construction of the national can be seen at least as far back as the eighteenth century, Sahlins contends, although, as evidence of the advanced stage of the transformation nevertheless, he emphasizes the 1820s and the 1860s as moments of heightened national identification on the part of both French and Spanish Catalan villagers. André Varagnac wrote of the death of a centuries-old historic rural society in the nineteenth century, marking an acceleration of the trend in the decades after 1870. Before then rural France had been alive with both change and continuities, but in important ways it had altered very little over the centuries. By the late nineteenth century, he argued, old practices and mentalities were dying and indigenously created new beliefs and customs were not replacing them, as had been the pattern in previous centuries.[10] This was the "dying land" evoked in René Bazin's sentimental regional novel, *La Terre qui meurt*.

Thus in the late nineteenth century the growth in interest both locally and in the big cities in holding on in some sense—a sense we need to analyze more deeply—to a France that seemed to be passing is not surprising. But cultural change did not give birth to cultural sciences in a simple cause-and-effect way. Changes in the constellation of political power and in political culture at the moment of

---

10. Maurice Agulhon, *The Republic in the Village: The People of the Var from the French Revolution to the Second Republic*, trans. J. Lloyd (Cambridge, 1982); Eugen Weber, *Peasants into Frenchmen: The Modernization of Rural France, 1870–1914* (Stanford, 1976); Peter Sahlins, "The Nation in the Village: State-Building and Communal Struggles in the Catalan Borderland during the Eighteenth and Nineteenth Centuries," *Journal of Modern History*, 60 (1988), 234–63, and *Boundaries: The Making of France and Spain in the Pyrenees* (Berkeley, 1989). André Varagnac, *Civilisation traditionelle et genre de vie* (Paris, 1948), 16–38, 64, explains the change by reference to the spread of industrial civilization. In contradiction to both Varagnac and Weber, Caroline Ford has persuasively argued that in at least one French countryside, lower Brittany, regional culture was by no means dying off at the turn of the century, but rather was creatively renewing its institutions and values in the face of heavy political obstacles from Paris. See Caroline Ford, "Religion and the Politics of Cultural Change in Provincial France: The Resistance of 1902 in Lower Brittany," *Journal of Modern History*, 62 (1990), 1–33, and her *Creating the Nation in Provincial France: Religion and Politics in Brittany* (Princeton, 1992).

republican consolidation permitted contemporary social scientists to see the transforming society with new eyes. In France they worked out their analytical assessments of the change within ideologically inspired paradigms framed and controlled by the newly defeated but intransigent monarchist right of the Third Republic.

The Politics of Roots

The defeat of monarchism and the social rooting of the republican state, although less obviously linked with the rise of French interest in folklore, nevertheless played a decisive role in the shaping of the definition of the field and of its problems in the case both of the regionalist advocacy and of the related interest in the life of those regions. One feature of late-nineteenth-century France, local in manifestation, national in import, has been decisive in the development of sociology, anthropology, and conservative political ideologies: when the jerry-rigged Third Republic began to appear as if it might last (1880s) and then was refounded on firm foundations by the Opportunist Republicans (1890s), disappointed supporters of monarchism (especially the legitimist strain) urged their friends to make the countryside the repository of their eclipsed idea of France, if not for immediate implementation of restorational hopes, certainly to tend there the banked fire of conservative consciousness. The advice and the strategy went well beyond the local chatelain showing himself to his people on the way to church on Sunday, or the idea of storing conservative aspirations against a long winter, the way country people store potatoes and turnips in their cellars. It was an active and sophisticated involvement with the farming population in the concerns of producing and marketing agricultural goods. "The antisocialist league formed by our *syndicats agricoles*," wrote the comte de Rocquigny, "will save the peasants from the socialist misleaders." By means of the Société des Agriculteurs de France and the regional *comices* and *syndicats agricoles*, rural notables could reintegrate themselves in French social life in a way that permitted the hope of exercising influence in the community and on the national level. Moreover, the church, the republicans realized, had to be humbled: with the political defeat of the variety of monarchisms, it was now the prime collector of oppositional energies, and continued to keep alive the conservative ethos.[11]

Some conservatives would neither accept the idea of defeat—at least not permanent defeat—nor save what they could by entering into the principleless marriage of convenience with rightist republicans which I have termed "the alliance of iron and wheat."[12] Neither, however, were many of them or of their organic intellectuals inclined to leave the *pays* around the Jardin de Luxembourg and the Bois de Boulogne, except perhaps in the winter for brief forays to inspire provincial audiences with lectures on rootedness and the compelling need to return to old values, and, of course, for summer vacations. Thus the self-appointed and often impious intellectual minions of the fallen ruling houses became the new radical rightists of French politics of the late nineteenth and early twentieth centuries. This is the paternity of the Action Française, for example, and the new monarchist politics it championed. But it also attracted other discontented and politicized intellectuals equally unhappy with the emergent republican culture. The totalizing idea expressing the far-rightists' discontents was—and had to be, as they had lost command of the state—that the present-day France of republican politicians, lawyers, businessmen, stock speculators, and Jews prominent in public life was not the True France. Catholic neo-traditionalists (of invented traditions, to be sure) such as Maurras— who himself neither believed in nor practiced religion—and his Catholic companions of the Action Française and their more secular and less monarchist coreligionists (such as Maurice Barrès, to name the most famous) needed an *intellectual* place of refuge, a mighty fortress against the onslaught of republican modernity.

They found it in this case in the ancient (it was already a part of the polemical battery during the French Revolution) ontological gambit of a True France as against a France that had erred. According to these new ultrarightists, the True France was a nation made up of many regional cultures but only one national one; it was a nation in which everyone had two *patries*, each commanding a differ-

11. Robert de Rocquigny, *Les Syndicats agricoles et le socialisme agraire* (Paris, 1893), 55, 334. On this topic see my *Alliance of Iron and Wheat*, 97–123.

12. Lebovics, *Alliance of Iron and Wheat*, 128–40.

ent kind of loyalty. Mistral, for example, as his great admirer Maurras pointed out, was as much a French nationalist as he was a Provençal patriot. And in fact the poet did belong to the right-radical Ligue de la Patrie Française. The work of the great southern poet, according to Maurras, "taught us not to be embarrassed for our homeland before the wretches who spoke to us more or less melodiously of cosmopolitan or universal anarchy."[13] French pacifists were, of course, traitors to the *patrie*.

Already a powerful political myth before World War I, the charge that the secular republic tried to destroy regional peculiarities with its cultural centralization, carried out primarily by the village schoolmasters, has recently come seriously into question. Jean-François Chanet, basing his conclusions on the preliminary results of an extensive survey of what in fact were the attitudes and practices of teachers toward the local patois, found little of that infamous crushing of the local language or of the children who spoke it. In surprising numbers of cases the teachers spoke the regional patois and used it in class as they needed it or as they found it pedagogically helpful. Moreover, the Ministry of Education began to encourage the teaching of the geography and history of the region after 1911—just before the same policy changes were undertaken in Vietnam, it should be recalled— and this suggestion was taken up by local teachers. Already in 1911 Mistral expressed a certain satisfaction with the support the schools were giving to regionalistic ideas. What republicans were trying to get at was less the local language than the clerical and conservative things said in it. So that even if local speech was not disappearing so rapidly, the new conservative interest in local ways in the late century makes sense on sociopolitical grounds.[14]

13. Charles Maurras, *Maîtres et témoins de ma vie d'esprit: Barrès, Mistral, France, Verlaine, Moréas* (Paris, 1954), 158, 163. The essay on Mistral was written well before World War II and Maurras's Vichy collaboration, and was published unaltered in this postwar volume. Maurras captures the spirit of right folklorism when he praises Mistral: "Toute la poésie divine qui sort des choses de la terre et des humbles rites de la vie domestique devint par Mistral manifeste, et tous ceux qui l'ont lu, tous ceux qui ont subi même indirectement le doux ascendant de cette pensée demeurent imprégnés dans leur intimité du bel honneur rendu à tout ce qui *assemble* et civilise *l'assemblage* élémentaire des hommes" (163; italics in original).

14. Jean-François Chanet, "Maîtres d'école et régionalisme en France, sous la Troisième République," *Ethnologie Française*, 18 (1988), 244–56.

In 1896 Frédéric Mistral opened his museum of Provençal life and culture at Arles as a place to conserve, revive, and continue regional cultural life—"a museum of ongoing life and of the stock of Arles"— in the face of modernity in general and the terrible centralizing engine of the newly refounded republican regime. His effort to revivify Provençal civilization was only the most published and publicized of several other such efforts to revivify interest in regional folklore in other parts of France.[15]

Whereas during the French Revolution the abbé Grégoire had sought to uproot local languages and customs for the sake of national unity, in the romantic aftermath of the revolutionary era, first the Académie Celtique (founded 1804) and then its successor, the Société Royale des Antiquaires de France (founded 1814), published materials on folklore with a more appreciative perspective.[16] But aside from a number of important and not so important historical thinkers of the middle decades of the century—the best known of whom were Jules Michelet, Edgar Quinet, and Ernest Renan—most intellectuals and scientists showed little interest in the truths about France which might be discovered in the study of the lore of the people.[17] The professionalization of the discipline of folklore and its self-definition in roughly its twentieth-century form occurred only

15. Fernand Benoît, "Le Musée Arletan et la campagne arlésienne," *Folklore Paysan,* 1 (1938), 15. The quoted passage is by Mistral; Benoît was the head of the museum in the late 1930s. Although the history of regionalism crosses that of the study of folklore, it deserves separate treatment, which I shall reserve for another time. The reader may find a useful introduction in the special issue of *Ethnologie Française,* 18 (1988), dedicated to regionalism. On the widening gap between the ideological vision of the southern countryside held by Mistral and his friends in the Félibrige and the changing life of Provence in the late nineteenth century, see Pierre Pasquini, "Les Félibriges et les traditions," *Ethnologie Française,* 18 (1988), 257–66.

16. Abbé Grégoire was a principled universalist humanist. He is remembered also for his powerful resolution in favor of the Jews in 1789, which described the Jews as "members of this same universal family that should establish fraternity among the peoples." In connection with the celebration of the bicentennial of the Revolution, the Socialist government of François Mitterand placed his ashes in the Panthéon.

17. Charles Rearick, *Beyond the Enlightenment: Historians and Folklore in Nineteenth-Century France* (Bloomington, Ind., 1974), 6–7, 18–19. Rearick treats the first marriage in France of history and the study of the culture of the common people. Among the less famous names about whom one may read profitably in Rearick are Augustin Thierry, Prosper de Barante, Pierre-Simon Ballanche, Claude Fauriel, Henri Martin, and Frédéric Ozanam. Maurras considered Renan one of his masters.

in the last decades of the century, coinciding with the years of consolidation of the new republic.

In the late century regional academies began actively to collect local artifacts, costumes, and stories. Museums dedicated to the celebration, or perhaps merely monumentalization, of local life began to spring up. Primarily because of his literary and political support in Paris, Mistral's was the most famous one, but there were others. And often at the cost of suppressing the pluralism of living local dialects, regionalists, who tended to come from the educated petite bourgeoisie, created societies to cultivate *the* reconstructed regional language, the correct usage of which they regulated.

The most famous of these bodies was the Félibrige, the literary society of Provence, created at mid-century but reaching its apogee around 1900, which worked for the revival of the culture of the Midi. Although membership included both reactionary Catholics (*blancs*) and more or less progressive republicans (*rouges*), in the great ideological transvaluation around the turn of the century a new generation of young southern conservatives came to the fore. The backward-focused values of contemporary folklore and regionalism melded with the frequently radical-reactionary dispositions of the younger regionalists to imprint the new disciplines with a rightist potential.[18]

Although the regionalists published local magazines devoted to regional cultural themes earlier in the nineteenth century, only in 1877 did Henri Gaidoz and Eugène Roland found *Mélusine,* the first national journal of folklore studies. In 1886 P. Sébillot, who headed the Société des Traditions Populaires, started the *Revue des Traditions Populaires.* The Musée d'Ethnographie du Trocadéro, although in existence since 1878, did not take French popular arts and traditions as such under its purview until 1888, when the curator Armand Landrin created a special section devoted to metropolitan spec-

18. Anne-Marie Thiesse, "Ecrire la France: Le Mouvement littéraire régionalist de la langue française entre la belle époque et la libération" (thèse pour le doctorat d'état, Université de Lyon II, 1989), 33, describes the typical regionalist writer as a person who was interested in literature (including local literature) as a youth, "went up" to Paris, there was mocked as a bumpkin for his literary tastes, and returned home not with lost illusions but rather determined to wear his literary regionalism as a badge of identity and of honor.

imens.[19] The museum's relative neglect of French artifacts, it is important to note, was part of a larger pattern that placed the study of French ethnology in the shadow of the anthropological disciplines in France concerned with comparative physical anthropology or foreign ethnographic studies.[20]

Moreover, in the years before World War I the study of the ethnography of the regions of France could not gain the university connection that would have both legitimated it and facilitated the systematic yet critical development of its own paradigm. Isac Chiva sees this failure as due to the *political* hostility of the Durkheimians.

> Rejecting the role ascribed to tradition and to folklore as manifested in particular in P. Saintyves et P. Sébillot, the school of *L'Année Sociologique* displayed a decisive ideological enmity [toward the direction they were giving the field]; at the same time these writers were criticized for their ideological opposition to republican consolidation, for their militant Catholicism, for the overblown role they ascribed to the aesthetic and the emblematic.[21]

Emile Nourry, who used the pen name Saintyves, had succeeded Sébillot in the forefront of folklore studies. He and his friends had been discussing founding a new folklore society since before the war, but the project had not yet been launched when the outbreak of hostilities pushed the idea into the background. Only in the late 1920s, after the founding of the Institut d'Ethnologie in 1925, when the Durkheimians felt more secure about their position in French intellectual life and were beginning to practice the kind of academic imperialism we saw in the Rivet-Marin correspondence, do we see the founding of a Société du Folklore Français. But still in the mid-1920s most of the great figures of the discipline moved outside the Durkheimian orbit; if the Durkheimians wanted to influence the

19. Faure, "Folklore et révolution nationale," 16–19; Nélia Dias, *Le Musée d'ethnographie du Trocadéro (1878–1908): Anthropologie et muséologie en France* (Paris, 1991), 191–94.

20. Isac Chiva, "Entre livre et musée: Emergence d'une ethnologie de la France," in *Ethnologies en miroir: La France et les pays de langue allemande*, ed. Chiva and Utz Jeggle (Paris, 1987), 20. See also chap. 1 above.

21. Ibid. See also Raymonde Courtas and François-A. Isambert, "Ethnologues et sociologues aux prises avec la notion de 'populaire,'" *Maison-Dieu*, 122 (1975), 20–32.

development of the paradigm(s) of this new field of social science, as they had done in sociology and were beginning to do in ethnography, they would have to engage in academic coalition politics.

In February 1929, under the patronage of Sir James and Lady Frazer, a new society, the Société du Folklore Français, held its first *assemblée générale* in—of course—Paris. The next year the directorate of the organization began the publication of the *Revue du Folklore Français*, which two years later became the *Revue du Folklore Français et du Folklore Colonial.*

The professionally coalitional and, in the strategy of the Durkheimians, potentially cooptive nature of the new organization (actually founded in 1928) may be read in the list of names of its principal founders. As was fitting, Saintyves, France's most distinguished folklore scholar, assumed the presidency, which he held until his death in 1935. Arnold Van Gennep, already writing his massive *Manuel de folklore français contemporain,* an intellectual loner, by conviction an anarchist but not affiliated with any scholarly or political circle,[22] supplied disciplinary ballast to the society. Another founding member was André Varagnac, nephew of Marcel Sembat, the radical politician and admirer of popular art. Varagnac had been a student of Marcel Mauss, and he shared with the Durkheimians both a great admiration of the works of Sir James Frazer and a leftist political orientation. He was in fact one of the rare folklorists politically on the left. Finally, in the inner circle we find the triumvirate of the Institut d'Ethnologie: Marcel Mauss, Lucien Lévy-Bruhl, and Paul Rivet.[23] Folklorists of divergent ideological outlooks accepted membership in the new society, but this agreement to provide disci-

22. Although he acknowledged affinities with Durkheimian theory and the members of the school tolerated his personal crankiness. See Arnold Van Gennep, "La Décadence et la persistence des patois," *Revue des Idées,* 8 (1911), 412–24. Here, for example, he writes about the role of the state and of capitalism in wiping out the patois of peasants and workers.

23. Chiva, "Entre livre et musée," 21; Faure, "Folklore et révolution nationale," 19–20. Before World War I Sembat himself had discussed with James Frazer the possibility of creating a society dedicated to French folklore, but he died soon thereafter. See Georges-Henri Rivière, "Les Musées de folklore à l'étranger et le futur 'Musée français des arts et traditions populaires,'" *Revue de Folklore Français et de Folklore Colonial,* 3 (1936), 66; Varagnac, *Civilisation traditionelle,* 12.

plinary structure to the field would not bring with it agreement on one dominant paradigm.

With Rivet taking over the directorship of the Trocadéro museum in the same year as the founding of the new folklore society, the modern institutional growth of folklore studies may be said to have begun. The chief architect of that development and the personal embodiment of a new cosmopolitan paradigm, different both from the ruralist essentialism of the conservatives and from the populist essentialism of the left, was the young man Rivet brought in as associate director in 1928, Georges-Henri Rivière.

Where Did You Do Your Doctorate?

One day in 1928, Paul Rivet, just named head of the old ethnographic museum, waited impatiently in his office for a young man he had summoned for an interview and who was late. When he finally arrived, Rivet looked him over. Before him, feeling out of his element, stood a thin, aesthetic-looking Parisian who appeared very much like other young men we see portrayed in the photographs of members of the city's avant-garde of the late 1920s, thin-faced, sensitive bordering on delicate, alert. Rivet asked Georges-Henri Rivière where he had done his thesis. "My thesis . . . I haven't got a thesis" was the answer. Rivet thought a moment. Never mind, he replied, he needed someone with Rivière's talents. "I'll do the science; you take care of the popular translation of this science. I am a man of the people. I intend to found a great museum of popular culture." So Rivière remembered the job offer.

Left over from a nineteenth-century exposition, the fifty-year-old museum of ethnography was grimy outside and grim within. Full of old unused and dead things, it needed a breath of life. Rivet could not expect the specialists in archaeology and ethnography in place nor those he could hire to supply the needed air of excitement. But he had singled out this young man he had just hired, the assistant to David David-Weill, the great collector and power in the museum world, because he had recently mounted—his first such effort—a splendid exhibition of pre-Columbian art at the museum. Rivet had realized that Rivière could improve the attractiveness of the exhibition and the popularity of the museum. Rivière, the new museum's director also realized, could connect Rivet to the world of *tout-Paris*, and with luck serve as the conduit of funds and, more likely, loan pieces owned by his collector friends for display in the underfunded state museum. The professor of natural history swallowed his surprise on learning that Rivière possessed only a high school diploma and hired him anyway. So began Georges-Henri Rivière's connection to the anthropology of France in the years before World War II, and with it questions of national and regional identity.

The Dandy

Georges-Henri Rivière, a thirty-one-year-old Parisian with no background in anthropology, no museum experience, a musician, was an unlikely choice for such a responsibility. He was born 5 June 1897 in Montmartre. His father served as a middle-rank civil servant in the Prefecture of the Seine. His mother—not his father's wife but a maid in the household—was a daughter of farmers in Picardie. Although Georges-Henri visited their farm in Vaux-le-Frestois on vacations, he grew up and went to school in Paris. His father died when he was fourteen. His uncle, Henri Rivière, a painter who worked in the then-fashionable Japanese style, assumed the aesthetic education of the young man. He invited his nephew to spend time in his circle of friends—artists, collectors, dealers, and publishers, for the most part. His uncle encouraged him as well to pursue his interest in music. Accordingly, after passing the *baccalauréat* examination in 1915, the only academic degree he would earn, he entered the Paris Conservatory, where he studied organ with Eugène Gicout and harmony with Marcel Samuel Rousseau. He had to interrupt his musical education in 1917, when in his twenty-first year he was called up to serve in an artillery regiment. During training a horse kick smashed his knee, sparing him from service at the front but also ending his hopes for a grand career playing a keyboard instrument. On his return from military service he resumed his musical education, studying counterpoint with Charles Koechlin for five years (1920–1925).

But after the war—probably because of its carnage—Rivière's interests turned away from the religious music that had first attracted him (in 1916–1917 he had briefly served as *maître de chapelle* of the Church of Saint-Louis-en-l'Île) to the rich Paris jazz scene. Josephine Baker's famous *Revue nègre*, which he first saw in 1924, bowled him over. He wrote his first popular song for Baker. A wonderfully campy photograph shows the two of them standing before a display of spears at the museum, she flashing a brilliant seductive smile, he hamming the fascinated seducer.[24] The next year he took a job at the Folies-Bergère. He also played piano at the Casino de Paris and wrote an opera with Jacques Fray and Tristan Bernard called *Le Loulou florentin*.

He branched out to the other arts. In 1925 he became the paid administrator and art consultant to the prominent collector David David-Weill, president of the Arts Council of the National Museums, a relationship he kept up until 1939. Meanwhile he immersed himself in the creative-*cum*-beautiful-people scene of interwar Paris. "On the advice of Georges Salles, from 1925 to 1928 I attended the Ecole du Louvre, began to frequent the people I called 'the cultured and smart upper crust,' and became at the same time a friend of the surrealists. I knew Aragon, Bataille, Leiris, Desnos. . . ."[25]

By neither training nor style—he was already known for the style of self-presentation evoked by Baudelaire in the France of his youth as the "dandy"—did he seem suited to serve as first assistant to the no-nonsense socialist physical anthropologist Paul Rivet. Christian Zervos, editor of the *Cahiers d'Art*, in which Rivière had published articles on art between 1924 and 1928, urged him to visit the ethnographic museum, where he would see "extraordinary things. All that Precolumbian art is marvelous."

"I had vaguely heard about it from the surrealists," he recalled

24. Reproduced in Isac Chiva, "Georges Henri Rivière: Un Demi-siècle d'ethnologie de la France," *Terrain*, 1985, 76.
25. Geneviève Breerette and Frédéric Edelmann, "Une Rencontre avec Georges-Henri Rivière," *Le Monde*, 8–9 July 1979, 16. See also J. B. Cuypers, "Georges Henri Rivière in memoriam," dossier "G. H. Rivière," in his papers deposited in the archives of the International Council of Museums in the UNESCO building, Paris.

many years later. He was indeed smitten by the pre-Columbian art housed at the museum. The refinement, elegance, high-cultural so-phistication, yet strangeness of these works moved Rivière first to write an article about them and then, in collaboration with Alfred Métraux, a former student of Rivet (and future leader of the 1934 Franco-Belgian anthropological mission to Easter Island), to install the exhibition of pre-Columbian art at the museum. Put on in 1928, the show was well received and won, as we have seen, Rivet's respect for his talents and a job as, in effect, director of exhibitions.

The two men set to their tasks with great energy. Rivet worked to upgrade the museum and politicked actively both in the field and with his political friends. Rivière set out to learn what he had to know about his new profession, and at the side of Rivet strode to turn the old "notions and sundries store" into "a great center both of popular education and of scientific research."[26] As we have seen, with the new interest of metropolitan colonial circles in winning the population to accept a Greater France, Rivet could and did promote his museum as a valuable resource for knowledge of the colonies.[27] The ethnographic museum played host to the delegates to Marin's international anthropological conference, held during the 1931 ex-position.

Rivière began immediately to put his rich avant-garde imagination to work at the task of bringing the old museum to life. He began to take down the masks, spears, and other weapons displayed sym-metrically on red cloth backdrops. The arrangement showed ar-

26. Breerette and Edelmann, "Rencontre avec Rivière," 22, quoting from the cata-logue of the exhibition created by Rivet's former co-workers held in his honor in September 1976; Nélia Dias, *Musée d'ethnographie du Trocadéro*, esp. 194–205. Rivet and Rivière accepted the characterization of the museum they had inherited as an old sundries store: Paul Rivet and Georges-Henri Rivière, "La Réorganisation du musée d'ethnographie du Trocadéro," *Bulletin du Musée d'Ethnographie du Trocadéro*, 1 (Janu-ary 1931), 25. Jean Jamin has greatly facilitated the work of historians of French anthropology, and my own, with a fine facsimile edition of these *Bulletins*, which appeared eight times between 1931 and 1935, stopping with the beginning of the remodeling of the museum structure. See Jean Jamin, ed., *Bulletin du Musée d'Eth-nographie du Trocadéro*, in his series Les Cahiers de Gradhiva (Paris, 1988). My page citations are to the Jamin edition.

27. "Rapport sur l'état du Musée d'Ethnographie du Trocadéro et projet pour sa réorganisation," Marin Papers, Archives Nationales, 317 AP, carton 170. See the passage quoted in Jamin's preface to his edition of the *Bulletin du Musée d'Ethnographie du Trocadéro*, xvii.

tifacts of other cultures elegantly—a bit like the trophies of a rich big-game hunter—but made sense neither ethnographically nor aesthetically. While the journalists' accounts were still in the public's memory, he also put on shows featuring the treasures brought back by the museum teams of the Dakar-Djibouti mission of 1931–1933 and by Métraux's Easter Island expedition of 1934.

His most culturally irreverent coup—an act conceived in the spirit of a museum administrator who had to use flair to supplement a thin budget and faithful to the aesthetic politics he learned from his surrealist friends—was his promotion of the boxing match at the Cirque d'Hiver on 15 April 1931 between the boxer Al Brown, world bantamweight champion (billed as an American but of Panamanian nationality), whom Jean Cocteau called *"la merveille noire"* (the black marvel), and a French fighter of his weight class; the take was to go to the museum to defray some of the expenses of the upcoming Dakar-Djibouti expedition. Rivière persuaded Brown to contribute his purse to the museum's expedition with the argument that "you'd be fighting for the honor of the culture of your ancestors." On the night of the fight Marcel Griaule, the anthropologist who headed the expedition, introduced Brown in the ring, flanked by four museum guards in uniform: "This man will box for African culture." In English Brown responded, "I am happy to box for African culture." Looking back on the event in 1974, Rivière remembered it with delight as "a great moment."[28]

Almost immediately upon assuming the museum's leadership and appointing Rivière, Rivet began to send his new assistant on trips throughout Europe. He wanted Rivière to learn something of the new developments in folklore museology in Sweden, Germany, and even Russia, to acquire or borrow works for Paris as opportunity permitted, and perhaps even to acquire a bit of political culture. In Sweden Rivière learned something of what was at the time the most advanced work being done in the display of aspects of national folklore—Skansen, in Stockholm, had been the first outdoor museum in Europe to open its gates to the public—and made important contacts for the Paris museum. Berlin was even more interesting. On 6 January 1932 Rivière wrote Rivet these New Year's sentiments: "I

28. Cuypers, "Georges Henri Rivière in memoriam."

have spent several intense days here. Never before have I been so involved in the lives of the ordinary people. The new friendships I have recently made in Berlin opened up to me a world I suspected existed but did not know. More and more I am gripped by my realization of the necessity of the march of our society toward communism." He went on to describe the loan objects he had procured from the Berlin ethnographic museum and the three items he had purchased from the Hamburg museum: "one magnificent lacquered tea chest from Siam, modern; a Tibetan vase for our exhibition; and one magnificent and very uncommon sculpted wooden figure of Micronesia, [which] I am sure Mr. D. W. [David-Weill] will donate to us."[29]

In writing to his friend Vera Bour he assumed a more frivolous style. He wrote her a few months later of the fascinating political conversations he had had with German diplomats that summer at Baron von der Heydt's summer home in Holland and how he looked forward to going to Berlin in August. He adjured her not to worry that the Germans had turned his head. "I'm not going to become a Nazi [followed by a crudely drawn swastika] and my German is improving quickly."[30]

Writing to Rivet from Leningrad on 15 August 1936, therefore during the Popular Front, he took the tone of the enthusiastic but serious political person.

> There is no need to tell you that I have been seduced beyond words by the USSR. You foresaw it even more than I did. I am not talking just about the museums, which are *humane*, profound, fertile, but also of the quality of life, of the concept they have of how to organize a society. I would not say that I have chosen, that happened a long time ago without my knowing it. But now I understand.[31]

What kind of man was Georges-Henri Rivière? We find in the correspondence and reports of his activities a person with great intelligence and charm, doubtless; clearly he was suave and astute

29. Some items from the correspondence of Georges-Henri Rivière from the archives of the Musée de l'Homme have been published by Jean Jamin. See Rivière to Rivet, 6 January 1932, *Gradhiva*, 1 (1986), 24.

30. Rivière to Vera Bour, 28 July 1932, Salle des Manuscrits, Bibliothèque Nationale de Paris, NAF 25124², fol. 813.

31. Rivière to Rivet, 15 August 1936, *Gradhiva*, 1 (1986), 26.

about people, especially people who counted. Here was a man with a highly refined aesthetic sensibility, well connected to the important avant-garde currents in the world capital of modernism; he was the avant-garde's man in the museum world.[32] In 1929 he had had the idea of creating a new magazine of modernist culture, which he persuaded Georges Wildenstein, the art dealer, to finance. *Documents: Doctrines, Archéologie, Beaux-Arts, Ethnographie* appeared for two years under the editorship of Georges Bataille. Bernard-Henri Lévy singles out Bataille, Leiris, and Caillois, along with Breton and Artaud, as extremely farsighted in having early understood and taken a stand against "the forces of regression of the age."[33]

Yet, for all his sophistication, Rivière had a politically innocent side: he seemed often to treat political engagement as one more social gambit or aesthetic coup. Would a paradigm of folklore which revealed the true essence of France appeal to him, whether that essence included workers as well as peasants, as the supporters of the Popular Front proposed, or just peasants, in accordance with the soon-to-be ideological orthodoxy under Pétain? Since his role in constituting the discipline became so important after 1937, knowledge of how he participated in the discourse of folklore and about the directions toward which he tried to move it will help us solve the puzzle of the political role of folklore in the succeeding years.

32. Jamin, in his preface to his edition of the *Bulletin du Musée d'Ethnographie du Trocadéro*, highlights very well the importance both for the discipline and for French society of the modernist direction the new ethnographic museum took under the influence of Rivière, with Rivet's close support (xvi, xviii–xix). See Jamin's "De l'humaine condition de 'Minotaure'," in *Regards sur Minotaure*, ed. Charles Georg (Geneva, 1987), 79–87, esp. 81. Rivière's desire to live like his friends of *tout-Paris* caused him to miscalculate in 1929, when he agreed to marry Nina Spalding Stevens, a wealthy American who wanted entrée to that world in exchange for her funding of a better lifestyle than he could himself afford. Apparently she was the only person in his circle not to understand that he was gay. They married in Paris on 26 January 1929. The marriage—which Rivière had understood from the start as a *mariage blanc,* but apparently the bride had not—broke up immediately and she returned to New York. His nephew, Jean-François Leroux-Dhuys, tells this intimate story as a comic episode in a biographical sketch, but paradoxically has little to say about the years 1941–1944. See Jean-François Leroux-Dhuys, "Georges Henri Rivière: Un Homme dans le siècle," in *La Muséologie selon Georges-Henri Rivière,* ed. Rivière (Paris, 1989), 22.

33. "Perhaps a key to understanding the century: the truly political—that is, literally antifascist—consequences of an ethic of literature": Bernard-Henri Lévy, *L'Idéologie française* (Paris, 1981), 123. On *Documents* see James Clifford's important article "On Ethnographic Surrealism," *Comparative Studies in Society and History,* 23 (1981), 539–64, esp. 548–53.

But we should note that he was not the first modernist aesthete to have, if not sided with the angels in his aesthetic engagements, at least avoided evil. I am thinking of, for example, the German symbolist poet Stefan George.[34] Nor was he the only aesthetic modernist of his generation to believe that he could come to a modus vivendi with the traditionalisms of fascist forces without being, if not compromised, certainly perceived as an opportunist. The attempt of Mies van der Rohe of the Bauhaus—director after the departure of his racially or politically undesirable colleagues—to continue working in the National Socialist state until his departure for Chicago in 1937 offers a sorry parallel to Rivière's problems with principles.[35]

Understanding Rivière's tastes and values matter, finally, for he became head of a new national museum of folklore in 1937, a major creation and legacy of the Popular Front. Such a museum was very much in keeping with the cultural agenda of the new left alliance. It was one of the few permanent creations of the Popular Front.

Open the Gates . . . Break Down the Barriers

Jacques Soustelle, in 1936 a young anthropologist on Rivet's staff and also a socialist, proposed that the cultural task of the Popular

34. George cultivated an aestheticism in an art and lifestyle akin to that of his French masters, Villiers de L'Isle-Adam, Verlaine, and Mallarmé. Although he attracted young men of the wealthy and educated Jewish bourgeoisie who entrusted to him their education for the beautiful life, his elitism, antiphilistinism, and hostility to party politics also made him interesting to later influential supporters of National Socialism. In 1933 he refused the Nazis' offer of the presidency of the German Academy and left for Switzerland. He died later that year. His desire to be buried in Switzerland, not in Germany, was a fitting gesture of refusal to permit identification of his life-poetical mission with that of National Socialism. In Germany, modernism's questioning of the (aesthetic) authorities of the past saved George and many in his circle from the embrace of the conservative revolution. See my discussion of the *Georgekreis* in *Social Conservatism and the German Middle Classes in Germany, 1914–1933* (Princeton, 1969), 79–108.

35. For the fascinating story of Mies van der Rohe's attempt to accommodate the Bauhaus and his own work to the fascist cultural apparatus in the first years of the National Socialist state, when the Nazis showed themselves to be more principled in their aesthetic loyalties than the last head of the Bauhaus, see Elaine S. Hochman, *Architects of Fortune: Mies Van der Rohe and the Third Reich* (New York, 1989).

Front was to "open the gates of culture. Break down the barriers that, like a beautiful park forbidden to the poor, enclose a culture reserved for a privileged elite." The goal of giving access to *the* culture was set largely by the Communists but shared by their alliance partners. No one, or no one in office, contemplated fostering new modes of creation. As Julian Jackson has pointed out, what was intended was "the democratization of an existing traditional culture." Pascal Ory, in what is now the definitive study of the cultural politics of the period, describes the agenda as a demand upon the bourgeoisie to give workers back their heritage (*"patrimoine"*).[36] *Regards*, the PCF picture magazine, treating culture as if it were a part of surplus value, urged workers to "take back what was stolen from us." The party's annual congress in 1937—held, significantly, at Arles—enthusiastically celebrated the works of the Félibrige.

Although the PCF must also be credited with actively promoting the major cultural innovation of the Popular Front, that of greatly and permanently enhancing the state's administrative and financial responsibility for cultural life,[37] its conservatism in respect to the contents of that culture was as puzzling as it was glaring. We can see that such a posture was not the inevitable result of the dead hand of Stalinist aesthetics by recalling the rich debates on Weimar Germany's left, notably Georg Lukács's advocacy of realism as the supreme art form recognized by socialist criticism (with Walter Scott, Balzac, and Thomas Mann as its heroes) versus Walter Benjamin's support of the epic theater of Bertolt Brecht. Writing during the Popular Front, Brecht in particular strongly condemned the political betrayal that went with the left's acceptance of the culture of the bourgeoisie: "He who in our time says 'inhabitants' rather than '*Volk*' and 'landed property' rather than 'the land' discredits many lies. He strips these words of their putrid mystique."[38]

The narrowness of the French Communist Party's preferences

---

36. Pascal Ory, "La Politique culturelle du Front populaire française (1935–1938)" (thèse pour le doctorat d'état, University of Paris X, Nanterre, 1990), 1654.

37. Ibid., 1636–39.

38. "Wer in unserer Zeit *statt Volk Bevölkerung* und *statt Boden Landbesitz* sagt, unterstützt schon viele Lügen nicht. Er nimmt den Wörter ihre faule Mystik." The passage is from Brecht's *Fünf Schwerigkeiten beim Schreiben der Wahrheit* and I quote it from Albrecht Betz, *Exil und Engagement: Deutsche Schriftsteller im Frankreich der dreissiger Jahre* (Munich, 1986), 111–13.

may have been the consequence of the old base–superstructure theorizing. In exchange for needed political cooperation with the progressive bourgeoisie in the face of the fascist threat, the PCF might have embraced the culture of the middle class, since culture was derivative of the deeper socioeconomic processes and in the end of secondary importance, or at least negotiable. But the German Communist Party didn't close itself off this way. And the PCF's embrace of French high culture from the party's founding to at least May 1968 cannot have been just opportunism, an adventure with the pretty harlot of the bourgeoisie.

The explanation lies, I believe, rather in the historic role of the party as an important mediator of social promotion. Itself often treated as an outsider in French life, the PCF sought to be accepted, to belong, and attracted to its ranks many gifted people with similar status concerns: immigrants, but also peasants from red regions, lower white-collar workers in private and state employ, and, of course, above all thoughtful workers. The only currency these people could acquire to pay for their full participation in the life of the nation was education. If they could immerse themselves and their children in the culture of France—the language, the arts, the things-that-go-without-saying—they would *be* fully French. More or less without interruption (except under Vichy) since the 1880s, that was the cultural version of the republican contract. It is still largely valid in today's France. How could the PCF encourage both cultural innovation—the serious zaniness of their temporary friends the surrealists, for example—and keep their rapport with their constituencies? How could immigrants be assimilated in a moving, confusing, avant-garde cultural scene? Better—more authentically French—to read the Molière and Racine assigned in the republican schools, to buy classics in handsome editions, display them, perhaps read some. Better to learn to appreciate the Gothic, Victor Hugo, champagne.[39]

In the mid-1930s, then, the organized left accepted the bourgeois culture and its institutions as normative. Socialist and Communist cultural criticism focused on increasing and democratizing access to

---

39. This hypothesis requires elaboration and support. I will provide both in a forthcoming article, but some of the social-historical evidence may be found in Bernard Pudal, *Prendre parti: Pour une sociologie historique du PCF* (Paris, 1989), 21–62, 115–20, esp. 41–43.

it. For Communists, wrote André Thirion in his memoirs of sur-realism, "family life, the artwork on French banknotes, movie serials, and modesty were as sacred as the verses of the International."[40] In 1937, on the three hundredth anniversary of the publication of his *Discourse on Method*, the Communist press joined heartily with the bourgeois press in praise of René Descartes's contributions to French civilization. And Rouget de Lisle, who composed the "Marseillaise" while on garrison duty in Strasbourg, also was celebrated in *L'Hu-manité*.

Important cultural spokesmen of the left, even in statements radi-cally assailing the inheritors of France, continued to think within the Maurrasian paradigm. Louis Aragon, now broken with his surrealist friends, described his and the PCF's literary politics this way: "I deny the quality of *Frenchness* to the prose of Coblenz [the émigré center during the French Revolution], to the prose of the *versaillais* [the people who crushed the Paris Commune], to the prose of the sedi-tious elements in 1935. Our French novel is French because it ex-presses the profound spirit of the French people. . . . It is the arm of the true French against the 200 families who run the banks, the gambling houses, and the brothels."[41]

Perhaps Jean Jamin has best marked the blind spot of 1930s French left cultural theory when he remarks that, while Rivet and many of his co-workers fought to demonstrate the equality of the races in the face of mounting racism, they never seriously ques-tioned the category "race."[42] So too with cultural essentialism.

Consider André Breton's reply to his former cultural revolution-ary companion in a talk he wrote for the Communist-called Con-gress of Writers for the Defense of Culture in Paris in 1935, but was not allowed to give because he had slapped Ilya Ehrenburg in the

40. André Thirion, *Revolutionaries without Revolution* (1972), trans. Joachim Neu-groschel (New York, 1975), 113. See further the paper by Denis Milhau, one-time member of the CPF, "Reflets de la crise du reflet," in the proceedings of the con-ference held at Saint-Etienne in 1979, *L'Art face à la crise, 1929–1939*, ed. Louis Roux (Saint-Etienne, 1980), 241–93, esp. the discussion of Maurice Thorez's thoughts on the mission of the French proletariat to replace the faltering bourgeoisie in defense of the national interest and of "our cultural heritage," 262.

41. Quoted in Ory, "Politique culturelle du Front populaire," 177, 191–219; Julian Jackson, *The Popular Front in France* (Cambridge, 1988), 113, 120, 126.

42. Jean Jamin, "Le Savant et le politique: Paul Rivet (1876–1958)," typescript, 1990.

face on the street a few days before its opening: "We remain opposed to any claim by a Frenchman that he possesses the cultural patrimony of France alone, and to all extolling of a feeling of Frenchness in France."[43] Breton, and under his influence the surrealist movement, never yielded to nationalism; the surrealists championed a principled internationalism in the interwar decades. As early as 1921 Breton and Aragon had staged a mock trial of Maurice Barrès for unbridled nationalism, with the Unknown Soldier testifying against him in German. And in the 1930s Breton and his circle followed Charles Maurras's writings in *L'Action Française*, where, in André Thirion's words, he "explained each morning . . . that there was a gap between the 'legal country and the real country' and that electoral opinions could not possibly represent the will of France," and they were infuriated with the echoes of that "shabby and antiparliamentary nationalism" in "at least half of the metropolitan press." Breton's and the surrealists' cultural pluralism extended from rejection of chauvinistic attitudes toward Germany and German culture to celebration of tribal peoples and their cultures as at least as valid as those of the Christian West and in many ways superior.[44]

Thus the organized left and right agreed that art for the people had once more to root itself in folklore, with the difference that the organized left wished finally to include workers in that idea of a fixed coherent national cultural heritage. But a small aesthetic left that was equally keen on popular imagination—Rivière and some of his friends in the arts—rejected the project of recovering a lost authenticity as both conservative and dangerous to humanity. In 1936 Rivière, like the surrealists, neither looked for the essential France nor understood culture hierarchically or nationalistically.

Rivet, for his part, created L'Association Populaire des Amis des Musées, which brought proletarian visitors to his museum, and also organized cultural events for worker audiences—the inauguration of the Musée de l'Homme, tours of factories, even group visits to Picasso's workshop. Michèle Cointet summed up the cultural pro-

43. André Breton, "Speech to the Congress of Writers (1935)," in *Manifestoes of Surrealism*, trans. Richard Seaver and Helen R. Lane (Ann Arbor, 1969), 237.

44. Clifford Broeder, *André Breton: Arbitrator of Surrealism* (Geneva, 1967), 14; Thirion, *Revolutionaries without Revolution*, 252, 330–31, 346.

ject: "Art for the people—*the right was equally persuaded*—had once more to find its roots in folklore."[45] And the vision of France held by both Frances overlapped remarkably, but this consensus beneath the civil strife proved fatal for the left's ability to mobilize against the minions of True France.

This, then, was the discipline of folklore and the forces in play around it in the 1930s. Now we must look at the institutional expression of this science.

45. Pascal Ory and Jean-François Sirinelli, *Les Intellectuels en France de l'affaire Dreyfus à nos jours* (Paris, 1986), 96–102; Michèle Cointet, *Histoire culturelle de la France, 1918–1958* (Paris, 1958), 107; italics mine.

True France or . . . ?:
Fulfillment and Disruption

Rather than move France toward Rivière's vision of a pluralist national culture, as we have seen, the Popular Front
became embroiled in another engagement of the Franco-
French civil war waged on the level of ideology over the question
who most represented the True France. With the help of the German occupiers, become under Hitler specialists on questions of national authenticity, the right finally overcame both the politics and
the cultural aspirations of this latest left alliance. In his proclamation
of French essentialism at the moment of defeat and transformation,
La Seule France (France Alone), Maurras celebrated the triumph finally of the *pays réel* in the rule of Marshal Pétain. "The government
of the army offers us the shining image of French unity. The government of the parties is the symbol of our divisions," he wrote in 1941.
In the new regime he hoped to recover the *pays réel* liberated finally
from its étatism and, "*stripped of accumulated artificial [cultural] pas-
tiches, returned to its natural organization.*"[1] The right looked to the
discipline of folklore for help in recovering the great buried trea-

---

1. Charles Maurras, *La Seule France: Chronique des jours d'épreuve* (Lyon, 1941), 19,
171. Isac Chiva has argued that in recent centuries French society has tended to react
to crisis by looking to nature, returning to the past, and embracing the local. This is
so. Vichy presents us with the paradox of both conforming to Chiva's description and
being technocratic, modernizing, and centralizing. See Isac Chiva, "Le Patrimoine
ethnologique," *Encyclopaedia Universalis. Symposium, 1990*, 229–41, esp. 235.

sures of the natural France. But were a discipline given its academic place during the Popular Front and a folklore museum created by a Popular Front ministry suitable instruments to carry out the cultural agenda of Vichy?

Not only had the Popular Front accepted the conservative paradigm's valuation of authenticity—with the difference of their own candidates for national honor—but upon its political demise, with search for the True France still an unquestioned *projet,* there surfaced the capacity, if not a necessity, for folklore and regionalism to fulfill the ideological and political agenda of the Vichy regime. That new order, after all, based its claim to moral and historical legitimacy on a return to the abandoned heritage of the True France.

Thus the intellectual organization of the field moved individuals within it closer to Vichy than their own subjective motivation might have impelled them to do, creating an overdetermined complex of influences, affinities, and temptations between such men as Georges-Henri Rivière and the political order created after 1940.

Accordingly, if we were to focus our analysis primarily on individuals' motives, we would gain few useful historical insights about why a new *science humaine* experienced the political career it did. But studying the development of the paradigms of folklore as their adherents employed them, rather than carrying out the analysis in a fashion that takes no account of the discipline's educational impact on its practitioners, will, I suggest, give us better clues about the historical responsibilities of the actors. So we must first look at the discourse of folklore to understand why individuals thought or acted as they did in the period of Vichy rule.[2]

Let us look at the development of folklore by focusing on, for us, the key years in the career of Georges-Henri Rivière, from 1937 to 1967, when he headed the Musée National des Arts et Traditions Populaires. As we have seen, in the shadow of the dominant paradigm of French cultural essentialism there had grown up on the cultural left another vision of culture that understood twentieth-century France to be socially variegated, syncretic, polyvalent, and that tried to break out of the ontological trap to see *populaire* in its

2. Michel Foucault's work has been a valuable influence in getting us to look at history in this way. See, e.g., his *Order of Things: An Archaeology of the Human Sciences,* trans. A. M. Sheridan French (New York, 1972), 344–87.

most inclusive, permissive, and variegated sense. This view of a possible France coincided badly with that of a France with deep foundations unearthed and restored by Vichy; and, as a consequence, it armored folklorists who embraced the nonessentialist vision while living in the very belly of the beast—such as Marcel Maget, who after the creation of the *Etat Français* worked in the Peasant Corporation, and even the controversial Rivière, who managed to come to terms with every regime under which he worked in his long career— against the seductions of taking up the political values of Vichy, while doing work favored by the regime. We must glance back in the institutional history of the new folklore museum to see how the politics of folklore evolved.

The Musée des Arts et Traditions Populaires

As we have seen, the rise of the left in the mid-1930s gave Paul Rivet even better access to the state's coffers in his efforts to have his renewed Musée de l'Homme built. In 1937 Rivet and Rivière took advantage of the opportunity presented by the rebuilding to create France's first national folklore museum, the Musée National des Arts et Traditions Populaires (ATP).

Occupying quarters with the ethnographic museum in the remodeled building, now renamed the Palais de Chaillot, the new ATP, as it soon became known, broke off from the parent institution's affiliation with the natural history museum—the origin of Rivet's professorial chair—to go with, for Rivière's tastes, the more appropriate Musées Nationaux administration of the Beaux-Arts, which reported then to the Ministry of Education. Rivière became its first chief curator. André Varagnac, who had professional competence in folklore studies, took the post of associate curator. First eight and eventually thirteen additional professionals completed the team of the "French Section of Folklore Ethnography," as the formal title of the organization read. As befitted the historical moment and the intention of its patrons, the decree creating the museum was dated and promulgated on May Day, 1937.[3]

3. Sources for the parliamentary and administrative history of the beginnings of the Arts et Traditions Populaires, as first a department of the Musée de l'Homme and

The ATP's first public activities were occasioned by the International Exposition of 1937, which was dedicated primarily to the arts and architecture. For the fairground, the main part of which was laid out on the Champs de Mars between the Eiffel Tower and the museum's own refurbished structure and also along the Rive Gauche, the ATP was asked to mount an exhibit on the architecture of rural dwellings and another on the open-air regional museum (*musée de terroir*) at Romenay en Bresse.[4] Staff members worked with the architects who designed the buildings representing the styles of the various provinces built along the river in the Centre Régional.[5] The museum facility itself, however, was still in the process of reconstruction and would not be ready to open its doors to the public until after the war.

For Rivet, Rivière, and the staff of researchers they had assembled, once the museum and research center attached to it had been organized, their most compelling immediate task was constituting the field of folklore studies. They began with the design of the new center for the ethnology of France and then created agendas for future research. First, let us see what Rivière intended the new Département des Arts et Traditions Populaires to look like. He reported on the progress of its creation to the first international

---

then a separate museum, may be found in the Archives de Direction des Musées Nationaux (hereafter cited as Louvre Archives): Direction Générale des Beaux-Arts to Minister of Education, n.d., headed "Création d'un Département des Arts et Traditions Populaires aux Musées Nationaux"; budget request, n.d., "Rapport Sommaire sur la création du Département de Folklore des Musées Nationaux, du Musée Français des Arts et Traditions Populaires et des Musées de Plein Air"; Georges-Henri Rivière to Henri Verne, 5 March 1937, listing the staff and their salaries; and "Création du Musée: Décret du 1er mai 1937," all in U ATP 1. See further in Archives Nationales, F21 4906; Christian Faure, "Folklore et révolution nationale: Doctrine et action sous Vichy (1940–44)" (thèse doctorat, Université de Lyon II, 1986), 20. On the political-administrative history of the foundation of the ATP we have Pascal Ory, "La Politique culturelle du Front Populaire française (1935–1938)" (thèse pour le doctorat d'état, Université de Paris X, Nanterre, 1990), 994–1017.

4. Georges-Henri Rivière, "Le Musée du terroir de Romenay," *Folklore Paysan*, 1 (1938), 11–13.

5. Faure, "Folklore et révolution nationale," 20n. The guidebook does not mention the pavilions to which Faure refers, but it has ten enthusiastic pages describing the various buildings of the Centre Régional. See *Exposition internationale des arts et techniques: Guide officiel* (Paris, 1937), 104–14. See further Archives Nationales, Exposition internationale des arts et techniques, Paris 1937, F12 12114.

folklore congress, held in Paris in 1937, in conjunction with the exposition.

In the Palais de Chaillot, Rivière had a space of approximately 2,000 square meters at his disposal. After entering a peristyle shared with the Musée des Monuments Français the visitor would come to the ATP's *vestibule d'honneur,* which would have an atmosphere "both solemn and intimate," in Rivière's words. These responses would be evoked by statues and images of patron saints of agriculture and of artisanal activities. Then off of an introductory hall that would provide a first educational overview, Rivière planned an *optional* circuit dedicated to various ecologies and human adaptations to them (*genres de vie*). First there would be a display on the forest and its related crafts and ways of life, followed by a hall dedicated to agricultural life. Next the visitor could see something of the ways of living and crafts of the mountains, the rivers, and the seas. In keeping with Marcel Mauss's recent writings, which had moved exchanges into the center of anthropological discussion, adjoining these ecologically defined halls Rivière planned a hall where visitors would see materials related to the processes and the places of exchanges: ports, roads, markets, fairs, boutiques, traders, and the like. Adjoining this room Rivière designed an exhibition on town life featuring "the neighborhoods and their celebrations" as well as urban craftsmen with displays of their tools. The hall on the town would be next to one on village life, dedicated to, among other things, country churches, social life, rural artisanship, and festivals. Rural architecture, an interest that became central to the ATP under Vichy, got its space, as did the work clothing and festive costumes of the regions of France. The ages of human life from the cradle to the grave and the progression of seasons would be evoked at the end of the tour. Throughout Rivière planned alcoves representing types of artisan shops and the interiors of peasant homes. Finally a gallery would be consecrated to changing exhibitions on the various regions of France.[6]

6. Georges-Henri Rivière, "Méthodes muséographiques du nouveau département des Arts et Traditions populaires," *Travaux du 1er Congrès International de Folklore, tenu à Paris du 23 au 24 août 1937 à l'école du Louvre* (Tours, 1938), 300–301. *Facultatif* is in italics in the original. In a letter of 6 June 1938 to his friend Jacques Carlu, chief architect of the reconstruction, Rivière described his idea of the layout of the museum and the contents of the halls much as he had described it the year before at the

In conjunction with the museum in Paris, Rivière hoped to create a series of open-air museums on the model of the Swedish Skansen. But Rivière realized that in view of the diversity of the French countryside and of styles of rural architecture, there could be no one type for the country such as Sweden had created. This part of his planning came to little before the war.

Although overwhelmingly rural and regional in emphasis, Rivière's ATP did not leave out the cities and urban skills. Nor did it neglect commerce. Indeed, its design evoked two quite contrary outlooks and the differing emotional responses appropriate to them. The first was that of the salvage paradigm, the notion that an old France was passing away: we must preserve and display *typical* examples of an epoch that is coming to an end.[7]

Although presented in the usual anthropological present—that is, ahistorically—the museum Rivière was building was not in fact out of time. It was an evocation of the rural France of his childhood—his peasant mother's home and the homes his collaborators had grown up in or, as in Rivière's case, visited on vacation from what must have been a tense Paris household in the golden decade and a half before the outbreak of World War I. It was the world that Varagnac wrote had stopped changing in those prewar decades, the society that Eugen Weber argued had been modernized out of its old culture in the late nineteenth century. Especially for Rivière, and to varying degrees for other ethnographers, it was a French version of Thomas Wolfe's sense of his North Carolina childhood, of not being able to go home again. This sensibility was the echo of the *Traditions* in the name of the museum. All this was in keeping with the dominant essentialist paradigm.[8]

The second orientation that Rivière planned for his new museum

folklore congress, except that he emphasized that the *salle des villes* would contain "*folklore ouvrier et corporatif*": Archives of the Musée National des Arts et Traditions Populaires, dossier ATP Musée, Historique, 1938.

7. James Clifford, "Of Other People: Beyond the 'Salvage Paradigm,'" in *Dia Art Foundation Discussions in Contemporary Culture*, no. 1, ed. Hal Foster (Seattle, 1987), 121–30. It is a perennial plaint. See, e.g., Pierre Alphandéry, Pierre Bitoun, and Yves Dupont, *Les Champs du départ: Une France rurale sans paysans* (Paris, 1989).

8. Madame Noëlle Gérôme (CNRS), who worked with Rivière at the ATP at the end of his career, considers the simple origins of his mother and the human link she provided to the countryside as especially important factors in his later attraction to all that was *populaire:* conversation with the author, Paris, 16 January 1990.

relates more to *Populaires* in its name. The moment of the ATP's founding was also the apogee of the Popular Front, in whose cultural politics his patron Rivet was then playing such a great role. One summer evening in 1936 when he and Varagnac were leaving their temporary offices at the site, they came on some of the construction workers involved in building the new museum grouped in a circle around a fire in which was burning a coffin representing the 48-hour week. The two men realized they were witnessing an amalgam of a ritual funeral procession and the kind of bonfire that country people lit on festive occasions, a *feux de joie*. Indeed, that summer, without having been given party directives, workers all over the Paris region were spontaneously creating scenes of comic marriages and burlesque funerals that echoed the triumph of Mardi Gras and its comic funeral the next day, though its celebration had long ago died out in the Paris region and few of them could ever have experienced it. The contents of urban folklore may have differed from that of the countryside, but, as Rivière and Varagnac appreciated, in this instance at least, the forms—continuations of ones perhaps expiring on the land—were very much alive and fertile.[9]

Rivière accepted the idea that folklore was made in cities as well as in the country and that it was constantly being renewed. Thus he always regretted the name given his museum, and would have preferred, say, "The Museum of France." He tried explicitly to promote this sense of his discipline as both the definition of the field and the agenda for its growth.[10]

That sense was an uncommon compound of three ways of thinking. First, he accepted the scientific conception of the field pressed

9. André Varagnac, *Définition du folklore* (Paris, 1938), 46–49, clearly includes urban and workers' folklore in its definition and argues for the mixed and variable qualities of folklore, its regional specificity as well as its international similarities. But, attempting to resist the right-wing's appropriations of the discipline, Varagnac pointed out that "les aspects strictement nationaux étant de beaucoup les plus rares" (strictly national aspects were much more uncommon) (28). Rivière wrote a strongly supportive preface. For more on the tension between the traditional and the popular in folklore studies, see Raymonde Courtas and François-A. Isambert, "Ethnologues et sociologues aux prises avec la notion de 'populaire,'" *Maison-Dieu*, 122 (1975), 20–42.

10. A valuable conversation on 22 January 1989 with Jean Jamin about Rivière and modernism led me to this way of treating the distinction between the traditional and the popular in folklore studies.

by both Rivet and the Durkheimians, though he put his own distinct spin on the science. Moreover, he accepted their socialist politics.[11] These two values—emphasis on science and democratic politics—were in effect part of the job definition Rivet gave him and his associates in the newly created Institute of Ethnology. When the ATP was created, Rivière, following Rivet's lead, included in the plan an ethnographic research center, called in France a *laboratoire*. He wanted the museum also to be the intellectual center of the new discipline. We already have a sense of his political engagements; they were those of the left-republican circle in the contemporary *sciences humaines*.

To those intellectual vectors Rivière added, third, his personal aesthetic modernism—reinforced by his contacts with the surrealists—which was manifested by his openness to cultural invention on all levels of society. We see the unlikely mix in a lecture that Rivière gave at the Ecole du Louvre in 1936, in which he reviewed definitions of folklore and argued for one that included the arts of city workers alongside those of the rural population. He noted that since the eighteenth century folklore museums have been "a real rallying place for oppressed peoples." Yet at the same time he celebrated the scientific accomplishments in the field of French folklore: "museums in continual growth, research work flourishing." That was the science and the politics.

But most important, he pointed out the speciousness of any notion of some pure folk tradition, for "exchanges are taking place constantly between popular art and the work of trained artists." And he acknowledged as his own Arthur Rimbaud's cosmopolitan tastes as the poet expressed them in *Une Saison en enfer:*

> What I liked were: absurd paintings over doorways, stage sets, carnival backdrops, billboards, bright-colored prints, old-fashioned literature, church Latin, erotic books full of misspellings, the kind of novels our grandmothers read, fairy tales, little children's books, old operas, silly old songs, the naive rhythms of country rhymes.[12]

---

11. Pascal Ory, "Georges-Henri Rivière, militant culturel du Front Populaire?" *Ethnologie Française*, 17 (1987), 23–28.

12. Arthur Rimbaud, *Complete Works*, trans. Paul Schmidt (New York, 1975), 204.

He accepted the whole range of art and artifacts, from the high art of the rulers of societies to kitsch, and he saw the discipline not as "an ineffectual contemplation of old ruins" but as a living discipline dedicated to the vital creativity of the people. In our age of almost complete divorce between the creative artist and the public, on one extreme, and of a "popular creation" that was at best "sporadic, aberrant, smothered" by hypertropic industrialism, he argued, a museum dedicated to the arts and traditions of the people can serve a valuable function. In the short term it can attempt to span these gulfs and strengthen popular culture by educating the public once more to appreciate the authentic and by supporting "all forms of living popular art."

But the long-term solution he accepted in 1936 required, he believed, the rational reorganization of the economy and the society so as to tame the machine, that uncontrolled sorcerer's apprentice of our day. As for the impact of French society's reformation on the culture, "it would result in an improved quality of production in a world that was no longer split into educated and popular strata and where humankind, finally, would reclaim its worth [dignité]. Then we could speak of truly collective cultures."[13] In short, ascribing differences in social power and in the valuation of high and popular culture to class differences, Rivière celebrated the elimination of the barriers between high and popular culture as the predictable consequence of the further democratization of French society.

From January to April 1938 the ATP sponsored a series of radio talks on folklore themes on Radio Paris. Lucien Febvre introduced the series and Rivière gave the concluding talk on popular arts and tradition in contemporary France. Among the others whom Rivière invited to speak were Marc Bloch (rural tools); Marcel Maget, the folklore specialist in the Ministry of Agriculture on detached service at the ATP (village artisans); André Schaeffner, the ATP musicologist who wrote the first French scholarly study of American jazz (music and folklore); André Varagnac (workers' folklore); and Guy

---

13. Georges-Henri Rivière, "Les Musées de folklore à l'étranger et le futur Musée français des arts et traditions populaires," *Revue de Folklore Français et de Folklore Colonial*, 3 (1936), 59–71.

Pison, an architect working with the National Museums (peasant architecture).[14]

Marshal Pétain's France

But the Popular Front fell apart, and after some scenes of political aimlessness, the German invasion and the defeat came as the deus ex machina in what was universally understood to be the flawed plot of the tragicomedy that was the last days of the Third Republic. In July 1940, meeting in Vichy, the Assembly conferred the leadership of *l'Etat français* upon the aged Maurrasian Henri Philippe Pétain. Defeat showed that France had gone astray; the task of the future was to reclaim the past. Folklore had come home.

Although research on the cultural politics of Vichy and on French culture in the years between 1940 and 1944 is still in its initial phases, the revolutionary nature of Vichy's traditionalism is manifest. The regime attempted to institutionalize France's first counterculture. In its early moments Pétain and the conservatives with whom he surrounded himself set out to uncover and to renew the True France of their imaginations. "Time was halted by a double move," judged Christian Faure, "resort to an anachronistic past and to an unquestioning atemporality."[15] Vichy traditionalists envisioned beliefs, customs, practices as somehow growing from nature; the historical signs of the work of human hands in their creation were

---

14. *Folklore Paysan*, 1 (1938), 17. Unfortunately, I have found only the titles of the talks, no scripts.

15. Faure, "Folklore et révolution nationale," 621, and *Le Projet culturel de Vichy: Folklore et révolution nationale, 1940–44* (Lyon, 1989), 52. Faure's work is strongest for the years 1940–1942. On the modernizing trends in the period, see the conference volume of the Institut d'Histoire du Temps Présent: Jean-Pierre Rioux, ed., *Politiques et pratiques culturelles dans la France de Vichy* (Paris, 1988), esp. Henry Rousso, "Vichy: Politique, idéologie et culture," 13–25, who discusses what he calls the paradox of "*la créativité en régime autoritaire*" (15). Anne-Marie Thiesse characterizes the cultural regionalism of Vichy as "*décor*" in "Ecrire la France: Le Mouvement littéraire régionaliste de la langue française entre la belle époque et la libération" (thèse pour le doctorat d'état, Université de Lyon II, 1989), 510–79.

obscured by the political mist that covered the new eternal order of the fields.

Nevertheless, although defeated, it was still France, after all: the state acted as the midwife at the rebirth of the old society.[16] The cultural apparatus encouraged and supported regional theater, music, and arts. In November 1940 Pierre Schaeffer, a young official with the national radio, initiated the founding of the organization Jeune France, which in the seventeen months of its existence worked to encourage regional diversity in the production of (high) culture— the first such attempt ever made in France. The Maison des Arts Libéraux of the Haute-Loire, which eventually merged with Jeune France, was another notable organizational effort to revive regional culture throughout its *pays*.[17]

Vichy people fostered folk dance and singing groups: they strongly emphasized cultural purity. There was to be no mixing of modern with antique; authenticity ruled. Groups in one region were discouraged from singing songs or performing dances that originated elsewhere. The performers had to be from the region they represented and costumed in what was deemed to be the traditional fashion. The two most famous such groups were southern. The Couqueto of Marseille, created in 1925, owed nothing to Vichy for its creation, but continued to perform in the new political setting. The other, La Capello of Arles, performed in public for the first time on 3 December 1940 to honor Pétain's pilgrimage to Mistral's town.

In addition to the important theater activities of Jeune France, independent regional theater groups presented plays on locally meaningful themes, often in the patois. The *théâtre d'oc*, its supporters hoped, would present plays in Provençal or French based on local history and legends which would infuse the peasants of Provence with pride in their culture and in their region. The prefect at Toulouse created an office to study ways to support local arts and artisans. He founded a school for drama and music coaches, a re-

16. Ory, "Politique culturelle du Front populaire française," 1610, 1619, makes clear the magnitude of Vichy's debt to the Popular Front in cultural policies.

17. On these groups, see Véronique Chabrol, "L'Ambition de 'Jeune France,'" in Rioux, *Politiques et pratiques culturelles*, 105–15; Faure, *Projet culturel de Vichy*, 57–65. Unless I note otherwise, the next few paragraphs draw on Faure's thesis and book, so far the most complete studies of the topic.

source center for people planning traditional festivals and ceremonies, a clearinghouse for choral groups, and a reading circle.

In music, of course, the goal was to detoxify the musical culture of
the sounds of Josephine Baker and Tino Rossi, of black jazz and
Latin rumbas. Better *L'Arlésienne* of the Jewish composer Bizet than
the music of savages, but best of all, folk music. Music, however—
even march music—was not one of the strengths of the National
Revolution. Not much could be done in the short time available for
the effort, and jazz, as we know, did not die in France.

The intent of Vichy's art project was exactly the reverse of that of
the surrealists. Whereas Breton and his friends had worked to pol-
iticize art and aesthetics, to reveal the lines of social power hidden
behind pretty or soothing images, Vichy artists, like their National
Socialist counterparts, tried to aestheticize the regime's politics.
Cheerful, harmonious, and above all nonconflictual natural-looking
images predominated. At least two specifically Vichy genres of popular art can be distinguished. First, there was the production of
quasi-cultural works glorifying Pétain, called officially "*imagerie du
Maréchal*" (Figure 24). The representation tended to be a kind of
sentimentalized realism—shall we call it fascist realism?—with primarily rural symbolism.[18]

The second type simply celebrated regions, the countryside, local
saints, customs, crafts, and the like. The best known of the artists
were G. Ambroselli, who did much marshal art, and Jean Chièze,
whose specialty was representing important people—saints, say, or
Pétain—in neo-medieval fashion, as bigger than other figures in the
picture. In December 1941 René Henry put on the first ever Salon
de la Paysannerie Française in the Boëtie gallery in Paris. The show
displayed art exclusively dedicated to the countryside and to the
land.[19]

Mass ceremonies of social bonding were encouraged by the new
order. Harvest festivals, other seasonal celebrations, and encamp-

18. See Laurent Gervereau and Denis Peschanski, eds., *La Propagande sous Vichy,
1940–1944* (Paris, 1990).

19. Faure, *Projet culturel de Vichy*, 144–62, 175. The point about aestheticization of
Vichy politics is Faure's, and, of course, before him Walter Benjamin's. See further
Laurence Bertrand-Dorléac, "La Question artistique et le régime de Vichy," in Rioux,
Politiques et pratiques culturelles, 89–98, and *L'Histoire de l'art: Paris, 1940–1944: Ordre
nationale, traditions, et modernités* (Paris, 1986).

24. Joan of Arc inspires Marshal Pétain and French youth. Photo Collection, Bibliothèque Nationale.

ments all intensified a long-stressed and much-threatened sense of community in the months after the defeat, and they continued to grow in the war years. Religious practice, especially populous pilgrimages, increased greatly. There was a return to traditional forms of religious enthusiasm. A massive pilgrimage of French youth marked the feast of the Assumption on 15 August 1942 in Puy-en-Velay, in the Haute-Loire. Another one was held the next year. Naturally, the cult of the Virgin Mary, the saint of twentieth-century reaction, waxed. Faure reports that the number of individuals in Lyon who discovered religious vocations increased.[20]

The new state strongly promoted local languages, beliefs, and customs in the schools, in youth organizations, and in the media. A ministerial decree issued on 24 December 1941 permitted teachers to give elective courses in local dialects. Since in the government's view the primary schools needed more teachers skilled in local patois, it instituted the appropriate language courses in the teachers' colleges, especially in the south. Training in local dialects was more readily done in the *lycées* and universities, since a number of teachers and courses were in place there already. French *scouts* and *routiers* in southern France, above all, organized study groups to learn about folklore. The Eclaireurs de France undertook archaeological digs and published their findings. The Guides de France set themselves to research the history and geography of country clothing. And the members of these youth groups participated in—animated, Faure argues—village festivals, dances, community encounters of all sorts. Their researches "transform[ed] the adolescents into folklorists."[21]

Finally, the news media propagated the idea of True France in every corner of True France. Vichy subsidized regional reviews and magazines. The *Corrèze*, created by the departmental commission of regionalist propaganda, offered a little poem by Félix Gras as a pithy statement of the magazine's calling:

> I love my village more than your village;
> I love my province more than your province;
> I love France more than anything.[22]

20. Faure, *Projet culturel de Vichy*, 194.
21. Ibid., 221–22.
22. G. de La Farge, *Corrèze*, November 1941, cited in Faure, *Projet culturel de Vichy*, 240.

The Vichy performance in the news media, although sincere, was uneven. Radio, both state and newly authorized private stations, broadcast regional folkloric programs in dialect, but not enough to please the Peasant Corporation.[23] After a massive purge of undesirables, the film organization turned out a number of documentaries celebrating the customs, tales, and ceremonies of the regions of France, but nothing as memorable as the Nazi film industry produced.[24]

The renewal of the essential France needed more time than the two brief years between 1940 and 1942, after which political desperation, Pierre Laval's lack of interest, and complete German occupation put back the effort. And it needed more than the energy an ancient warrior sprung from the soil of France could mobilize.

Rivière's Vichy

To the surprise even of its leadership, membership in the Société du Folklore Français, instead of shrinking because of the disruptions of war, occupation, and territorial division, expanded, especially in the nonoccupied zone.[25] The organization continued to meet at the Palais de Chaillot. And despite Vichy ideology and the German occupation, it retained its integrity and even manifested a new interest in urban life. In May 1943 Pierre Louis Duchartre and René Saulnier, the first an officer in the secret army of the resistance, spoke on "Parisian prints containing folkloric themes from the fifteenth century to the Second Empire." In February 1944 Albert Soboul gave a talk, with slides, on "un type de civilisation rurale: Louzaret (Cévennes)," which had grown out of his work with the *chantiers intellectuels*.[26] The new regime also showed an interest in

23. Hélène Eck, "A la recherche d'un art radiophonique," in Rioux, *Politiques et pratiques culturelles*, 177–91.

24. Christian Faure, "Le Film documentaire sous Vichy: Une Promotion du terroir," *Ethnologie française*, 18 (1988), 284–90.

25. *Revue de Folklore Français*, 13 (1942), 174.

26. Thus the Société, although by no means a center of resistance to Vichy, was also not its ideological partner. The meeting announcements for the war years may be found in "Rapport d'activités des chantiers des A.T.P., mai 1943," Louvre Archives, U ATP 2, 1943–10 juin.

reviving traditional regional architecture.[27] Here Rivière took the initiative.

The *Chantiers Intellectuels*

While in one part of the building the circle of resistants around Boris Vildé—"Jews, Freemasons, foreigners, citizens made French by the grace of the Popular Front," as Jacques Ploncard characterized them in his collaborationist publication, *Au Pilori*—worked actively against the German occupation, in another part Rivière and his team continued to prepare the halls of the folklore museum for its eventual opening, and began to organize for the great investigations of rural life which they coordinated under *L'Etat Français*.[28] The *chantiers intellectuels* (literally, intellectual work sites) were intended to provide employment for intellectual workers who had lost their jobs in the economic disorder caused by defeat and occupation, and at the same time to carry out study projects not normally funded by republican governments. When Rivière was given the opportunity to participate, he immediately saw the benefits that such projects would have for his enterprises.

Rivière himself launched four of them. The largest both in scope (both zones of France) and in personnel (approximately fifty professional participants at its height) was Chantier 1425, a project on rural architecture started in late October 1941. There had been serious interest in rural architecture in folklore circles as early as 1937, during the international exposition. It had been a topic of the radio series sponsored by the ATP in 1938. The amount of energy and resources devoted to it in the Pétain era, however, went far beyond previous efforts. From 1941 to 1943 architects traveled through the regions of occupied and Vichy France to investigate the

27. Faure, "Folklore et révolution nationale," 242–613.

28. This specimen of essentialist characterization appeared in *Au Pilori* in November 1941; cited in Patrick Ghrenassia, "Le Musée de l'Homme dans la Résistance," *La Quinzaine Littéraire*, 1 August 1987. Although there is no evidence that Rivière and ATP people took part in resistance activities, Rivière, who was competent in German, attempted (unsuccessfully) to intercede with the German authorities on behalf of the resistants at the Musée de l'Homme who were sentenced to death: interview with Marcel Maget, Paris, 27 January 1989.

construction of traditional houses in villages and small towns, and generated voluminous dossiers of photographs, sketches, architectural drawings, and documentation. Perhaps in the setting of newly occupied France the manifest apoliticality of the topic recommended itself to a man and a museum that had become important under the patronage of a well-known leftist political figure such as Rivet, who at the moment was in flight from the Gestapo.

Two other *chantiers* sent investigators all over France. In April Chantier 909 was launched to document, photograph, make rubbings, and otherwise collect data on traditional rural furniture. By May 1942 forty-five investigators were at work on this topic. In November 1942 the ATP, again in collaboration with the Ministry of Agriculture's Service de l'Artisanat and its Service de Folklore Paysan de la Corporation Nationale Paysanne, undertook a project (Chantier 1810) on the crafts and traditions of the peasantry. Finally, in July 1941 the museum created Chantier 1817, comprising eight specialists, who worked to finish the organization of the ATP and whose task it was to process the abundant reports, drawings, photographs, and documentation produced by the other *chantiers*.[29]

The rural focus of the ATP *chantiers* opened them to the charge of strengthening the peasantist ideology of the regime: "So under Vichy rural France became an ethnic territory of high cultural status. Thus both implicitly and explicitly folkloric ethnography connected to the Vichy paradigm in its affirmation of the superiority of rural over urban France."[30]

To be sure, with the number of researchers connected with the projects, along with those who were there for the job or possibly for the professional experience in this first professionally organized fieldwork project in domestic ethnology, there were individuals who shared the thinking of the regime. While fighting was still going on in Paris (22 August 1944), the resistance group Lewitsky-Vildé, made up of staff members of the two ethnographic museums and named

29. Georges-Henri Rivière, "Notes sur les chantiers 909, 1187, 1425 et 1810," 3 June 1943, Archives of the ATP, dossier ATP ORG APP, Centres de formation professionnelle, Chantiers 909, 1187, 1425, 1810. On the *chantiers intellectuels*, see Faure, "Folklore et révolution nationale," 26–40, and *Projet culturel de Vichy*, 33–52. The documentation collected in the course of these projects may be found in the archives of the ATP. Only a part of it has been organized and most of it is not published.

30. Faure, "Folklore et révolution nationale," 42–43.

after their executed co-workers, "informed" the *conservateur-en-chef* that "the presence" of three project members at the museum was "considered undesirable." After some discussion Rivière did as he was asked and dismissed the tainted staff members.[31]

But only three people were thus denounced, and we know of individuals who worked with these projects who considered themselves men of the left. There was Jean Amblard, a Communist by conviction and an artist who lovingly sketched scenes from the life of his *pays*, the Auvergne, for the ATP. Henri Lefebvre, later to become famous as a philosopher of the left, worked on Chantier 1810. Albert Soboul, who in postwar France was recognized as the (last) great Marxist historian of the French Revolution, before his departure soon after the liberation, served briefly as deputy director of research for the projects. He had researched rural cadastres for the survey of rural architecture. André Varagnac worked briefly on the *chantiers*. Eager to get out from under Rivière's command and motivated more by ambition to have his own shop than by any idea of going over to Vichy ideology, in August 1941 he left for Toulouse to direct the newly created superprefecture's Bureau de Régionalisme, where he remained during most of the war, encouraging manifestations of local folklore.

And then there is the case of Rivière, which is like that of neither the convinced who worked with Vichy nor some of the leftists who opposed it out of their own essentialist vision. Rivière claimed after the war that one of the intended functions of the *chantiers intellectuels* was to spare individuals from deportation to Germany and the German labor service. Contemporary witnesses support the claim.[32] It

31. "Rapport général mensuel d'activité présenté à Monsieur le Directeur des Musées nationaux et de l'Ecole du Louvre, mois d'août," signed by Marcel Maget, Louvre Archives, U-2A, ATP 1944—22 septembre 1944. I have no information on the culpability or innocence of the project members and no evidence of legal proceedings with judgments. On the Musée de l'Homme and the ATP at the moment of the liberation in August 1944, see my brief edition of the key documents in "La Libération du Musée de l'Homme et du Musée des Arts et Traditions Populaires, août 1944: Un Conjuncture dans l'histoire événementielle de la science de l'homme," *Gradhiva: Revue d'Histoire et de les Archives d'Anthropologie Publiée par le Musée de l'Homme* (Paris), forthcoming.

32. "Liste des enquêteurs: Chantiers 909, 1425, 1810, 1187, 3.164," 1944, archives of the ATP, dossier ATP ORG APP, Centres de formation professionnelle, Chantiers 909, 1187, 1425, 1810. Soboul and Amblard participated in Chantier 1810: ibid.,

was characteristic, however, that, in contrast to the resistants in another part of the building, he labored in this good cause while enhancing his administrative empire.

Where Does Collaboration Begin?

To understand how the dominant folklore paradigm worked to encourage participation in Vichy's designs, we must go beyond the categories of collaborator, opportunist, and resistant which have governed the discussion of Vichy until recently and see in what ways the logic of a discipline—here, folklore—conformed to or repudiated certain political visions.[33] This simple moral trinity—collaborator, opportunist, resistant—cannot contain what we now are beginning to know about the elaborate and subtle scale of responses and initiatives—both structurally facilitated and individually essayed—which made up public life under Vichy; nor does it help us follow the conjunctural and the momentary in the politics of French culture.[34] Most important, as Klaus Schreiner points out in his incisive study of the fate of German medieval history under National Socialism—a not unsuitable parallel to this inquiry—we have to see what in the paradigms of the field, or which paradigms, disposed

---

dossier ATP, Chantiers généralités. This dossier contains many communications from Rivière to various authorities documenting his claims to need to keep various of his investigators at their tasks rather than have them drafted into the German-created obligatory labor service. There are as well letters from some investigators thanking him for his intervention. It is marvelous, if curious, to find such a thick dossier in an otherwise very slim record of his and the museum's activities during the war. Faure, "Folklore et révolution nationale," 40, vigorously disputes Rivière's claim (made in *Ethnologie Française*, 3 [1973], 9–14) to have had the labor service in mind when he organized the museum's projects, arguing that the *chantiers* were started before the Germans started to requisition the young men of the classes of 1940–1942. On Varagnac's activities to promote the revival of folklore in the south, see his "Rapport sur les activités au Bureau du régionalisme de la région de Toulouse," Paris, 17 June 1942, Louvre Archives, U ATP 2-A, 1942—24 août.

33. Henry Rousso does this admirably in *Le Syndrome de Vichy, 1944–198* . . . (Paris, 1987), esp. 313–22.

34. Together with the fundamental works of Robert Paxton and Richard Kuisel, we have the newer scholarship in the essays presented at the November 1987 conference on culture in Vichy France in Rioux, *Politiques et pratiques culturelles.*

researchers before the change of regime to take a path that would lead them and their discipline to come to terms with an authoritarian dictatorship, or, as in the case of Rivière, not to do so.[35] The main path that led to Vichy—or the factor that weakened the will of social thinkers to resist taking that path—was the search for the essential, the authentic, the True France.

Rivière's role under the *Etat Français* was not unambiguous. So, for example, although he was willing to serve as *conseiller scientifique*, he otherwise kept the Comité National du Folklore at arm's length from his museum to keep its amateur and partisan activities in the post-1940 folklore enthusiasm from tainting what he defended as the scientific field.[36] Or what can we make of his audience—the purpose of which we do not know—with Marshal Pétain on 8 September 1942, along with Charles-Brun and Pierre Louis Duchartre? Charles-Brun, entertaining great hopes for his beloved regionalism, supported the new regime; Duchartre, however, is remembered as an undisputed hero of the resistance.[37]

Always a man of his time who accommodated himself to circumstances to accomplish his goals, Rivière wrote nothing about workers' folklore under Pétain; he now played only country tunes, and these in the salvage/let-us-rescue-what-we-can-before-it-is-gone mode.

35. Klaus Schreiner, "Führertum, Rasse, Reich: Wissenschaft von der Geschichte nach der nationalsozialistischen Machtergreifung," in *Wissenschaft im Dritten Reich*, ed. Peter Lundgreen (Frankfurt am Main, 1985), 163–252, esp. 167–69.

36. Even in 1943, when he and Charles-Brun worked with the leadership of the Comité National du Folklore to devise a plan for a Corporation Nationale du Folklore, Rivière insisted on keeping the scientific and research activities the preserve of the ATP, the professional organization (the Société du Folklore Français), the *chantiers intellectuels*, and the Ecole du Louvre, leaving the practical action and the burden of Vichy ideological practice to others. See Faure, *Projet culturel de Vichy*, 32, 88–89.

37. Clipping from *Paris-Soir (Lyon)*, 10 September 1942, Archives of the ATP, ATP Musée, Rivière, Georges-Henri, Presse. Anne-Marie Thiesse, "Ecrire la France," 179–82, paints Charles-Brun as a fellow traveler who showed almost no hesitation about the Vichy regime yet refused to countenance anti-Semitic sentiments, as he had consistently done among his rightist friends since the turn of the century. Agnès Humbert, an art historian who worked at the ATP with Rivière during the war, wrote critically of accommodations made under the German occupation—books removed from the library, German authors added, a volume by Montandon placed on the shelf near the works of Lévy-Bruhl, free passes for German soldiers, etc. But this sort of evidence supports charges of opportunism or even discretion more than of fascist conviction. See Agnès Humbert, *Notre Guerre* (Paris, 1946), 22–23.

Writing programmatically on peasant folklore studies in 1942, he spoke in terms of "our heritage in folklore (which is indeed one of the essential conditions of our survival)." As a result of all the great revolutions—agricultural, political, and industrial—that have swept over France, "the question of the life or death of our traditions" is posed. He now defined "the mission that has fallen to the artisans of folklore: to maintain and to exalt peasant civilization, which is at once unified and diverse."

But in his heart the enthusiast for peasant life continued to be the urban aesthete who still loved jazz and who defined a rural ceremony as "less a spectacle presented to a public by a number of specialists than an aesthetic activity of the community as a whole." He continued to refuse to privilege older traditions in folklore at the expense of the contemporary practices and beliefs of the countryside. Nor did he wish to isolate the folklore of peasants from other cultural currents in the nation, from urban culture.

Despite his yielding to the Vichy rhetoric of "health," "vitality," and even at times "authenticity," and his apparent lack of resistance both to the Germans and to Vichy rule, Rivière's folklore was not the French version of *Blut und Boden*. Rather it continued to echo, however cautiously, the hope of a creative, syncretic cultural community. Soon after mounting his 1941 display of Norman farmhouses in the Grand Palais, he wrote that he had wished to exhibit the joining of the peasant heritage with the "forms of a new life."[38] The interpenetration of folk and urban cultures, he proposed the following year, "would be perhaps one of the most effective means of bridging the abyss that little by little has opened up between art and the people, and to encourage a healthy, living, real art among the peasantry."[39]

Lest there remain any doubt that, despite adventures in opportunism and moments of weakness, Georges-Henri Rivière clung to the avant-garde, progressive, and humanist values of the 1930s under Vichy and the occupation, the text he and Marcel Maget contrib-

38. Georges-Henri Rivière, "Logis de la ferme normande," *La France Européenne: Revue Mensuelle de l'Exposition du Grand Palais*, no. 1 (June 1941), 23. As usual in this period, his use of the words "new life" is ambiguous to a fault. However, his modernizing instincts here revealed themselves before the Vichy technocrats changed the direction of the state from the one Pétain had given it.

39. Georges-Henri Rivière, "Le Folklore paysan: Notes de doctrine et d'action," *Etudes Agricoles d'Economie Corporative*, 4 (1942), 291–316.

uted to the *Journées d'études de l'habitat rural* in June 1944 provides the necessary testimony. Largely the intellectual work of Maget, this first appreciation of the work on the rural architecture project took a thoroughly modernizing line in respect both to this genre and to rural life. Rejecting the attitude toward rural life which wished to see the population frozen into miserable life forms of the past, Rivière and Maget refused "the transformation of the peasantry into a kind of zoo for the pleasure of tourists." Nor did they accept economic isolation and quasi-autarkical regionalism as a way of keeping rural culture intact. Peasants should not be condemned to eke out poor existences in quaint peasant towns on mountaintops, for example, moved there centuries before to protect the villagers from dangers that no longer existed: "*only tradition* has kept populations living in utter poverty while clinging to infertile or marginal land." Taking up an agenda consistent with the socialist strivings of the Popular Front, promoted then by Vichy technocrats, and one that would continue to guide the postwar reconstruction of France and its thirty years of radical economic modernization, they wanted to see peasant housing as a part of a peasant life integrated "in the context of a totally planned economy." They wished to see rural architecture and the rural culture that engendered it conserved so far as possible, but not at the price of condemning fellow citizens to live "like Indians on their reservations." They wanted to help the countryside adapt to modern life, and even— "certainly the most important problem"—to innovate culturally and aesthetically. Then "a new beauty will come forth from the industrial revolution, finally freed of its contradictions."[40]

The End of the Eternal Order of the Fields

The conference for which Maget and Rivière wrote their report expressing their modernist views for the future of rural France was

40. Marcel Maget and Georges-Henri Rivière, "Habitat rural et tradition paysanne," *Journées d'études de l'habitat rural, 13 au 17 juin 1944* (Paris, n.d. [1944?]), 1–9; italics mine. On the technocrats and the continuity of the plan, see Richard Kuisel, *Capitalism and the State in Modern France: Renovation and Economic Management in the Twentieth Century* (Cambridge, 1981).

held a week after the first Allied soldiers came ashore at Normandy. After the liberation Rivière planned to embark on an ambitious series of special shows at the ATP, now finally opened. But the end of the war also brought him grief: André Varagnac denounced him to the Commission d'Epuration des Beaux-Arts as a collaborator.

The events at the museum at the moment of his accusation are worth telling. Because of the unsettled military situation, Rivière decided as of 19 August 1944 to remain at the museum day and night. The afternoon of 21 August the ATP and the Musée de l'Homme were "occupied" by the resistance group Lewitzky-Vildé (Front National), made up of the staffs of the two museums. Guy Pison, an architect and head of the *chantier* on rural architecture, assumed the leadership of the ATP contingent, while the musicologist André Schaeffner led the other museum's group. On the twenty-second they proceeded to purge the three undesirables, as we have seen, and the same day the head of the National Museums sent over some FFI (Forces Françaises de l'Intérieur) armbands, which went to the ATP group and to Schaeffner and Michel Leiris for the Musée de l'Homme. On Friday, 25 August, the Lewitzky-Vildé group at the ATP invited Rivière to join them at an "intimate gathering" to celebrate what Marcel Maget called in his report "the victory of the Paris Uprising." Shells were still falling in Paris on the twenty-sixth.

On the twenty-eighth, in the heat of the liberation, then, Rivière received a phone call informing him that he was being charged with collaboration. The next day the director of the National Museums appointed Maget and Pison to run things and asked both Rivière and Varagnac, then assistant curator, to leave the museum until further notice.

On 14 March 1945, having been suspended from his post for nearly eight months while the investigation was held, Rivière received a letter of recall. Nothing had been found to merit prosecution of the case; the inquiry decided "de ne donner aucune suite à l'enquête" (to close the file), and he was restored to his post.[41] Vara-

41. "Rapport général mensuel d'activité présenté à Monsieur le Directeur des Musées nationaux et de l'Ecole du Louvre, mois d'août," signed by Marcel Maget, Louvre Archives, U-2A ATP 1944—22 septembre 1944. Rivière reported the text of the letter as reading, "décidé de ne donner aucune suite à l'enquête ouverte à son sujet par le Conseil supérieur d'enquête et invité à reprendre ses fonctions sans délai":

gnac returned at the same time but soon left the museum to head an archaeological project of his own.

Since the records of the purge investigations are sealed, not to be opened in our lifetime, and Varagnac has died, it is unlikely that we will learn much more of this puzzling episode very soon. Knowledgeable people such as Marcel Maget, who directed the museum during the period of Rivière's suspension, although making strong counterarguments to the charges of Christian Faure that folklore studies veered toward the Vichy ideology between 1940 and 1944, will say very little about Rivière's activities in those years. He considers the charges made, and dropped, in 1945 a matter judged and closed. It may have been a kind of attempted palace coup by, according to all testimony, a disgruntled coworker, who, chafing under long and forceful administration, tried to exploit Rivière's less than brilliant political showing during the war.[42] Yet we may draw certain conclusions from this episode; here, as in Rivière's aesthetic and museum world, the surface reflects more light than we could find by attempting to plummet the depths of the human heart.

It is unlikely that Rivière compromised his principles or helped the German cause. He was on good terms during the war and, as we saw, immediately after with men of anti-Vichy convictions. After the war he continued to be accepted in the ranks of the leaders of French social science. He persuaded Charles de Gaulle and André Malraux, France's first minister of cultural affairs (both essentialists themselves in respect to French culture), to build a new splendid Musée National des Arts et Traditions Populaires in the Bois de Boulogne. Claude Lévi-Strauss gave it his blessing; a text by the great anthropologist introduces the visitor to the halls of the collection. And even after Malraux forced him to retire from the leadership of the ATP in 1967, just before the opening of its new quarters, Rivière continued to work creatively in his field.[43]

"Rapport général mensuel . . . mars 1945," signed by Rivière and dated 30 April 1945, ibid., U-2 ATP 1945. See also Jean-François Leroux-Dhuys, "Georges-Henri Rivière: Un Homme dans le siècle," in *La Muséologie selon Georges-Henri Rivière*, ed. Leroux-Dhuys (Paris, 1990), 26–27.

42. Conversation with Jean Jamin, Paris, 22 January 1989; interview with Marcel Maget, Paris, 27 January 1989.

43. See also Lévi-Strauss's praise for his postwar work on behalf of French museology at the ceremony at which Rivière received the Fondation de France's Science

Indeed, in the style characteristic of his efforts in cultural production, in 1966 he pioneered the French regional *écomusées*. These were regional parks, but not vast empty storehouses of salvaged greenery and animals in what was until recently the American mode. The ecomuseums, which multiplied rapidly in the next decade, contained villages and villagers; they were devoted to showing people living and working in the ecological setting of the region. They were planned and built by local authorities in collaboration with the government, and the local population was actively encouraged to participate in their management.[44]

A Premature Postmodernist?

After the war, too, Rivière regularly contributed articles on folklore to the PCF's *Almanach de l'Humanité*. He wrote simple popular pieces, but many of them were dedicated to the cultural theme to which he had been loyal throughout his career. In 1973, for example, in a contribution titled "Paysans de France: Créateurs de culture," he expressed the hope that someday he would see in contemporary society "an amalgam of rural and urban culture, of the mechanical and the manual, stripped of dreary uniformity."[45]

So, although it was true that under Rivière's leadership in the early days of Vichy folklore studies lost interest in workers' folklore, and that he stayed and worked within that repugnant regime, Rivière nevertheless never gave up the cosmopolitan turn he had promoted during the 1930s. Indeed, despite his opportunism and his unsure grip on left-wing political ideas, Rivière's very commitment to a polyvalent syncretic idea of French culture wrapped up in

Award for 1977, "Allocution de M. Claude Lévi-Strauss à l'occasion de la remise du Prix Scientifique de la Fondation de France à Monsieur Georges-Henri Rivière," Rivière papers in the archives of the International Council of Museums (ICOM), which he headed for many years, in the UNESCO building (rue Miollis), Paris. I could not discover the reasons for Malraux's ungenerous action.

44. Isac Chiva, "Georges-Henri Rivière," *Terrain*, 1985, 79.

45. Georges-Henri Rivière, "Paysans de France: Créateurs de culture," *L'Almanach de L'Humanité, 1973* (Paris, 1973), 193–203, esp. 203. See further Rivière's obituary in *L'Humanité*, where his career is very positively assessed. A copy, along with an equally friendly appreciation of his work in *Le Monde*'s death notice, may be found in the Rivière papers at the ICOM archives. The ICOM files also contain many letters written after the war by democrats and even leftists in praise of the head of the ATP. However, his otherwise detailed CV and other lists of activities are either very skimpy or silent on the period 1940–1944.

his vanguardist modernism held him back from falling for Pétainist agrarian mystification, for a mythic True France, whether it included workers or not.

It is interesting and important to note in this respect how ambivalent the Vichy regime was about the modern art and the artists that had been the glory of the previous decades in France, as if fearing contact with so powerful an antidote to retrograde fantasies about the future of French culture. It chose instead to promote a "pictorial traditionalism," or, with the great artists of the 1930s in exile or pushed to the side, a conservative continuation of the school of Paris carried out by safe artists.[46]

The work especially of Laurence Bertrand-Dorléac on the plastic arts under Vichy is beginning to illuminate this fascinating subject. She has pointed out, for example, that the German censors contented themselves with making sure that artists who were Jewish, Freemasons, or known Communists were neither written about nor shown; but they never concerned themselves with art that in Germany would have been deemed somehow subversive for formal reasons. As in other matters, the French government went beyond the Germans in the strictness of the canons applied to art acquisitions in the years between July 1940 and August 1944. If we omit pieces difficult to classify—admittedly nearly half the purchases—the artworks acquired by the French state were almost exclusively landscapes, still lifes, portraits, and waterscapes. Moreover, in a preliminary study, Bertrand-Dorléac has expressed skepticism as to whether the artists of the group Jeune Peinture de Tradition Française can be seen as aligned with the resistance because they consciously embraced the "French tradition" in painting, used bright colors and the colors of the national flag, and returned to portraying the human figure after its long banishment by the innovators of the interwar years. Yet finally Vichy's more remarkable innovation in the plastic arts was the creation of a special staff of artists who created images of the marshal in all media (*l'art-maréchal*).[47]

46. Laurent Gervereau, "Y a-t-il un 'style Vichy?'" in Gervereau and Peschanski, *Propagande sous Vichy*, 147; Laurence Bertrand-Dorléac, "La Question artistique et le regime de Vichy," in *La Vie culturelle sous Vichy*, ed. Jean-Pierre Rioux (Paris, 1990), 137–60, and by the same author, *L'Histoire de l'art*, 25–48, 115.

47. Bertrand-Dorléac, "Les Arts plastique," in Gervereau and Peschanski, *Propagande sous Vichy*, 222; Anne Sefrioui, "Laurence Bertrand-Dorléac, les artistes des années sombres," *Art Press*, 156 (March 1991), 64–67. A new volume on Vichy art by Bertrand-Dorléac will soon be published.

Rivière's story serves as a morality play expressing our contemporary concern to find a way to justify—anchor if possible—judgments of political justice, the values of cultural tolerance, and above all living with the consequences of a world without fixed values. True, by rejecting a reactionary essentialism Rivière held back from accepting the fundamentalist anthropology of a Louis Marin (who was a member of the governing *conseil* of the Société du Folklore Français), for example, or the racialism that some of the Vichy anthropologists cultivated.[48] Yet his career reveals no signs of resistance to *any* authorities; operationally, he accepted the world of state power as he found it, whether that were the Popular Front, the German occupation, Vichy, or de Gaulle, benefiting as possible from each to further his concerns. In matters of cultural value his pluralism was ballasted by a valuation of aesthetic excellence. But what ballasted his ethical values?

In his last years on a table in his modest apartment, furnished with simple functional furniture, he kept a kind of absurd museum containing among other things a beautifully lathed children's top given him by a Provençal craftsman, a sculpted ashtray in the shape of a cat, and—perhaps added after Malraux forced his retirement in 1967—a glass ball full of blue-tinted water, which, when turned upside down, dropped snow upon a miniature statue of Charles de Gaulle.[49]

Rivière's career of being all things to all regimes illuminates the dark side of Max Jacob's rejection of centeredness even in the individual; as he put it in his *Art poétique*, "une personalité n'est qu'une erreur persistente" (a personality is only a persistent error). Ironically—the voice he and his avant-garde friends preferred—Jacob was captured late in the war and died in a concentration camp on the eve of the liberation. The career of Rivière, a premature postmodernist, poses all the questions but suggests few encouraging answers to the perplexities that arise from the relinquishing of essentialism for postmodernity.

48. Archives Nationales, 317 AP Marin Papers, carton 58.
49. Leroux-Dhuys, "Georges-Henri Rivière," 25.

Conclusion

A paradigm of essentialist cultural identity dominated French cultural and political life from the second founding of the Third Republic and the Dreyfus affair until the dissolution of Vichy rule. Soon after its apotheosis in Vichy it exploded into bits. Forged from intellectual pieces and social practices of a narrowed vision of the possibilities of French culture in the late nineteenth century, a conservative way of thinking, what after Foucault I would call an episteme, took on its modern, militant, and political form at the beginning of the twentieth. We have seen how essentialist social science and politics worked in the first half of this century, from their new conservative construction to the struggles to break out of that heritage in the most recent decades.

Our conclusion has to be that the construction of an exclusive, unitary, and fundamentalist concept of French cultural identity was a conservative political project that took in good people and that, for the democracy of the Third Republic, it was a disastrous one. When we reflect on the framing of the discourse of essentialist cultural identity, on the efforts to persuade the French to accept an imperial sense of Frenchness and to persuade colonial people to return to French-nurtured roots so that by becoming more native they could be more French, and finally, on the creation of a domestic cultural definition of what it was to be French which could benefit only the most regressive sides of national life, we find that True France has been deconstructed to reveal its consequences in cultural narrowness and political reaction. But deconstruction is only a mental operation, finally only another verbal victory that scholars like to celebrate over the powerful. Visions of cultural identity may be theorized in libraries, but they function in the world and finally must be contested there.

In the end, the project of True France failed for four powerful reasons, two having to do with changes in the culture and two with the misfiring of the politics of identity. First, on the level of the culture, as the twentieth century developed and even under the technocratic phase of Vichy, its authoritarian paradigm was rendered increasingly irrelevant in a world of emptying villages, triumphant market agriculture, the decline in religious sensitivity, better communications between country and city, between France and the world, and the accompanying dethronement of local notables and of the remnants of deference. Since World War II a new European consciousness has arisen as an alternative to a narrow nationalism, whether it flies Jacobin or integralist colors. The places for the practices of True France are disappearing.

Second, as we have seen, there had always been a republican True France, a project to complete the republic, and however much it partook of the cultural closedness, intolerance, and even elitism of what the right found in the French cultural heritage, it nevertheless promoted its own episteme, an essentialism of democracy, social justice, and egalitarianism.[1] Republicans and the left lost much in sharing the vision of one authentic nation, but however handicapped, they could at least contest the most retrograde aspects of the paradigm from within it, as true Frenchmen.

Third, Hegel's court of world history continues to meet and render judgments; its rulings are still the most powerful texts of the age.

---

1. Claude Nicholet, *L'Idée républicaine en France: Essai d'histoire critique* (Paris, 1982), 503. Foucault's adaptation of Bachelard's idea, also fruitfully employed by Thomas Kuhn in his notion of a scientific paradigm, should not be so narrowly understood as to allow for only one episteme in any epoch. I want to contribute to the discussion of Foucault's question how epistemes are challenged and change: in the twentieth century a ragtag collection of socialist, psychological, primitivist, aesthetic, scientific, economic, and anticolonial ideas and practices successfully challenged the episteme of True France so that in the years after 1945 French people became increasingly aware of cultural choices open to them.

The conjunctural defeat of the ideas and the practices of Vichy *in history* discredited the enterprise of True France, the promised land to which Pétain tried to return France. Its association with failure has made the Vichy definition of France suspect.

Finally, and more as the result of cultural developments throughout the West than of political agendas, the very definition of the self of people altered. The growing awareness that personal identity and the *patrie* were not so intertwined, that different citizens could experience the nation differently, just as there could be many facets to a person's identity, have done the work of tearing apart essentialism. But—and this was the blind spot of structural functionalism in anthropology, which insisted upon the unity of a culture—the triumph of multiplicity in life has not automatically eliminated True France from common sense, social sciences, and social practices. In certain ways, postmodernity has intensified the desperate efforts of many individuals and groups to fulfill the felt need for an end to anomie and for fixity in social life by fastening onto something eternal, or at least guaranteed to last until the crisis passes.

Like the buildings from which bits of ancient columns have been salvaged in the Mediterranean world to hold up parts of more modern structures, the old structure has fallen down; but some parts of it continue to be important. Today both in the United States and in Europe, now especially in Eastern Europe, writers, movements, and institutions continue to promote old-sounding national traditions, values, ways of thought, and social relations as a way of anchoring behavior and belief in an age of apparent value randomness. In the United States the followers of Leo Strauss, among other university-based intellectuals, wish to bring us back to a fixed and venerable heritage of values and learning, while the religious right wants to bring us back to God. In my own Suffolk County in 1989 a legislator of Italian descent tried—unsuccessfully—to persuade his colleagues to make English the official language of the county. In California, not long before, a public figure of Japanese descent put his might—successfully—into making English the official language of the state. As the United States population grows more Hispanic and more Asian, we will continue to have to deal with our own nativism, our own ideologies of Americanism.

When I was a student in Berlin in the early 1960s I heard much

talk about the need "to overcome" or "to deal with" Germany's recent past (*"die nächste Vergangenheit bewältigen"*). A quarter of a century later, the attempts by conservative German historians to close
the book on National Socialism, as well as the disputes about the
orientation of a new German history museum, are disquieting. For
the right it is a return to nationalist roots (with the episode of National Socialism in brackets). At issue is a new highly mythologized
definition of the nation, which as a truncated political entity had
existed only from 1871 to 1945, a brief time as we measure history,
and then in only fifteen of those years, 1919–1933, enjoyed democratic government. Principled social scientists such as Jürgen Habermas, and in the arts Günter Grass, to name just the best known
outside Germany, refuse to allow German conservatives to invent
such bad-faith traditions unopposed.[2]

The annexation of East Germany to the Federal Republic has
intensified to white heat the politics of national identity in the German cultural area of Central Europe. If, as has been suggested in the
pages of the prestigious *Frankfurter Allgemeine Zeitung*, the assimilation of East Germany requires Germans to embrace once more the
idea of a "national community," if the role of the new German "nation" will be to comfort us in a changing and heartless world, to serve
us as "a refuge," then we are right to ask if the politics of identity
might not once more trouble German—and therefore European—
politics.[3] German unification seems to have benefited the conservative historians' version of the story of the nation.

Today in France, too, the digging for roots continues, but like
Jean-Paul Goude's outlandish bicentenary July Fourteenth parade,
with the distracting dissonance of many different drumbeats.[4] One

---

2. On the *Historikerstreit*, see Charles Maier, *The Unmasterable Past: History, Holo-
caust, and German National Identity* (Cambridge, Mass., 1988).

3. The *Frankfurter Allgemeine Zeitung* wisely left it to a Briton teaching in an American university to express what, as a result of the historical criticism of Hans Ulrich
Wehler and his colleagues of the Bielefeld school, was a sentiment that dared not in
German letters speak its name. See Harold James, "Die Nemesis der Einfallslosigkeit,"
Frankfurter Allgemeine Zeitung, 17 September 1990, 36. See further Carl Schmitt's
argument that democracies must suppress diversity and difference to succeed: *Parle-
mentarisme et démocratie* (1923; Paris, 1988), 106, cited in Gérard Noiriel, *La Tyrannie du
national: Le Droit d'asile en Europe, 1793–1993* (Paris, 1991), 311.

4. Goude created a postmodern parade in which African drums vied with French
peasant drums, jazz percussion with a solemn marching beat, and everyone was
weirdly garbed.

search has an official address. In 1981 newly victorious and with great plans for a Socialist renewal of French cultural life, the Socialist Ministry of Culture encouraged the creation of a Direction du Patrimoine to look after France's endangered cultural heritage. Architectural evidence of its work may still be seen everywhere in work sites of restoration and repair of ancient churches, châteaus, and houses. But regional music, costumes, and practices were also targeted with the creation of a Commission du Patrimoine Ethnologique. The commission, chaired until 1989 by Isac Chiva, was created with the blessings of Claude Lévi-Strauss. It publishes an excellent journal dedicated to French ethnology, which, with the ATP's *Ethnologie française*, adds a second major periodical to a small field.[5]

That is one *projet* of national definition. Its formation recalls—the way French culture often returns to unresolved issues, if in *aufgehobenen* ways—the left's struggle for the True France of the years of the Popular Front once again. But this time one lesson has been learned: beyond its ethnological contributions, the Direction du Patrimoine has functioned, at least to the change in government in 1993, to preempt the invention of another *pays réel* by contemporary rightists at this moment of cultural confusion.[6] In this sense, the work of the Mission du Patrimoine Ethnologique is closer historically to that of Rivet and Rivière than to the cultural project of Charles Maurras or Louis Marin. The first such struggle in the century ended in tragedy; what will be the long-term results of this battle, now that the onetime president of the Ecole des Hautes Etudes en Sciences Sociales, Marc Augé, has finished his term of leadership, and the government has changed, is not yet clear.[7]

In other quests after national identity in France, political leaders

5. The new directions within the Ministry of Culture were initiated in 1979 by the previous government, but the Socialists made the project their own, increasing the cultural budget impressively to carry out the task of conservation and renewal.

6. The minister of labor, Jean-Pierre Soissons, told an anti–Le Pen meeting at the Sorbonne on 12 March 1991 that the left had "to raise the question of 'national identity' clearly" but with care not to fall into the rightist trap contained in the idea: "Let us not leave ourselves open for the National Front to take our heritage, our history, or we risk losing our future to it as well": *Le Monde*, 15 January 1991, 15.

7. The first head of the Commission for the Patrimoine (1979–1989) was Isac Chiva, a leading anthropologist of French life and a close collaborator of Claude Lévi-Strauss. The Durkheimian family resemblances of this effort to that of the Institute of Ethnology and the Folklore Society—whatever the theoretical differences—are striking.

of the indigenous populations of New Caledonia and Tahiti wish to revitalize their culture. For the political front of the Canaques, the FLNKS, according to one of its spokesmen, Rock Wamytan, "culture is the foundation of political action." They do not want a melting pot, at least not for the moment; that might come later. To prepare for the political independence that will come in 1998, the FLNKS wishes first to affirm Canaque culture and then to promote it in all ways possible.[8] This is a return to roots, like that of other conquered peoples, which is difficult to oppose despite all the ambiguities and risks we can foresee.

Still other cultural projects in present-day France seem to have much less substance, even if they have violent ways of speaking and acting to make their case. After several years of nonlethal protests, the Corsican nationalists have escalated their campaign to reclaim their Corsican *patrimoine* by threatening with violence any Corsican who collaborates with the French occupier, and they have blown up tourist facilities. So they fight for a "Corsica for the Corsicans."

The cause of the Front National of Jean-Marie Le Pen continues to flourish, and now, because of a new electoral strategy, it works most actively both on the local level and in the European parliament, where even its allies on the German radical right, headed by a former SS man, have reproached Le Pen for his racism. Unfortunately, the Front National's "France for the French" and Le Pen's new accusation that "the Jewish International" and "Freemasonry" have created "antinational feeling," however unrepresentative politically of the larger population, are signs of issues still unresolved in the history of the chase after identity in France and in the hinterland governed from Paris.[9] With the resentments of the *pieds noirs* continuing to fester, with the animosity toward North Africans on economic grounds (they "eat the bread of the French"), and with the decline of the Communist Party as the catchbasin of *ressentiment,* the Le Penist movement will continue to flourish. Not to increase its membership might be a more terrible sign than its growth in past years, for it would mean that the current mainstreaming of radical right agendas was succeeding.

In his provocative book *L'Idéologie française,* which critiques the

8. "La Culture canaque et le FLNKS," *Le Monde,* 10 August 1989, 6.
9. "Après les déclarations de M. Le Pen sur 'l'internationale juive,'" *Le Monde,* 13–14 August 1989, 5.

dominant strains of French belief today as Marx did those of German philosophers in the 1840s, Bernard-Henri Lévy speaks of the hunger after roots as a kind of racism without race: "The particular marvel of this racism of the real France is that it has so well made itself a part of our common sense, so artfully grounded in our countryside and our soil, that it has become a weltanschauung, a philosophy of society, a whole architecture of the Pétainist polity of yesterday, of the day before yesterday, and perhaps one for tomorrow."[10]

But other voices and other forces continue to try to mediate the growth of a more open French culture. Speaking at a large conference sponsored by the Direction du Patrimoine in 1987, not long before he assumed the leadership of the agency, Marc Augé drew a sensitive distinction between two pluralisms. An anthropologist specializing in Africa, he once wrote that he could relate better to the ways of thinking, fears, and hopes of someone from the Ivory Coast who got off the Métro with him at Sèvres-Babylone than to the most sophisticated ideas of a man in his building with whom he spoke occasionally and who reads the Catholic newspaper *La Croix*. He could do this, I think, because he reveled in what he called a "glorious pluralism" that comes from the rich fertilization of cultural life by the encounters, crossings, and syncretisms of different civilizations. It is the richness Lévi-Strauss wrote about in *Race and History* or, as Augé has remarked, the creativity produced by the explosive expansion of cultural exchanges which we know as the European Renaissance.

But Augé distinguished another pluralism, a negative one, "a pluralism of deprivation." It is that of Third World societies that have lost their heritages and live in a postmodern grab-bag world of cultural churning. It is that of the French-born children of Algerian backgrounds who are in anguish about who and what they are. "Because I believe in the glorious pluralism, I will take the liberty of expressing the hope that there never will come a day when we find ourselves reproaching these children of Africa and of France for refusing, or not knowing about, what we never truly offered them, or didn't offer them effectively or clearly enough."[11]

10. Bernard-Henri Lévy, *L'Idéologie française* (Paris, 1981), 125.
11. Marc Augé, remarks at the plenary session, *Actes des colloques de la Direction du Patrimoine: Patrimoine et société contemporaine*, held in Paris 7–11 October 1987 (Paris, 1988), 55–57.

Today three challenges to the sense of national identity fill many of the population with misgivings and, if not mastered, could have deleterious consequences for French democracy and cultural tolerance. First and most troubling is the problem of the North Africans. If the question continues to be put not as Marc Augé expressed it, as how to empower a glorious pluralism, but rather as Braudel understood it, as how to *integrate* the Islamic population, on the model of the other ethnic groups that have been made into *les français*, the values of Le Pen, if not necessarily his movement, will certainly continue to spread in ways that could threaten French democracy.

The Muslim population of France and, to varying degrees of poignancy, many others of immigrant origins are caught in what Gérard Noiriel has called an "impossible choice": by the decision to become French they accept the republican contract of citizenship, but that decision requires them to abandon their ancestral heritages. The social aberrations and unhealthy passions such a dilemma has given birth to—from the Dreyfus affair to the recent national debate about whether Muslim girls may wear religious head coverings in public school—has brought recruits to the project of True France. For to reconcile the republican contract with the claims of place and kind requires immigrants, colonials, even provincials either to abandon their first identities (few can easily see themselves as "Afro-French" or "Arab-French") or to be wrapped up in the straitjacket of a state-approved identity that since the Third Republic has excluded the religious dimensions of people's lives. The need is to accept immigrants into a new, less restrictive idea of what is French, or better, a new project for a more open, polyvalent culture, perhaps with a new, less rigid understanding of the possible relations of religion and the state; that project is only now in the process of creation.[12]

Second, there is the fear of Americanization. This word summarizes many processes of modernization as well as the decline of France as a world power. It is certainly correct to criticize the baleful influence in the world of American arms, American usages, and American marketing dressed up as American culture. Nevertheless, French-made adult sitcoms, for example, are not obviously truer

12. On the history of citizenship written on a comparative basis see William Rogers Brubaker, "Immigration, Citizenship, and the Nation-State in France and Germany: A Comparative Analysis," *International Sociology*, 5 (1990), 379–407, and *Citizenship and Nationhood in France and Germany* (Cambridge, Mass., 1992).

than the American imports to the best aspects of the French cultural heritage or to its most creative possibilities. Barring American products—cultural and otherwise—will not make French ones better, and there is always the risk that such a defense of national values and national production might be used as a cover for a reactionary antimodernism or simply defensive policies that give French people fewer material and cultural choices.[13]

Finally, however haltingly, the European Community continues the economic consolidation of its twelve member countries. With this move the locus of citizenship has become increasingly problematic. Fear of loss of national identity in many of the member states has banished talk of any European superstate emerging from economic integration. Nevertheless, the free movement of goods, labor, and capital—and values and ideas—across national boundaries will continue to raise ever more acutely the question what it is to be German, French, or British. To the threat to "historic" identity from immigration and modernization will be added that of internationalization.

Introducing a conference he had agreed to chair dedicated to the theme, Claude Lévi-Strauss commented ironically that "if we were to believe certain individuals, the crisis of identity would be the new *mal du siècle*." He expressed skepticism about the value of this idea: "the forces of nature and of history [are] supremely indifferent to our autism."

And even after having heard many fine papers by specialists in the natural and social sciences, anthropologists predominating—several of whom chafed under the strict observance of structuralism—Lévi-Strauss continued to refuse any notion of a "substantial identity." He proposed, rather, that the common denominator of the *problématique* of foreign societies and our own is not this postulate that we all have an identity and must search for its expression but rather the need to question the idea of identity with the aim of reforming or reconstructing the society.[14]

Identity or changing societies: that is the opposition Lévi-Strauss

13. See Richard Kuisel's book on the Americanization of France, *Seducing the French: The Dilemmas of Americanization* (Berkeley, 1993).

14. Opposed to what he termed *"un substantialisme dynamique,"* Lévi-Strauss admitted the concept of identity as "a virtual center of focus to which we must refer to explain a certain number of things, but which has no real existence": *L'Identité: Séminaire interdisciplinaire dirigé par Claude Lévi-Strauss, professeur au Collège de France, 1974–75* (Paris, 1977), 9–11, 330–32.

focused upon. His critique of the idea of identity, I believe, had more behind it than the resistance of this master thinker of the structuralist paradigm to inroads by methodological heretics. He saw the profoundly conservative uses of such a concept in the enterprise of understanding societies—all over the world—and in people's struggles to change those societies to make them more (dare we say) human. The American anthropologist Renato Rosaldo reminds us that today "all of us inhabit an interdependent late-twentieth-century world marked by cultural borrowing and lending across porous national and cultural boundaries that are saturated with inequality, power, and domination."[15] I would add that there are no more purely local civil wars, local ecological crises, local economic problems, or even local creation in the arts. And I hope that allusions to cultures other than France have made the point that with varying degrees of intensity most contemporary cultures are experiencing anguish and conflicts over cultural identity and cultural pluralism.

The paradox of the contemporary world is that once-oppressed peoples often feel that they need essentialist constructions of their cultural identities for survival, while the once dominant must abandon exclusionary self-definitions if they are to hope to master potential disorder in the state. The explanation has two parts.

First, agonies of cultural identity originate, as I have argued, as direct results of conquest and political rule, and indirectly from economic expansion. The "discovery of the world" and its colonization, the tracing both overseas and at home of political boundaries that ignored cultural, linguistic, and historic affinities, and, most recently, the accelerating massive *Völkerwanderungen* from the peripheries to the world's metropoles have resulted in a cultural and political crazy quilt in each place and all over the world. The free movement of labor in the Common Market will just continue the global trend. White European males have created a heterogeneous world that they no longer can govern with their own essentialist ideologies, even if many are loath to relinquish control. The disin-

---

15. Renato Rosaldo, *Culture and Truth: The Remaking of Social Analysis* (Boston, 1989), 217. Rosaldo, although himself deeply involved with Chicano cultural issues, resists an anthropology of essentialism. He proposes we talk about culture in a narrative mode (127–43).

tegration of the East European and the Soviet order held together by the Soviet army and Marxist-Leninist-Stalinist culture is just a sensational version of the end of ideologies everywhere. These passing hegemonies—in the former Eastern bloc as in the West—have been replaced by fundamentalist religion and varieties of cultural and national essentialisms. No armies, no schools, no central culture ministries can halt these centrifugal processes. Unitary hegemonic identities no longer serve as sources of political legitimacy. The dominant who caused the peoples to be gathered together have had cultural pluralism imposed on them for their sins, and if there is to be any order in states, they must make their peace with variety.[16]

Second, cultural essentialism, especially in a highly urbanized modern society such as France, has become largely irrelevant as a way for even the dominant population to construct a sense of a collective self, to give meaning to their lives. A French person may well see herself as an Arlesian, for example; in language, in diet, in dress, in social practice, and in kinship, this identity made up an important part of her definition of self a century ago. Mistral thought so. But today her sense of being a woman, perhaps a divorcee, a computer programer, a European even, a fan of *Dallas*, with relatives and close friends—not so distinguishable in importance anymore—all over the world makes for different constructions of the self and for different collective entities seen as matching new self-definitions. In a word, individuals of Algerian descent, born and educated in France, may well not wish to, perhaps cannot, assimilate Frenchness, and yet may still be French in some meaningful way, or Algerian, should they emigrate to Algeria.[17] But what is certain is that in a world in which increasing numbers of the population are

16. See, e.g., William Pfaff, "Defining World Power," *Foreign Affairs*, 70 (1991), 34–48, esp. 38–39, where Pfaff links acceptance of the new great ethnic migrations with acknowledgment of "a world [that] is moving towards a restored pluralism of power."

17. Jean-Loup Amselle has persuasively argued that this diversity has always existed, even in such highly communitarian societies as those of historic Africa. He rejects those social analyses he terms "ethno-substantialist, which isolate conceptually and therefore politically, vulnerable groups in societies." Rather than "a multicultural society" of American liberal ideology and French new-right enthusiasm, which in its extreme version yields orders such as apartheid, he speaks rather of "an originary syncretism": *Logiques métisses: Anthropologie de l'identité en Afrique et ailleurs* (Paris, 1990), 28–66, 248.

seen as marginal wherever they may live—in some cases a near majority, as with the African-American, Spanish-speaking, and Asian population of the United States—we have to rethink our ideas about who belongs and who is marginal. Or more important, the paradigm of "belonging" requires rethinking.[18]

Here, as in the Enlightenment, France might set itself once again to fostering an emancipatory project that recognizes diversity and yet holds to a vision of a nonrepressive unity of humankind. Because of both its ideology and, often, its history of being the second home of humankind, the heartland of cosmopolitanism as it were, France has contributed greatly to the creation of a global culture of modernity which combines tolerance, nonexclusivity, openness, and the ethics of humanity. If it can be made to grow in this time of pandemic identity politics, such a public cultural project would make a world in which people had multiple identities and in turn would tolerate others with different mixes of self-defining qualities without the need to create fortresses of unique self-definition.

Moreover, there are, I believe, two traits specific to French culture which make it especially well suited to foster thinking through, and to collaborate in creating, a new world that transcends variety—without suppressing it—to achieve new unities and syntheses of cultural life. For, first, however tolerant of difference French culture becomes, it should be clear that French universalism will never yield to any ideology of incremental pluralism such as the United States proclaims with each newly recognized ethnic group being taken into the polity after overcoming the bigotry and the poverty that held it back. Nor is it likely that French people will accept the word "mosaic," as it is employed in Canada, for example, to make sense of the diversity of the population of contemporary France.

France has historically had one quality since at least the Reformation, we may even qualify it as a kind of identity—for even Lévi-Strauss admits the possibility of employing some such idea as a way of focusing a number of social qualities that need explanation—a universalist pluralism that has set it off from other nations and yet has marked it as the special seat for the hopes of humankind. Students of French civilization cannot ignore a certain French intol-

18. A welcome study on this theme is Noiriel, *Tyrannie du national,* esp. 307–24.

erance for diversity which some contemporary observers trace back
to the French Revolution. Notwithstanding the funeral-festival for
the death of the Revolution which has been celebrated since 1989,
and which seems to have a sufficient supply of ideological fuel to go
to 2015, it would be intellectually profitable to look to the long-term
origins of some of our present mischief before 1789, perhaps in the
works of the ancien régime. Louis Marin's totem, Saint Louis,
earned his heavenly spurs in no small part by his vicious persecution
of the Jews. Although the conclusion of the French religious wars in
the wake of the Reformation at least raised the possibility of toleration as a state policy, not so long after the reign of Henry IV another
king reasserted a sole religious identity for his subjects. Louis XIV
cannot be said to have been influenced by Jacobin fanaticism when
he cruelly expelled many of his Protestant subjects. On the whole,
balancing the acts of revolutionary intolerance against the attack on
established religion and church power, the emancipation of the
slaves, the opening of the question of women's rights to discussion,
the granting of civil parity to the Jews, and the beneficial spread of
its values beyond the borders of France, the 1789 revolution furthered a golden pluralism more than it closed options for France. In
brief, the Maurrasian paradigm of True France has long historical
antecedents, if an especially vicious twentieth-century articulation.

The emergence of the idea of a tolerant and pluralist France has
been interspersed with strange and ill-assorted chapters: the Protestant upheaval and Henry IV's solution to it; the tolerant Enlightenment, which invented the first, humanist anthropology and gave us
the great tract on toleration, *Candide;* the French Revolution for the
slaves, Jews, women, and many Europeans living as subjects of
kings; the polyglot revolutionaries of 1848 and the Commune; the
defeat of political bigotry in the time of Dreyfus; the magnificent
and noble pluralism of André Breton and his surrealist friends (the
uncrowned heroes of our story); French decolonization; and, recently, the acceptance of the idea of Europe in all its manifestations.

What are the possibilities in present-day France? Change is think-
able now, for the historical situation—the world our fathers made—
which permitted the thought of True France has begun to pass. As
we have seen, the conservative anthropological paradigm, *qua* system, died with Vichy. Greater France has disappeared with the de-
volution of most of the colonial empire, and by the same token,

there is currently no national agenda to persuade intellectuals of the former colonies of anything. If any period marks the coming to a close of France's cultural passage to modernity, it is those three glorious decades of economic growth and social transformation following the end of the war. Paris and the provinces have changed their relations, and decentralization, or perhaps simply the continuing homogenization of the country, has ended the old national dialectic of center and periphery. The European Economic Community is on the way to forging a European culture, however uncertainly, of which France will be not the master, as in the Enlightenment, but an important part.[19]

Jacques Derrida, to take a prominent though not unique proponent of the new intellectual current, is ready to rethink French universality in a new Europe and a freer world. He speaks of a law of universality, a law that has no exceptions, that gives meaning to the particular:

> Cultural identity appears not as the opaque body of an untranslatable language but rather as the irreplaceable *inscription* of the universal in the singular, the unique *testimony* to the human essence and to the singularity of humankind. At every moment, we must speak the language of *responsibility:* I have, the unique "I" has, the responsibility to stand witness for the universal.[20]

A second theme in the history of French culture is appropriate to this historical moment. As one of the most language-sensitive cultures in the world, France can lead in what André Fontaine, editor of *Le Monde,* has called the "reunification in our language."[21] With the changes in Russia and Eastern Europe, and the mortal blow to the deceptions of fulfilled production targets and universal

19. Philip Schlesinger, "On National Identity: Some Conceptions and Misconceptions Criticized," *Social Science Information,* 26 (1987), 220–26.

20. Jacques Derrida, "L'Autre Cap," *Libre* (supplement to *Le Monde*), October 1990, 11–13; italics in original. The uniqueness of Europe, Derrida argues, lies in the fact that it does not close itself off in a narrow identity, but is always open to others, always unfinished. For a parallel analysis focusing on the idea of Central Europe today, see Michael Geyer, "Historical Fictions of Autonomy and the Europeanization of National History," *Central European History,* 22 (1989), 316–42.

21. Quoted in Ralf Dahrendorf, *Reflections on the Revolution in Europe* (New York, 1990), 13–14.

social welfare, of Cold War lies on both sides, a space is opening up where we can begin the free democratic dialogues that Jürgen Habermas has placed at the heart of his project for a democratic order. Words will still need to be translated, but there is now a chance that "democracy," "cultural freedom," "rights of minorities," "economic democracy," and many other concepts may begin to have similar meanings in a greater part of the world. The fascination with both the tyranny and the uncertainty of language, after fine wines one of France's major exports to the world's intellectuals, can now aid us in constructing an internationally understood language of democracy. The universality of which Derrida writes might be spoken of, and so could be worked for.

The cultural and political project I am proposing here would be the necessary postpluralist response to the globalization of knowledge, to the new opportunities in many parts of the world to create new public orders, to a newly triumphant and unbridled world capitalism, and to the dangers of the new American political colossus. It is true that if we remain divided, all our pluralisms will persist, but at the price of becoming historically trivial. It is one of those rare cases in history in which thinking may make it so.

Bibliographical Essay

Although the French national character, like all national characters, is illusory, I have tried to document it by employing original sources and printed evidence where they could be found. Chapter 1, on Louis Marin, rests on Marin's scholarly papers, hitherto unexploited, at the Archives Nationales in Paris (Louis Marin 317 AP). On the Colonial Exposition as images (Chapter 2), beyond the written records retained by the Archives de la France d'Outre-mer in Aix-en-Provence there is an abundance of published photographs, contemporary postcards, and commemorative volumes, as well as the volumes of the final report. There are no studies of the imagery of the fair. Chapter 3, on the political activities of the Vietnamese students and the colonial administration's response, rests primarily on documentation in the Archives Nationales, section Outre-mer, especially those of the police charged with surveillance of the natives of the colonies living in France (SLOT-FOM, CAI, and the Sûreté). Finally, on folklore (Chapter 4) there are the archives of the Direction des Musées Nationaux, of the Musée National des Arts et Traditions Populaires (now located in the Bois de Boulogne), the papers of Georges-Henri Rivière in the archives of UNESCO in Paris and those in the Musée de l'Homme (some of them published in *Gradhiva*), and interviews and reminiscences of co-workers and contemporaries.

In each chapter, usually in the first few notes, I give the important secondary literature for the topic, very often with comments on the utility of the titles cited. What follows is a readers' and researchers' guide to facilitate further work.

One of the pleasures this investigation has brought me has been the opportunity to read or reread theorists who I thought might help me do better historical work, but whom I had not yet tried out, as it were. Because the topic crosses disciplinary boundaries, my reading has necessarily been very rich. I cite in the body of the work my particular debts to individual writers and note the writings from which I have especially profited. In particular, this investigation has helped me appreciate the value of the corpus of Michel Foucault's work, as well as its limitations for historical research. My intellectual debt to Pierre Bourdieu should also be evident. Because they are less well known among historians, it is worth citing a few of the titles that proved valuable here: Pierre Bourdieu, "Le Champ scientifique," *Actes de la Recherche en Sciences Sociales*, 2/3 (1976), 88–104, and "Les Conditions sociales de la production sociologique: Sociologie coloniale et décolonisation de la sociologie," in *Cahiers Jussieu n° 2, Université de Paris VII: Le Mal de voir: Ethnologie et orientalisme. Politique et épistémologie, critique et autocritique*, ed. Pierre Bourdieu (Paris, 1975), 416–27. For an introduction to Bourdieu's theoretical framework, see his *Outline of a Theory of Practice* (1972), trans. Richard Nice (Cambridge, 1977). The reader will find in context the references to Jean Baudrillard, a brilliant thinker underneath some of the silly formulations framed, I think, to shock the reader to engage with his theme. Roland Barthes helped me understand how signs worked. I shall continue to recommend Antonio Gramsci for the study of culture. The Hobsbawm-Ranger idea of the invention of tradition is capable of rich development. The formulation of the question of cultural domination by the state as a "hegemonic project" is fruitfully employed by Ian Lustick in his *State-Building Failure in British Ireland and French Algeria*, Research Series of the Institute of International Studies, University of California, Berkeley, No. 63 (Berkeley, 1985), and in David Laitin, *Hegemony and Culture: Politics and Religious Change among the Yoruba* (Chicago, 1986).

At the crossroads of literature, philosophy, and anthropology metatheory, the works in James Clifford and George E. Marcus, eds.,

Writing Culture: The Poetics and Politics of Ethnography (Berkeley, 1986), have been very stimulating. On changing the relationship between anthropologists and subject peoples in language see James Clifford, *The Predicament of Culture: Twentieth-Century Ethnography, Literature, and Art* (Cambridge, Mass., 1988). For a meditation on the theme of the anthropologist as author, and the possibilities of a new postcolonial anthropological discourse, see Clifford Geertz's Harry Camp Lectures at Stanford, *Works and Lives: The Anthropologist as Author* (Stanford, 1988). See, too, his earlier *Interpretation of Cultures: Selected Essays* (New York, 1973).

On the history of the social sciences in France the reader should know about the Société Française pour l'Histoire des Sciences de l'Homme, connected to the Centre A. Koyré at the Muséum National d'Histoire Naturelle. An indispensable review is *Gradhiva*, published out of the Musée de l'Homme by Jean Jamin and his CNRS team, devoted to the history of anthropology. George Stocking publishes an annual collection of articles on the history of the discipline, *The History of Anthropology*, with the University of Wisconsin Press (vol. 1, 1983). Useful articles often appear in *Isis*.

Studies of French anthropology are given in the notes to Chapter 1; see especially note 6. See further Georges Condominas, "Notes on the Present-Day State of Anthropology in the Third World," in *The Politics of Anthropology*, ed. Gerrit Huizer and Bruce Mannheim (The Hague and Paris, 1979), 187–99; and Paul Mercier, *Histoire de l'anthropologie* (Paris, 1966). The classic statement of the new mission of the discipline to act as the advocate of formerly colonial peoples in the postcolonial world was written by Michel Leiris: "L'Ethnographie devant le colonialisme," *Les Temps Modernes*, 6 (1950), 357–74; see also Talal Asad, ed., *Anthropology and the Colonial Encounter* (New York, 1973). An international colloquium on the present state and future of anthropology organized under the auspices of the CNRS was published in 1979: Georges Condominas and Simone Dreyfus-Gamelon, eds., *L'Anthropologie en France: Situation actuelle et avenir* (Paris, 1979). On conservative anthropology, aside from the few studies on Le Play and his followers mentioned in note 11 of Chapter 1, little historical material has been published on him, although there seems to be some interest again in his theoretical style. Some sifted biographical data on Louis Marin are found in Fernande Marin, *Louis Marin, 1871–1960: Homme d'état, philosophe et savant* (Paris, 1973). William D. Irvine, in his *French Conservatism in Crisis: The Republican Federation of France in the 1930s* (Baton Rouge, 1979), has done a valuable political study employing the section of Marin's papers dedicated to that aspect of his career.

The best general study of French colonialism is now Jacques Marseille, *Empire colonial et capitalisme français: Histoire d'un divorce* (Paris, 1984); see also Charles-Robert Ageron, *France coloniale ou parti colonial?* (Paris, 1978), and Raoul Girardet, *L'Idée coloniale en France de 1871 à 1962* (Paris, 1972). On putting colonies on view and on constructing colonies from the imperial countries, see Robert W. Rydell, *All the World's a Fair: Visions of Empire at American International Expositions, 1876–1916* (Chicago, 1984). On French colonial expositions there is William H. Schneider, *An Empire for the Masses: The French Popular Image of Africa, 1870–1900* (Westport, Conn., 1982). For suggestive new approaches see Fredric Jameson, *The Politics of Post-Modernity; or, The Cultural Logic of Late Capitalism* (Durham, N.C., 1991), 101–29; Debora L. Silverman, "The 1889 Exhibition: The Crisis of Bourgeois Individualism," *Oppositions: A Journal for Ideas and Criticism in Architecture*, 8 (1977), and the appropriate pages of her *Art Nouveau in Fin-de-Siècle France: Politics, Psychology, and Style* (Berkeley, 1989); and Patricia Mainardi, *Art and Politics of the Second Empire: The Universal Expositions of 1855 and 1867* (New Haven, 1987). On the 1931 fair see Ministère des Colonies, Le Gouverneur-Général Marcel Olivier, Rapporteur Général, Délégué Général à l'Exposition, *Rapport Général: Exposition Coloniale Internationale de 1931*, 7 vols. (Paris, 1933). Most recently on 1931 we have the beautiful picture book by Jacques Marseille, *L'Age d'or de la France coloniale* (Paris, 1986), and the look backward by Charles-Robert Ageron in "L'Exposition coloniale de 1931: Mythe républicain ou mythe impérial," in *Les Lieux de mémoire*, ed. Pierre Nora, vol. 1, *La République* (Paris, 1984), 561–91.

On education and politics in Vietnam we have the splendid but unpublished thesis by the late Gail Paradise Kelly, "Franco-Vietnamese Schools, 1918–1933" (University of Wisconsin–Madison, 1975), and her "Colonial Schools in Vietnam: Policy and Practice," in *Education and Colonialism*, ed. Philip G. Altbach and Gail

P. Kelly (London and New York, 1978). Scott McConnell, *Leftward Journey: The Education of Vietnamese Students in France, 1919–1939* (New Brunswick, N.J., 1989), has attempted—unsuccessfully, I think—to overthrow Kelly's argument. The articles by Daniel Hémery cited in Chapter 3 are still valuable. On the moral economy school see Brooke Larson, *Exploitation and Moral Economy in the Southern Andes: A Critical Reconsideration*, Columbia–New York University Latin American, Caribbean, and Iberian Occasional Papers, no. 8 (New York, 1989).

We are just beginning to get studies on French domestic anthropology—that is, folklore, cultural museology, and the cultural politics of the 1930s. For the discipline of anthropology we have Isac Chiva, "Entre livre et musée: Emergence d'une ethnologie de la France," in *Ethnologies en miroir: La France et les pays de langue allemande*, ed. Isac Chiva and Utz Jeggle (Paris, 1987). We will also soon be able to read a Berkeley Ph.D. thesis by Richard Gringeri on French culture and French anthropology. The most important work on cultural politics in the era is Pascal Ory, "La Politique culturelle du Front Populaire française (1935–1938)," 5 vols. (thèse pour le doctorat d'état, Université de Paris X, Nanterre, 1990). Beyond the notices and short texts cited in Chapter 4, in particular Pascal Ory, "Georges-Henri Rivière, militant culturel du Front Populaire?" *Ethnologie française*, 17 (1987), 23–28, there are no biographies of Rivière.

On culture, cultural policy, and Vichy we are beginning to get some valuable work. We have Christian Faure, *Le Projet culturel de Vichy: Folklore et révolution nationale, 1940–44* (Lyon, 1989); but it is still worth reading his more detailed thesis, "Folklore et révolution nationale: Doctrine et action sous Vichy (1940–44)," 2 vols. (thèse doctorat, Université de Lyon II, 1986). See the conference volume of the Institut d'Histoire du Temps Présent: Jean-Pierre Rioux, ed., *Politiques et pratiques culturelles dans la France de Vichy* (Paris, 1988), especially the essay by Henry Rousso, "Vichy: Politique, idéologie et culture," 13–25. Anne-Marie Thiesse characterizes the cultural regionalism of Vichy as *"décor?:"* "Ecrire la France: Le Mouvement littéraire régionaliste de la langue française entre la belle époque et la libération," 2 vols. (thèse pour le doctorat d'état, Université de Lyon II, 1989). On art in the largest sense as propaganda see Laurent Gervereau and Denis Peschanski, eds., *La Propagande sous Vichy, 1940–1944* (Paris, 1990).

As the reader can see, most of the topics treated in the text and in this essay have just begun to interest French scholars. The questions are fresh, the sources are just now becoming accessible. There is much to do.

Index

True France: The Wars over Cultural Identity, 1900–1945 by Herman Lebovics